Entering Torah
Reuven Hammer

ENTERING TORAH

Prefaces to the Weekly Torah Portion

REUVEN HAMMER

gefen
publishing house
JERUSALEM ◆ NEW YORK

Design & Typesetting: Marzel A.S., Jerusalem
Cover Design: S. Kim Glassman
On the cover: Ark curtain by Raḥel Hammer
for Fuchsberg Jerusalem Center.

ISBN 978-965-229-434-0

1 3 5 7 9 8 6 4 2

Gefen Publishing House, Ltd.   Gefen Books
6 Hatzvi Street, Jerusalem 94386, Israel   600 Broadway, Lynbrook, NY 11563, USA
972-2-538-0247   516-593-1234
orders@gefenpublishing.com   orders@gefenpublishing.com

www.israelbooks.com

Printed in Israel   *Send for our free catalogue*

To my children and grandchildren in love and admiration. They have allowed me to enjoy the blessing found in the Psalm:

...may you live to see your children's children.

May there be peace for Israel! (Psalm 128:6)

Contents

NUMBERS

DEUTERONOMY

Foreword

Studying the weekly Torah portion — *Parashat Hashavua* — is an ancient Jewish practice that is enshrined in codes of Jewish Law. For Judaism the Torah is not only divided into five books, known as the Ḥumash from the Hebrew word for "five," but into fifty-four portions, some of which are combined when there are less Shabbatot than that available for reading in the Jewish year. This division was the result of the ancient practice of Jews in Babylonia, who read the entire Torah in a one-year cycle. A knowledgeable Jew, therefore, is much more likely to say that an event or a passage is found in a certain *parashah* than to refer to the numbered chapter. Each portion has an inner logic, a beginning and an end, making it a distinct unit. The chapters and their numbers originated in Christian circles.

For the believing Jew today, no less than for the believing Jew in the past, the study of the weekly portion is a religious experience. For this reason it is customary to consider the section along with the words of traditional commentators from medieval times and those from even greater antiquity in the rabbinic midrash (interpretations). It is important to know not only what the Torah meant when it was written, but also what it has meant within Judaism since then. It is also important to distinguish between the two for the sake of intellectual honesty. Moderns have the advantage of using the results of linguistic studies and comparative studies of other ancient texts, as well as archeological findings, to help us understand the text.

Viewing the Torah as a work that reflects ancient traditions and that contains the teachings of Moses — even though according to the consensus of modern Biblical scholarship, it was finally completed only in the time of Ezra — rather than as a book dictated letter by letter by God to Moses, does not detract from the sacredness of the text. For a religious Jew it remains the repository of spiritual truth and the root from which the entire tree of Jewish belief has sprung. As the ancient sage Ben Bag-Bag said, "Scrutinize it over and over again, for everything is in it" (*Pirkei Avot* 5:24).

There is much that can be learned from the Torah concerning the history of the origins of the Jewish people, but even more important are the moral, ethical and theological truths that are contained therein. It reflects an entire worldview concerning the nature of God and of human beings, the task of Israel and the way in which the people of Israel are to live. Thus it is an ancient text that is ever new and always renewing itself. One studies it not only to learn what was, but also to discover what we are and how we are to live.[1]

It is in that spirit that these prefaces were written. They are not exhaustive and are not meant to replace study of the portion, but to guide one in understanding the portion by pointing out important ideas found therein and raising problems and questions for consideration. One can read them and read the verses cited and then go on from there to study the entire section and ponder its many meanings. Obviously this format means that only certain parts of the portions will be discussed while others are not commented upon. Thus this work serves only to open the door to study, not to exhaust the many possibilities. In the words of Hillel: *zil g'mor* — now go and learn it (Shabbat 31a)!

The genesis of this book lies in the columns on *Parashat Hashavua* that I wrote for the *Jerusalem Post* over many years. I have taken the ideas there and expanded, reworked and enhanced them for *Entering Torah*. I want to thank my editor, Deena Glickman, for her careful work and helpful suggestions. As always, my deep appreciation to my wife, Raḥel, who over the years patiently read, critiqued and improved my work.

In the words from Proverbs 3:17–18 that we recite at the conclusion of the Torah service, "It is a tree of life for those who grasp it and those who uphold it are content. Its ways are ways of pleasantness and all its paths are peace."

Reuven Hammer
Jerusalem 5769

---

1. In writing about God I have sometimes used the conventional masculine language, referring to God as "He" and so forth. I should like to make it clear that Jewish belief does not ascribe any sexual identity to God — neither masculine nor feminine. However I find it awkward to constantly avoid pronouns or to use expressions such as He/She. Therefore please take it for granted that any such inferences are incorrect.

GENESIS

B'reishit

B'reishit   בראשית

Genesis 1:1–6:8 | בראשית א:א-ו:ח

1. Creation

The first section of the Torah takes us on a grand sweep from the creation of the world to the story of Noah. In between we read of the first sin, the first birth, the first murder, the branching out of the human race and its failure to live up to God's expectations. Each of these is a magnificent theme worthy of contemplation and discussion. Let us first concentrate on the story or stories of Creation found at the very beginning.

Much ink has been spilled over the question: does the Biblical account of Creation square with scientific theories? What are we to do with six days referred to in the Bible versus the millions of years that evolution took according to all the best evidence and theories that are held today? I should like to posit the idea that we must make a distinction between science and belief, between Biblical poetry and scientific fact. The Torah is not a book of science. It serves to teach us beliefs and values which cannot be dealt with by science. The account of Creation in Genesis teaches us, first of all, that the world is God's creation. This is encapsulated in the opening three Hebrew words of the Torah: *B'reishit bara Elohim*, variously translated as "When God began to create" or "In the beginning God created" (Genesis 1:1). Thus we are told that the world was created and that it was created by God — one God. This is a belief that can neither be proven nor disproved. The believing Jew can, of course, give rational reasons as to why this seems to be true and the atheist can offer good arguments as to why it is not. But in the end it is belief and not reason that will determine what one thinks. As for the rest, the details of how this was accomplished, I am perfectly willing to turn to science to

5

learn the latest theories, which may or may not prove to be true, but I am not at all concerned as to how they fit into the Biblical story. On the other hand, if I want to have an account of the creation of the world that will inspire in me feelings of awe and majesty, I can do no better than to read the magnificent poetry of the first chapter of Genesis which, in addition to teaching me that the world is a creation and not accident or chaos, also instills in me the belief that God has given us a good world, a world made for blessing and for our benefit: "And God saw all that He had made, and found it very good" (Genesis 1:31).

As the Biblical scholar Nahum M. Sarna wrote:

> Biblical man, despite his undoubted intellectual and spiritual endowments, did not base his views of the universe and its laws on the critical use of empirical data. He had not, as yet, discovered the principles and methods of disciplined inquiry, critical observation or analytical experimentation. Rather, his thinking was imaginative, and his expressions of thought were concrete, pictorial, emotional and poetic. Hence, it is a naive and futile exercise to attempt to reconcile the biblical accounts of creation with the findings of modern science. (*Understanding Genesis*, [New York: Shocken, 1970] pp. 2–3)

The Sages long ago realized that the Torah need not be taken literally. One example will suffice. On the verse "Therefore He rested on the seventh day" (Exodus 20:11), the *Mekhilta* (*Baḥodesh* 7) comments:

> And is [God] subject to tiredness? Does it not say of Him "He is neither tired nor weary" (Isaiah 40:28)?...How then can the Torah record "therefore He rested on the seventh day"? Rather it is as if He permitted it to be written about Him that He created His world in six days and rested on the seventh so that we should infer: if He who is not subject to tiredness wrote about Himself that He created His world in six days and rested on the seventh, surely human beings — of whom it is written "Humans are born to toil" (Job 5:7) — must rest on the seventh day!

Our studies of the ancient world and its literature have taught us to see the Torah against the background of the beliefs of its time. There is little doubt that the Biblical account of Creation is a polemic against the pagan beliefs that were rampant then. Those ancient stories of Creation always posited the Creation as the result of cosmic battles between various gods and forces. The most well known of these, the Babylonian epic known as *Enuma Elish*, for example, tells of a fierce battle in which the god Marduk led a force of other gods against the sea monster Tiamat, slew her and then sliced her in two, creating the heavens from one half of her carcass and the earth from the other. Later on, Marduk created human beings with the purpose of serving the gods who would otherwise have had to toil unceasingly in menial labor.

How pure and refreshing Genesis seems after this story. There are no groups of gods, no primordial forces, no battles, no mythic tales of the lives of the gods — just the one God who creates by His word, who made human beings so that they would rule the good world He had created and not in order for them to be His slaves. This story sweeps through the ancient world like a breath of fresh air.

Creation is one of the central pillars of Jewish belief, repeated over and over in our prayers and in the Biblical writings. It remains as important today as ever and we should never tire of reading the Biblical account which relates it so magnificently.

2. Human Nature

Like a bolt of lightning, Genesis shattered ancient myths and replaced the chaos of paganism with the light of the belief in one power — one God — whose will is supreme, as we have seen. These opening chapters of Genesis created a revolution in religious thinking that eventually caused the collapse of ancient ideologies and their replacement with monotheistic beliefs.

But in addition to revolutionizing our concept of God, these chapters also offer us profound insights into the nature of human beings. The legendary figures that appear here have shaped our thinking about ourselves: Adam — man — a creature formed from the earth but created in the image of God; Eve — the mother of us all; Cain — the first human being created by human beings and the first killer; Abel — the first victim, destroyed by his own brother.

What does the Torah tell us about the nature of human beings? By definition humans are flawed, imperfect. If they were not, they would be divine. Anything other than God cannot be perfect. And so the very first thing that humans do is break the rules, thus demonstrating that they have free will and that this free will is allowed to override the divine will. But this has consequences. On the one hand, free will is what makes humans human. On the other hand, the incorrect use of free will casts us all outside of Eden.

The nature of the human being is the subject of the story of Cain and Abel and is especially emphasized in the description of the nature of Cain. What kind of person was he? What caused him to act as he did? In his book *East of Eden*, John Steinbeck portrayed Cain in sympathetic terms. He was the rejected son who longed for the love of his parents but could never seem to do the right thing, a truly tragic figure.

The Biblical Cain is a much more enigmatic figure. We know little about him. His mother must have been inordinately proud of him — or was she merely proud of herself? When she names him she proclaims, "I have produced a man with [the help of] the Lord!" (Genesis 4:1). The Hebrew word "produced" contains the letters of the name Cain. Eve herself was created by God from the body of a man. Now she has produced a man from her own body. This was indeed a terrific accomplishment and every mother must feel that pride and that wonder. But how did Cain feel to be the first truly human child?

We get an indication that Cain may have been callous, perhaps a spoiled child. His offering to God is described tersely as being "from the fruit of the soil" (Genesis 4:3) while that of his younger brother Abel is "from the choicest of the firstlings of his flock" (Genesis 4:4). Since the Torah does not waste words, we can assume that adding "from the choicest" was intended to indicate the contrast between the two offerings. Cain's is, if not begrudging, then at least not particularly generous. And for this reason God rejects it. Abel gives with a full heart.

Cain, the proud firstborn, is devastated by this. Perhaps this is the first time that he has faced a rebuke. God attempts to use this to teach him a lesson — a lesson about human beings in general and how they should conduct themselves. God tells him that "sin crouches at the door. Its urge is toward you yet you can be its master" (Genesis 4:7). Temptation is an integral part of human nature but it can be overcome. As human beings we have the ability to resist, although it is not always easy. Unfortunately Cain does not learn the lesson. Instead he continues to look for privilege and to succumb to the temptation to use any means to attain whatever he wants.

Cain quarrels with his brother. We do not know why. In one of the most puzzling verses in the Torah we read, "Cain said to his brother Abel" (Genesis 4:8), but there is no record of what he said! All we know is the consequence: Cain killed his brother. The midrash, as is its wont, fills in the lacuna and suggests several things that he might have said, several causes for a controversy between the two brothers:

- They quarreled over how to divide the wealth of the world, over who would get ground and who would get movable goods.

- They quarreled over in whose territory the Temple would be built.

- They quarreled over women. (*Genesis Rabbah* 22:4)

Indeed all of these remain causes for contention and strife. To this day we still kill our brothers over these things.

Nevertheless it seems clear that the Torah deliberately leaves this space blank because it wants to indicate to us that it matters not what they are fighting over. Quarrels can arise over anything and over nothing and when they do they result in bloodshed. There is no excuse for the bloodshed. As King Claudius, who has murdered his brother King Hamlet, says in the play, "O my offence is rank, it smells to heaven! It hath the primal eldest curse upon 't; a brother's murder" (*Hamlet*, act 3, scene 3). Every murder, says the Torah, is the murder of a brother. Every victim is an Abel, every killer a Cain. And the answer to the famous question, "Am I my brother's keeper?" (Genesis 4:9) is an emphatic "Yes!"

Cain is punished not by death but instead is made a wanderer. Perhaps God takes into consideration the fact that Cain has never seen death and may not understand the full consequences of his action. His punishment — the soil will no longer yield its products to him — is doubly appropriate: In the first place he was a farmer — and now his very way of life has been taken from him. In the second place, the ground has been contaminated with the blood he shed and therefore will no longer respond to his efforts.

The lessons of these stories are difficult ones and not always pleasant. Perhaps they teach us more about ourselves than we would like to know. But they do teach us the most important thing any human being can know: sin crouches at the door, but we can overcome the temptation. To be truly human is to learn how to do that and how to prevent oneself from becoming Cain.

Noah   נֹחַ

Genesis 6:9–11:32 | בראשית ו׃ט-יא׃לב

1. Noah: The Righteous

The wickedness of the human race has brought God to the drastic decision to begin all over again, destroying all humans in a great flood. However instead of creating a new creature from raw material, as He did with Adam, God will save one family and from that family the earth will be repopulated — a second Adam and Eve. How to choose the family worthy of surviving the catastrophe? The Torah does not depict God as having any problem with that. The last verse of the portion of *B'reishit* states simply "But Noah found favor with the Lord" (Genesis 6:8) and the first verse of the next portion explains why: "Noah was a righteous man; he was blameless in his age" (Genesis 6:9). How different this is from the flood stories found in other ancient Near Eastern literature. There too one human is saved when the gods decide to exterminate the human race, but no reason is given. There is no moral dimension involved. A god saves someone who happens to be a favorite. Nor is there a moral dimension behind the bringing of the flood. In the Akkadian epic, for example, we read that the reason was that "the god [Enlil] was disturbed by their uproar." The Torah, on the other hand, is concerned with righteous behavior, not with keeping quiet so that the gods can sleep better. Humanity is destroyed because of corruption, lawlessness and violence (Genesis 6:11) and Noah is saved because "you alone have I found righteous before Me in this generation" (Genesis 7:1).

Nevertheless, the question of exactly what kind of a man Noah was and the extent of his righteousness remains to be determined. The Sages themselves debated the question of the nature of Noah (*Genesis Rabbah* 30:9).

They seized upon the words of the Torah that Noah was "blameless *in his age*" (Genesis 6:9, repeated in 7:1) and asked: Does this mean that he was considered blameless and righteous *only* in his age but that in a better generation such as that of Abraham he would have been nothing special? Or does it signify that *even* in his age, an age of wickedness, he was able to maintain his righteousness and integrity?

It is difficult to say, but it is certain that the Torah does not think of him as being as righteous as Abraham. He is a stepping-stone, not the goal. Even the story that is told of him after the flood, in which he becomes inebriated (Genesis 9:21), indicates that he is far from perfect. Compare also his silence when informed that God is about to destroy all of humanity (Genesis 6:22) with Abraham's reaction when told that God intends to destroy the wicked cities of Sodom and Gomorrah (Genesis 18:23–32). Nevertheless there is a profound truth to be found in the insight that states that it is extremely difficult to be righteous when society is so evil and that one who manages to do so even in the midst of evil deserves great praise. Consider, for example, those righteous people of all nations who during the time of the Shoah saved Jewish lives. They risked their own lives and went against the prevailing opinions and actions of the society in which they lived. That is not an easy matter, but it serves as a lesson to us all that we must be willing to stand up against evil, against injustice, against prejudice, even when that stance is not popular.

Noah's importance is unquestioned. He plays a pivotal role in the Biblical scheme. There are ten generations from Adam to Noah and ten generations from Noah to Abraham. His name — *Noah* — gives us a clue, stemming as it does from the Hebrew root meaning "to rest," *lanuaḥ*. On one level this is connected to the story of the flood itself, in which we read that at the end of one hundred fifty days "the ark came to rest [*vatanaḥ*] on the mountains of Ararat" (Genesis 8:4). The Torah also gives a specific interpretation to the name, deriving it from *l'naḥem*, to comfort: "This one will provide us relief [comfort us, *y'naḥamenu*] from our work and from the toil of our hands, out of the very soil the Lord placed under a curse" (Genesis 5:29). Not only is Noah a second Adam in that all humanity will be descended from him; he also will cancel or mitigate the curse that Adam brought upon humanity. He is Adam reborn, humanity's second chance.

Unfortunately, Noah's descendants are little better than Adam's, as we see from the story of the Tower of Babel (Genesis 11). Thus ten generations later

God chooses Abram — later Abraham — to found a people that will be an example to the rest of humanity of what it means to walk with God in justice and mercy. Noah is merely one stop along the way, but an important stop because with him comes God's promise never to destroy all of humanity again (Genesis 9:11) and an attempt to discipline and control the human inclination to evil through the regimen of laws (Genesis 9:3-6).

One thing is certain. Noah must have been extraordinary. Even if he did not measure up to Abraham, he was righteous and he was worthy of being saved. He resisted joining the mob to participate in the violence that was all around him. That may not be perfection, but it is still worthy of praise and emulation.

2. Human Evil

One of the perplexing questions that we ask ourselves concerns the existence of human evil. This is the subject that lies at the core of this Torah portion, continuing the discussion that began already in *B'reishit*. The discussion is not conducted in the form of a philosophical treatise, but through a story and through God's words in reaction to human conduct. The answer we receive may not explain it to our complete satisfaction, but it gives us a method of dealing with it.

As we saw earlier, human beings are imperfect. By definition, this is as it must be, for the only perfect being is God. But what is the nature of this imperfection? We saw it demonstrated already in the previous Torah portion where Adam and Eve were revealed as disobedient (Genesis 3:14-24) and where Cain was unable to rule over "sin [which] crouches at the door" even though he was told that "its urge is toward you yet you can be its master" (Genesis 4:7). The result was the murder of brother by brother, a sin that continues to haunt our lives throughout human history.

But now evil has manifested itself in an entire civilization. "The Lord saw how great was man's wickedness on earth, and how every plan devised by his mind was nothing but evil all the time" (Genesis 6:5). This is such an extreme condemnation of human beings that it is not surprising that it led God to the conclusion that the creation of humans was a mistake and that therefore they should all be blotted out (Genesis 6:6). It is not quite so clear why other forms of life were also to be included in this terrible decree. Rashi quotes the rabbinic midrash to the effect that the beasts too had become corrupted but also offers the possibility that, since all these creatures had been created for the benefit of human beings, if people were to exist no more, there was no need for the animals.

The evil that warranted destruction is spelled out in greater detail in this portion: "The earth became corrupt before God; the earth was filled with lawlessness" (Genesis 6:11). Instead of evolving into an ever more righteous society in which social justice reigned, civilization was fraught with violence, creating a world in which corruption stained all human institutions. This was not the world that God had intended to create.

It is vital for an understanding of the Torah's message that we appreciate how deliberately the sin of humanity is spelled out. The flood story was an ancient one, told in the mythologies of all the nations of the Near East. But in none of them was there any indication that the flood was brought because of the moral corruption of human beings. Here we are told that all flesh had become corrupted: "Every plan devised by his [man's] mind was nothing but evil all the time" (Genesis 6:5). Everyone had succumbed to the temptations that sin places at the door.

Yet, as God had told Cain, "you can be its master." It is in the nature of humans to be tempted. There are urges within us — this *yetzer*, the impulses within us that need to be controlled — that can lead to evil or, when properly channeled, can lead to good. This is made explicit in God's utterance after the flood: "Never again will I doom the earth because of man, since the devisings [*yetzer*] of man's mind are evil from his youth" (Genesis 8:21). What a strange reason to pledge not to destroy humans. Because we have this impulse to evil, God will tolerate us! On the contrary, is that not a good reason to eliminate us? The text means to tell us that God realizes (as it were) that the creature He created has this flaw through no fault of its own. It is inherent in creating even the finest of creatures. There can be no perfect saints. Therefore this possibility of evil must be tolerated but it must also be fought against. It cannot be eliminated but it can be controlled.

It is no accident that immediately following this statement the Lord gives Noah, the new Adam, explicit instructions concerning how humans are to live — stressing the sanctity of human life (Genesis 9:1-7). The rabbinic understanding of the Torah expanded this concept into the "Seven Noahide commandments" — not worshipping idols, not blaspheming God, not murdering, not committing adultery, not robbing, not eating flesh from a living animal, establishing courts of justice (*Sanhedrin* 56a). It is through these commandments — through a commitment to the basic laws of morality — that humans can subdue their impulses and create a true civilization. This concept goes one step further when Israel takes upon itself the entire range of commandments, the purpose of which is "to purify human beings" (*Genesis Rabbah* 44:1). We can purify ourselves from the impulse toward evil if we adopt a disciplined life.

In a sense God has devised a new plan, a new strategy to meet the problem of evil that is inherent in human beings. The first plan — pre-Noah — was really no plan at all. Human beings were virtually given free reign. They were told to "Be fertile and increase, fill the earth and master it" (Genesis 1:28). The assumption is that they would know what to do and what not. Now God introduces discipline, rules and regulations that are realistic and take human weakness into account. God may be likened here to a parent who understands that giving a child total freedom is not doing that child a favor. The child needs rules and regulations that are flexible yet provide guidance.

It is unfortunate that many view the commandments as ends in themselves without seeing that they have a greater purpose. Blind observance with no thought as to the purpose of this observance becomes a kind of meaningless religious behaviorism.

The evil in us is not an outside force or an irresistible impulse. It is inherent in human nature. It can lead, as we have seen all too often, to terrible acts of cruelty, death and destruction. We cannot delude ourselves into thinking that it does not exist. It must be fought against and not tolerated, but the first battle is within ourselves. We can overcome it, we can purify ourselves and we can make this a world that God will not regret having created.

Lekh Lekha

לך לך

Genesis 12:1-17:27 | בראשית יב:א-יז:כז

1. The Journey

Jewish history begins with a journey. Jewish history begins when a husband and wife — Abram (exalted father) and Sarai (princess) — set out for a land unknown, answering a call which is both a command and a promise: *Lekh lekha* (Go forth)! Perhaps this is more of a request than a command. Perhaps, as the Sages pointed out, the second word — *lekha* (literally "to you") may indicate "at your free will," please do this. In any case, the instruction is freely carried out, an indication of their willingness to obey God and to trust Him. Actually, as recorded at the end of the previous portion, Abram's father Terah had begun a journey to Canaan — but stopped along the way at Haran, where he died. Thus Abram seems to be continuing that which his father had begun. And yet there is no indication here that Abram knows where he is going. Rabbinic tradition always depicts Abram and Terah in opposition. Terah is the idol maker, Abram the idol breaker. The simple text of the Torah, however, gives no indication of this.

Nevertheless it is certain that Abram's quest is unique. God does not speak to Terah. Terah is never commanded to leave Ur; he simply goes. Is he unhappy there? Is he seeking better economic conditions? Does he oppose the way of life there? We shall never know. But Abram feels the call of God. He goes because of the divine word. From God's point of view there is a definite goal and purpose in Abram's journey. He is to become the father of a new nation, a people that will be dedicated to God's ways. That is the meaning of the promise "I will make of you a great nation and I will bless you" (Genesis

12:2); that nation will have an effect upon all nations: "And all the families of the earth shall bless themselves by you" (Genesis 12:3).

Biblical history is schematic. There are ten generations from Adam to Noah and ten from Noah to Abram. God's disappointment with His human creations reached a climax with Noah's generation. God's attempt at disciplining human beings began then with the commandments given to Noah and his children that stressed the sanctity of human life — indeed of all life (see Genesis 9:1–6). Now there is a further step — the creation of a family-nation that will serve as an example to others of God's will. This begins with the selection of Abram and Sarai — Abram's children from other women are not part of this process — and will climax with the covenant at Sinai when this family becomes God's holy nation.

Twenty-four years after God's first call to Abram, God makes His plan much more explicit. God's first word to Abram had been simply "walk" (*lekh*, Genesis 12:1). Now God has a greater and more difficult command, the demand for moral perfection — *lekh lefanai*: "Walk before Me and be blameless. I will establish My covenant between Me and you" (Genesis 17:1–2). God then changes Abram's name to Abraham and Sarai's to Sarah, reiterates His promise to grant a land to their offspring and commands circumcision as a physical, tangible sign of the new covenant between them. The change of name always indicates a significant change in the nature and destiny of the person. In this case the letter *heh* has been added, probably representing the divine Name itself.

The Sages pointed out that whereas this verse (Genesis 17:1) says, "Walk *before Me*," regarding Noah the Torah states, "Noah walked *with God*" (Genesis 6:9). Noah went along with God, but Abraham served as a herald who walks *before* the ruler and both clears the way for him and announces his coming (*Genesis Rabbah* 30:10). Thus Abraham is to be seen as greater and more worthy than Noah, the one who will instruct mankind in a new relationship to the Divine.

The covenant with Abraham represents a further step toward the Sinai covenant. As many Biblical scholars have pointed out, the covenant with Abraham, which created a new people with a special relationship with God, falls under the rubric of a "covenant of grant." That is, it is a reward given to Abraham for his qualities and his service to God, rather than a covenant in which demands are made upon the recipient. That occurred later at Sinai.

This is an unconditional covenant; it does not say — as the Sinai covenant does — that if you take certain actions you will receive a specific reward. Rather it promises certain things to Abraham, much as a king might grant someone a knighthood together with an estate and certain privileges that will be his and his progeny's for all eternity. As God says to him, "Your reward shall be very great" (Genesis 15:1). Of course the expectation is that just as this person has been a loyal servant to the king up until now, so he and his descendants will continue to be loyal to the king in the future. When a male child is born, at the circumcision we say that the child is entering into "the covenant of Abraham our father," and thus continues the chain that began with Abraham.

It is difficult for us to assess the greatness of Abraham from the stories that are found in this portion alone. The great trials are yet to come. Rather we must assume that his worthy qualities were known by God even at the beginning. Abraham does not appear to have been a religious revolutionary in the same sense that Moses was, but he certainly developed an exclusive loyalty to his God whom he recognized as "God the Most High, Creator of heaven and earth," a title that was also used by Melchizedek the king of Salem (Genesis 14:19, 22).

Hundreds of years later when the story of Israel's history was retold, the Levites proclaimed, "You are the Lord God, who chose Abram, who brought him forth from Ur of the Chaldeans and changed his name to Abraham. Finding his heart true to You, You made a covenant with him" (Nehemiah 9:7–8). Thus the choice of Abraham is explained. Indeed, throughout his life Abraham demonstrated extraordinary loyalty to God.

This early stage in the development of what eventually became Judaism was critical. In many ways it determined the very nature of our culture and our religion. We are indeed a family, "a great nation," bound together by ties of history and mutual experience, descended from one couple. Even those who are not biological descendants of Abraham and Sarah become their spiritual descendants when they join the Jewish people. As Ruth said, "You people shall be my people, Your God shall be my God" (Ruth 1:16). We are a people before anything else — but we are a God-centered people. And we are still continuing the journey begun by Abram and Sarai toward the kingdom of God.

The third step in God's search for human beings who will be loyal to Him has begun. First there was Adam, then Noah and now Abraham who will become the father of a people dedicated to God's ways on earth.

2. The First Patriarch

In a sense Abraham is the first person whose portrait is painted completely by the Bible. He is the first for whom we have a complete life story, from birth to death, with so many major milestones in between. True, there is also something almost mythological about him as well. Consider his name — Abram, in Hebrew *Avram*. *Avram* is more of a title than a name. It has a meaning — exalted father. It does not sound like the kind of a name a parent would bestow upon a newborn infant. Yet it certainly suits the father of our people. Other stories about him also have a mythic character: his mystic vision (Genesis 15:1-21) and the story of the sacrifice of Isaac (Genesis 22:1-19). Yet he is also a completely human personality with strengths and weaknesses, with a wide range of human emotions. The trials of his life, the rivalry between Sarah and Hagar (Genesis 21:9-13), the sending away of Ishmael (Genesis 21:14), all portray a man of flesh and blood, of human feelings and emotions.

As Nahum Sarna has written:

> The Hebrew patriarchs are not mythological figures, not gods or semi-gods, but intensely human beings who appeared fairly late on the scene of history and whose biographies are well rooted in a cultural, religious and legal background that ought to be verifiable. (*Understanding Genesis*, p. 85)

Archeological finds from the city of Ur bring a feeling of reality to the founders of our people. We can see and touch figurines, perhaps idols, such as those that might have graced Abraham's childhood home, jewelry similar to that which Sarah might have worn. These are no longer mere literary figures, but real people.

One of the most problematic stories about Abraham concerns the time when he and Sarah had to go to Egypt because of a famine, an obvious prefiguring of the later descent of Jacob's family into Egypt under similar conditions. Abraham asked Sarah to say she was his sister and not his wife because he was afraid that his life might be in danger if the truth were known (Genesis 12:10-20). A similar story is told again later on about a trip to Gerar (Genesis 20:1-17), only in much greater detail. There Abraham explains, "I thought surely there is no fear of God in this place, and they will kill me because of my wife" (20:11). The fact that Sarah was indeed his half-sister does little to mitigate the situation. One must assume that these incidents have some basis in truth, for if one were looking to write a totally flattering biography of Abraham, it is doubtful if they would have been included.

Was Abraham justified in what he did? It is hard to say. One may take many steps to preserve one's life, including telling a falsehood. But did he not also endanger Sarah? Fortunately God saw to it that no harm came to either of them. The thirteenth-century Spanish commentator the Ramban — Rabbi Moshe ben Naḥman — roundly condemns Abraham for doing so and suggests that he should have relied on God's help. Indeed in the end it is only because of God's help that the situation turned out as it did. This, incidentally, is surely one of the motifs of the story — that God was with Abraham and Sarah at all times and protected them.

Abraham was faced with a great moral dilemma. Having to travel to the courts of kings and great rulers together with a wife of great beauty, in a civilization in which it was so easy for a ruler to kill a husband in order to take such a woman for himself, telling the truth was a certain path to death for him and dishonor for her. One has only to recall the story of David and Bathsheba to see that even a "righteous ruler" could succumb to such a temptation. Telling this lie would protect his life and might or might not succeed in protecting her. He chose what he believed to be the lesser of two evils.

I think that it is helpful to compare these stories with an incident in the life of Abraham's nephew, Lot. There are many instances in which we are meant to compare the values of these two men. In each instance, Abraham emerges as the one with greater ethical concern, while Lot appears not as a wicked man — but as one who is not totally righteous either. The incident to which I refer is that of the strangers who came to his home in Sodom, strangers who were really angels, although Lot did not know it. When they were in danger of being sexually molested by the men of Sodom, Lot offered his daughters to the men of Sodom in place of these men. Once again, only supernatural intervention prevented a catastrophe (Genesis 19:4-11).

It has always seemed to me that the terrible story of Lot's daughters sleeping with their father after the destruction of the wicked cities because they are afraid that only thus will the human race be preserved (Genesis 19:30–38) is connected to Lot's own behavior. What lesson could his daughters have learned from his willingness to sacrifice their virtue but that anything is permitted?

To return to our comparison, both Abraham and Lot are faced with dangerous situations. Both of them take steps to keep away the danger, but Lot goes much farther in violating the code of morality.

The saga that begins in this reading is a lengthy one. It marks the beginnings of Jewish history. This beginning is grounded in reality and portrays real people against a real background, struggling with dilemmas that are not very different than those we meet today. Seeing how they acted can help us in determining our own actions, knowing both what to emulate and what to avoid.

Vayera ‎וירא

Genesis 18:1–22:24 | ‎בראשית יח:א-כב:כד

1. Caring for Others

The first section of this portion seems to be little more than a prelude to the difficult trials that are depicted later on, yet it is an important part of the story of Abraham. Three divine messengers have come to him in the guise of simple human beings, passing wayfarers. Abraham not only greets them by inviting them into his tent but also presents them with a feast and an opportunity to rest and refresh themselves, waiting upon them personally (Genesis 18:1–8).

The twentieth-century commentator Benno Jacob maintains that from the very beginning Abraham knew who his visitors were. He points out that the story begins with "The Lord appeared to him" (Genesis 18:1) and in the third verse Abraham addresses them as "Adonai," meaning "my lords" which is also an appellation of God. E. A. Speiser and most modern commentators, on the other hand, take the same position as the midrash, that Abraham thought they were human beings. Speiser is certain that it is not until verse 10 that Abraham understands that it is God and not men speaking to him. "Adonai" here may well be a double entendre. Abraham uses it as a way of addressing humans, but we — the readers — know that God, "Adonai," is there.

Why does God choose to convey His message through these beings rather than speak directly to Abraham? It is not as if He has not addressed him directly before. The midrash portrays Abraham as upset that because of the heat of the day there were no strangers passing to whom he could offer hospitality (*Genesis Rabbah* 48:8–9). Perhaps this is the key to the matter. By sending "men" to Abraham, God is conducting another of the tests that Abraham must undergo, a test to see how he treats strangers.

Now that Abraham has been made aware of God's special relationship to him and his progeny, how will he deal with others — not his own kin? Will "chosenness" spoil him and lead him to arrogance and selfishness? What better way to test that than this?

Obviously Abraham passes the test with flying colors. Not only does he extend his hospitality to these strangers. He — a rich sheik — invites them personally to partake of his hospitality. The narrative stresses his concern with verbs such as "he ran" and "Abraham hastened." In the midrash Rabbi Joshua uses this as a lesson that important people should be willing to serve those less important than themselves (*Sifre Deuteronomy* 38).

It is significant that only after Abraham has demonstrated his care for others is he informed that next year Sarah will bear him a son. Having passed this test, he is worthy of that miracle.

Later rabbinic tradition laid much stress upon the importance of hospitality to strangers and found in Abraham the prototype of the generous person. "Whoever possesses three qualities is numbered among the disciples of our father Abraham: a generous spirit, a humble soul and a modest spirit" (*Pirkei Avot* 5:21).

2. Two Trials

Vayera could be titled "The Trials of Abraham." It is the central portion of the narrative of Abraham's life and describes several events in which his character is put to the test. When we have completed reading this section we understand why Abraham was worthy of being the beloved friend of God (Isaiah 41:8) and the founder of God's treasured people, Israel. He shows himself not only to be generous and hospitable, but also kind and loving, a champion of justice and mercy, capable of sacrifice and devotion to God. The section ends with the last trial — the binding of Isaac (Genesis 22:1–19).

The two trials that are depicted here are the most crucial events in the life of Abraham — the binding of Isaac and the story of the wicked cities of Sodom and Gomorrah. It is not accidental that these two are found together. As a matter of fact the story of the wicked cities interrupts the narrative of

Isaac's birth and subsequent history. There is a deliberate juxtaposition of these two events for they contain the very paradox and essence of Abraham's character. In the one he argues passionately for justice. In the other he submits silently to the will of God. Neither story is simple to comprehend but both are important for an understanding of Judaism.

The first of the two trials is in regard to the fate of the cities of the plain where Abraham's nephew Lot has chosen to settle. These cities, Sodom and Gomorrah, are wealthy and prosperous. They are lush, watered oases, "like the garden of the Lord, like the land of Egypt" (Genesis 13:10). That is why Lot chose to live there. But they are also the seats of moral corruption (Genesis 13:13). Violence is a way of life; theft, sexual immorality, corruption, contempt for the poor and the weak are the fabric of this "civilization." Just as earlier God had decided to bring the flood when humankind became corrupt (Genesis 6:11-13), so now the Lord determines to cause the destruction of these cesspools of immorality (Genesis 18:20-21). But before doing so, God decides to involve Abraham in this decision.

We might have thought that Abraham would be involved because of his family connection, but to our surprise that is not the case at all. Rather God says, "Shall I hide from Abraham what I am about to do, since Abraham is to become a great and populous nation and all the nations of the earth are to bless themselves by him? For I have singled him out, *that he may instruct his children and his posterity to keep the way of the Lord by doing what is just and right*" (Genesis 18:17-19). These amazing verses instruct us not only about the great respect in which Abraham is held by God, but also concerning the task that is his and that is ours as his descendants. It is no less than keeping "the way of the Lord" which is immediately defined as "doing what is just and right." If you want to know what it means to be a Jew, a descendant of Abraham, here you have it as concisely and clearly as you could desire.

The decision of the Holy One to punish the two cities is not capricious. Rather — as in the case of the flood — the Torah makes certain to let us know that it is based on moral and ethical considerations. The Torah even depicts God as saying that He will "go down to see whether" or not they are truly guilty of immoral conduct (Genesis 18:21), emphasizing God's concern for justice and teaching us, as the Sages understood, that we must be very cautious in making judgments.

Abraham is about to receive a lesson in the meaning of justice and concern for human life. Just as parents who are concerned with the moral development of their children will seek opportunities to demonstrate to them the meaning of morality, so God opens before Abraham the moral dilemma of justice and mercy in the concrete case of these cities and waits to see how Abraham will react.

Abraham's reaction is immediate. God had said that Abraham's task was to teach his children to do that which is just and right and Abraham demonstrates that his concern is exactly that. He dares to question the justice and the righteousness of God's decision. Unlike Noah who uttered not a word when he was told that all of humankind was to be destroyed (Genesis 6:22), Abraham — politely but firmly — says, "Will You sweep away the innocent along with the guilty?" and begins to bargain with God concerning the minimum number of righteous people that would justify a decision not to destroy the cities (Genesis 18:23). He starts with the number fifty — a number that God is willing to accept (Genesis 18:24-26). Considering the fact that there must have been at the very least a few thousand inhabitants there, the ratio of righteous to wicked is rather small — and yet Abraham would consider that justice! As he says, "Shall not the Judge of all the earth deal justly?" (Genesis 18:25).

The midrash very cleverly indicates that actually Abraham is asking not for justice but for mercy. He wants the entire city — with all the wicked in it — to be saved if there are even ten righteous people in it. Thus the midrash reads verse 18:25 not as a question, as the *pshat* (simple meaning) has it — "Shall not the Judge of all the earth deal justly?" — but as a statement: "The Judge of all the earth *shall not* deal justly" but mercifully. You cannot have it both ways — either there will be full justice or there will be a world. For the world to continue to exist it must be judged with mercy (see *Genesis Rabbah* 49:9). This discussion with Abraham must be exactly what God had in mind. He wants Abraham to be critical, to search for justice and mercy — even if it means questioning God — and to bequeath this as a legacy to his descendants. It is this story which serves as the basis for the concerns of such prophets as Amos and Jeremiah for justice in the conduct of human affairs and for the right to question God in the name of justice, as did Rabbi Levi of Berdichev in the famous "Kaddish," in which he asks God why He brings so much suffering upon His people Israel.

Abraham's concern for human life is astounding. He has no personal interest in the people of these cities. If his care were for Lot he could have said, "Save Lot and his family — they do not deserve to die," but he did not. Incidentally we should note that God's plan is to save the innocent in any case. That is why the angelic messengers are sent to Lot's house to rescue him and his family (Genesis 19:12). Rather Abraham is concerned with a just and merciful world and cannot conceive that the God he worships would have it any other way. We can contrast him not only with Noah who showed no concern for human life or for justice or mercy but also with Jonah who was appalled at the thought that the wicked might be saved by the simple act of repentance (Jonah 4:1-3).

How pleased God must have been with Abraham's dialogue, as pleased as a parent when the child demonstrates moral concern. Here was a man of faith and belief who did not hesitate to challenge God Himself when he thought that an injustice was being done. Here was a man who cared not only for his welfare and the welfare of his family but for total strangers. Here was a man who would prefer to see thousands of wicked people spared rather than have a few innocent people perish.

The other story, that of the trial of Abraham, when he is commanded to "offer him [Isaac] as a burnt offering" (Genesis 22:2), stands in contrast to Sodom since here Abraham offers not a word of protest. He remains silent and never once speaks to God during this entire ordeal. Perhaps his silence may be explained by the fact that here the action involves him and his family (considered as one entity) and not other people. Thus Abraham will argue with God about others, but if a demand is made of him directly, he will obey — as he did when told to leave his home and journey to an unknown land.

The midrash offers quite a different picture; although it depicts Abraham as saying nothing until the story is almost finished, at that time he does question God and even makes demands of Him as a compensation for what God has put him through (*Tanhuma Vayera*). The very fact that the rabbis went so far in reinterpreting the story may indicate that they too were disturbed by the moral dilemma it presents. The story itself has always been troubling to commentators, ancient and modern. Why should God demand such a thing, and why should Abraham be willing to do it? Perhaps Abraham should have refused.

It may help if we try to understand this story against the background of its time and of ancient beliefs and practices. The sacrifice of children was practiced in many ancient cultures and, in certain places, even well into more recent times. Later on the prophets denounced the pagan practice of offering children to the god Molech and Micah asked, "Shall I give my firstborn for my transgression, the fruit of my body for my sins?" (Micah 6:7).

It is suggested that the story of Abraham's trial accomplished three things: First, it taught that God does not want human sacrifice. Abraham's action of sacrificing a ram without even being commanded to do so (Genesis 22:13) established the precedent that animal sacrifice was sufficient and would become the norm in Israel. This is especially important in view of the fact that the place where this happened would in the future be identified as the site of the Temple. Secondly, the story would answer the questions of pagans who might say, "We are more god-fearing than you. We are willing to sacrifice our children for our gods and you only bring animal offerings!" to which Israel could reply: "Abraham would have done so if God had really wished, but he was taught that this is not God's will." Thirdly, it provides a reason why God should have bestowed His special blessing upon Abraham. It was because Abraham demonstrated complete obedience and loyalty to God even under the most difficult circumstances: "Because you have done this...I will bestow My blessing upon you" (Genesis 22:16–17).

"The deeds of the ancestors serve as an example for their children," taught the rabbis, and in the life of Abraham we see this clearly. In pursuing justice and loving mercy, all the while being willing to follow God's commands, we prove ourselves to be the true children of Abraham. No wonder such a man was fit for the task God had given him. Is it not an honor for us to be the descendants of Abraham and to have the task of bringing to reality the ideal of doing that which is just and right?

Ḥayei Sarah   חיי שרה

Genesis 23:1–25:18 | בראשית כג:א-כה:יח

1. Abraham Prepares for the Future

In *Ḥayei Sarah* the Torah devotes an inordinate number of verses to two
events that at first glance might not seem all that important. The first is the
purchase of a burial place for Sarah, the second the finding of a wife for Isaac.

Regarding the first, we read an elaborate tale of bargaining between Abraham and Ephron the Hittite for a burial plot in a cave in Ephron's field in
Hebron, then called Kiriat-arba. Obviously this story has practical and
symbolic meaning far beyond the respect that was to be shown to Sarah, our
first Matriarch.

On one level we see here an example of polite bargaining in which the
seller offers the product as a gift — at the same time managing to mention the
price — and the buyer, understanding the subtleties of trading, insists upon
paying for it (Genesis 23:3-16). But on a deeper level something more is
involved. Abraham is not merely seeking burial rights, nor would he have
accepted this as a gift — even if it had sincerely been offered. Rather he is
determined to make a legal purchase of a portion of land in Canaan, land that
would then belong to him and his progeny after him. Modern Biblical scholars have pointed out that the terminology used regarding the sale, such as "at
the full price" and "at the going merchant's rate," is the same as that used in
Near Eastern court records of that period. Indeed the conclusion of the sale
(Genesis 23:17-19) could well be a legal contract. Abraham, as a "resident
alien" (Genesis 23:4) has no legal way of buying land and so he has to
convince Ephron to make an exception for him. The reason is that Abraham
wants to anchor God's promise, the promise to grant him the land of Canaan,

in reality before he dies. He may not possess the entire land, but he has at least a portion in it.

Although rabbinic legend taught that Abraham wanted this specific place because he knew it was the burial place of Adam and Eve (*Genesis Rabbah* 58:4), the Torah itself ascribes no particular importance to the place. By stating at the very beginning "Sarah died in Kiriat-arba — now Hebron — in the land of Canaan" (Genesis 23:2), the Torah may be indicating that since that is where she died, Abraham sought there a place in which to bury her. What was truly important was that it was "*in the land of Canaan.*" Thus, paradoxically, the death of Sarah becomes the occasion for the fulfillment of the promise of a land for the children of Abraham and Sarah. Abraham may be a man of faith, but he is also a practical man who wishes to take the steps necessary to insure the future of his family and of the people his family will eventually become. In order for God's plan to become a reality, human beings must undertake the necessary actions.

The second story, occupying a full sixty-seven verses in Genesis 24, is similarly concerned with assuring the future. After purchasing land, Abraham seeks an appropriate wife for his son Isaac for he knows that "it is through Isaac that offspring shall be continued for you" (Genesis 21:12). Here too there is a divine promise that awaits fulfillment. Although it may be that marriages were usually arranged in Biblical times, it is to be noted that there is no indication of this with Abraham and Sarah and certainly not concerning Jacob and Rachel, a true love match.

Yet there are two factors that compelled Abraham to send his servant back to Abraham's family in order to return with a wife for his son. One is the passive nature of Isaac. Of all the Patriarchs he is the least adventurous. He is not a pioneer like his father nor a wanderer like his son Jacob. Perhaps his one adventure in life — the three-day journey he took with his father to Mount Moriah — was enough to make him cautious of further journeys. Or perhaps he was meant to spend his entire life in Canaan in order to symbolize the fact that this land was to belong to Abraham's seed. Isaac remains there as a living symbol of the claim to the land. This explains why Abraham tells his servant that no matter what, he is not to take Isaac back to Abraham's native land (Genesis 24:6, 8). The woman must come to Isaac in Canaan and not vice versa. The other factor is that Abraham does not want Isaac to marry someone from the natives of the land who, as the Torah makes clear elsewhere, do not live up to the moral standards Abraham wanted. For example we read in Leviticus 18:3, "You shall not copy the practices of the land of Egypt where you dwelt, or of the land of Canaan to which I am taking you." Later on Isaac too would not permit Jacob to take a wife from among the Canaanites (Genesis 28:1).

So it is that with the last important actions of his long, exciting and fulfilling life, Abraham takes the practical steps needed to insure the future — the acquisition of the land, instilling the importance of dwelling in the land in his son, and guaranteeing that his son will marry a proper wife so that they will be able to continue the tradition and pass it on to the next generation. This is neither a failing on the part of Abraham nor an indication of lack of faith in God's ability to fulfill the promises made to him. Judaism teaches that we are not to wait passively for miracles but take the steps needed to bring about the fulfillment of our destinies. We are active, not passive, partners with God in creating the world and perfecting it. Having taken all of these steps, the Torah could write as his epitaph, "And Abraham breathed his last, dying at a good ripe age, old and contented; and he was gathered to his kin" (Genesis 25:8). No one could ask for more.

2. The Matriarchs

Hayei Sarah, perhaps more than any other portion, directs our attention to the role of the Matriarchs — the mothers of Israel — in our history. It begins with the death of Sarah and continues, as we have seen, with the story of the way in which the second Matriarch, Rebekah, was chosen to be the wife of Isaac.

Sarah is unique and is granted greater attention and respect in the Scripture than any of the other Matriarchs. Her death and burial are not only recorded, but the exact years of her life are spelled out: "Sarah's lifetime — the span of Sarah's life — came to one hundred and twenty-seven years" (Genesis 23:1). The death of none of the other Matriarchs is recorded in this way. Only the years of the lives of the Patriarchs and other important men are so inscribed. Her importance is shown further by the fact that earlier on Abraham is told by God to listen to her advice (Genesis 21:12). She is the only woman in the Bible whose name is changed by God (Genesis 17:15). The prophet Isaiah mentions her by name in such a way as to equate her with Abraham: "Look back to Abraham your father and to Sarah who brought you forth" (51:2). The story of the purchase of a special burial place for her indicates her importance. And, perhaps most of all, the fact that when her son Isaac marries it says that "Isaac loved her, and thus found comfort after his mother's death" (Genesis 24:67) indicates her special importance, as well as the importance of mothers and wives in general.

And yet for all that Sarah remains somewhat elusive. What do we know of her? She was Abraham's half-sister (Genesis 20:12) — a relationship that later would have been forbidden for marriage according to Torah law. She was an exceedingly beautiful woman (Genesis 12:11, 14). It is interesting that the Torah goes out of its way to tell of this, and later on to mention specifically Rebekah's beauty (Genesis 24:16) even though Proverbs says specifically "Beauty is illusory" (31:30). Sarah's reaction to the news that she will have a child in her old age is problematic. She laughs and the laughter is understood as lack of belief — for which she is mildly rebuked (Genesis 18:13-15). Her action in insisting that Abraham send away Hagar and Ishmael (Genesis 21:10) "distressed Abraham greatly" (Genesis 21:11) and leaves an impression that Sarah was a hard woman who made Abraham's life difficult. This impression is enhanced by the fact that Abraham goes out of his way to treat Hagar and Ishmael kindly. The Torah, however, supports Sarah's action. And of course the midrash totally justifies it by describing Ishmael's actions as either idolatrous, immoral or dangerous (*Genesis Rabbah* 53:11). In this case one might say that Sarah represents the "quality of justice" while Abraham exemplifies "the quality of mercy." There may indeed be times when justice, even if it be harsh, is required.

All in all there is something remote about Sarah. Her very name — which means princess — indicates that she is royalty as far as our people is concerned. Royalty generally remains distant and aloof. Her dedication to Abraham is unquestioned. Her willingness to put herself in danger for his sake is proof of that. She surely shares his values and joins in his adventure.

The story of the second Matriarch, which begins in this portion, is somehow a much more human portrayal. We meet Rebekah performing the most humble task — drawing water (Genesis 24:16). She too is described as being very beautiful. We immediately see that she is also kind and generous and has that quality that was so much a part of Abraham — welcoming strangers (Genesis 24:25).

The description of the first meeting of Rebekah with her intended groom, Isaac, is a brief but moving love story — the first love story in the Torah. In fact the Torah goes out of its way to tell us that "Isaac loved her" (Genesis 24:67), a most unusual comment for the Torah. The marriage may have been arranged, but it was much more than a business matter.

In the following portion we learn much more about Rebekah and we see her as a strong and determined woman, no less so than Sarah, who also fights for what she understands to be the rights of her beloved son. The resemblance to Sarah is not only in her outward beauty, but also in her nature — though only in part.

The story of the servant's search for a bride for Isaac is instructive of a number of points. It illustrates how important it was that the woman be of good character. She is viewed not merely as an instrument for childbearing and someone to take care of the cooking, but as one who has enormous influence in the household and over the upbringing of a child. Abraham goes to all of this trouble to find Isaac the right wife specifically because he understands that with the wrong wife, Isaac will not be able to continue on his father's path of righteousness. We also see in this story that although the rights of women were far from equal with those of men — as unfortunately is the case even today in many societies, including our own — she did have certain rights, including the right to say "no" regarding her marriage partner (Genesis 24:57-58). It was on this basis that rabbinic law determined that a woman may not be married without her consent (*Genesis Rabbah* 60:57 and Rashi on that verse).

It would be a falsification of history and of the sacred text to say that the Matriarchs played the same role in the history of our people as did the Patriarchs. The covenant with its promise of blessing is made specifically with Abraham, Isaac and Jacob individually, not with Sarah, Rebekah, Rachel and Leah. Nevertheless it should not be forgotten that of Sarah God said, "I will bless her so that she shall give rise to nations; rulers of peoples shall issue from her" (Genesis 17:16).

The laws of the Torah, for all their concern with women, reflect a society in which men dominated and in which women were dependent upon their husbands in many ways. The laws of inheritance discriminate against women

(Numbers 26:53, 27:6–11). A husband can annul his wife's vow (Numbers 30:2–17) and only men can grant divorce (Deuteronomy 24:1). Many rabbinic enactments attempted to enhance the rights of women, but were far from granting them equality, although there is no question but that they are treated with respect in our tradition. As Prof. Judith Hauptman, an expert on Talmudic law, has pointed out, women at that early time did not expect equality but protection.

The depiction of these women in the Torah as more than stock figures, but as real people who played an important role in our history, is indicative of Judaism's general attitude toward women. Upon this basis it is possible to build an attitude of respect and to work toward the goal of creating a society in which the rights of women will indeed be equal to those of men.

Toldot תולדות

Genesis 25:19–28:9 | בראשית כה:יט-כח:ט

1. Isaac: The Planter and Builder

The story of Jacob and Esau with which this portion begins and ends is so compelling that we often ignore the part that deals with the life and actions of Isaac. After all, the portion does begin with the words "This is the story of Isaac" (Genesis 25:19). True, Isaac sometimes seems to be an uninteresting figure, a passive personality first dominated by his father and then manipulated by his wife, Rebekah. He appears also to be the perfect example of "the sandwich generation," wedged between his father, the great founder, and his son, the great adventurer. What did he ever do in his life? Abraham circumcised himself at the age of ninety-nine (Genesis 17:24). Isaac was circumcised when he was eight days old (Genesis 21:4). Later he permitted his father to bind him on the altar and nearly sacrifice him. He waited at home while his father's servant went in search of a wife for him and, in the latter part of this portion, he permits himself to be deceived by his wife and his son. One can also question Isaac's judgment in preferring Esau over Jacob (Genesis 25:28) — even if Isaac had a taste for venison — and in wanting to give a blessing to Esau rather than to Jacob. His blindness seems to be a perfect symbol of his life. And yet this man deserves another look.

The first thing that he does in this portion is to plead for his wife before God "and the Lord responded to his plea" (Genesis 25:21). One should contrast this with a similar story concerning Jacob and Rachel. We know how deeply in love Jacob was with Rachel, yet when she is barren and cries out "Give me children, or I shall die" Jacob is "incensed at Rachel, and said, 'Can I take the place of God, who has denied you fruit of the womb?'" (Genesis

30:1-2). Jacob could have learned tenderness and concern from his father. The fact that Isaac could intercede with God also indicates his status. The same word "intercede" was applied to Abraham: "He is a prophet, he will intercede for you" (Genesis 20:7). Isaac, then, is a kind and loving husband. As we saw, although the marriage was arranged, the Torah does say, "Isaac loved her" (Genesis 24:67). He is the only one of the Patriarchs to have only one wife. He is a prophet as well, given access to God as was his father Abraham.

Isaac was also a man of peace who made a pact of friendship with the inhabitants of the land (Genesis 26:27-31), taking the initiative to avoid hostilities. The most important thing that Isaac did was to plant wheat and to dig wells. Wells had been dug previously by Abraham, but the Philistines had stopped them up. Now Isaac dug them again and dug new ones in other places in the land (Genesis 26:15-22). To the last Abraham had remained a wanderer, caring for sheep and other animals but never settling down. In contrast, the Torah tells us "Isaac sowed in that land and reaped a hundred-fold the same year" (Genesis 26:12). The herdsman became a farmer. The wanderer became a man of the land. In other words, Isaac solidified what his father had begun and fulfilled what God wanted of him when He told him that he was not allowed to leave Canaan (Genesis 26:2-5). He settled the land, worked the land and prospered thereon. Not everyone can be first. Perhaps it is just as important to know how to build upon that which came before, to solidify it and to expand it. Knowing how to settle down is no less important than knowing how to take a journey.

So let us give Isaac his due. He may not have been perfect, he may not even have been charismatic or exciting, but he was a solid individual who carried forward the work of establishing the people upon the land they had been promised.

2. Jacob: The Enigma

This portion introduces the third and most complex of the Patriarchs — Jacob. If Abraham is "the great father" and Isaac the quiet, passive successor, Jacob is the wanderer, at times the deceiver and ultimately the struggler. The two main incidents that are related in this portion both feature him in a negative light. In the first he takes advantage of Esau's nature to persuade him to sell his birthright as the firstborn of the twins (Genesis 25:30-34). It can be argued here that Jacob did not really deceive or coerce Esau. Nevertheless it hardly seems like a shining example of brotherly love!

The second incident is much more problematic since it does indeed contain real deception. Under his mother's urging, he disguises himself as Esau, pretends to be him and even answers when his father asks him, "Who are you, my son?" "I am Esau, your firstborn" (Genesis 27:18-19). True, a midrash takes advantage of the Hebrew text and parses it differently as if it said, "I [i.e., It's me]. Esau is your firstborn" (*Genesis Rabbah* 65:18) — but this is by no means the simple meaning of the text.

The Torah's moral judgment of Jacob's actions will become apparent in the subsequent portion, in which the deceiver is deceived by Laban (Genesis 29:25-27) — a punishment that fits the crime (in rabbinic parlance *midah k'neged midah*). The prophets also used Jacob as an example of improper conduct, playing on his name so that it came to mean one who acts crookedly or takes advantage of a brother. "The Lord...punished Jacob for his conduct, requiting him for his deeds" proclaimed Hosea (12:3) and Jeremiah similarly used Jacob's name as a symbol of crooked behavior (9:3).

It is abundantly apparent in the Biblical narratives that the Matriarchs and Patriarchs were after all human beings, subject to the same weaknesses and temptations as all of us; this is often pointed out by the classical commentators. To be human is to err and Judaism knows no human beings who are above that. The Matriarchs and Patriarchs were neither evil nor were they scoundrels. Therefore we must wonder what it was that caused Jacob and, even more so, Rebekah to practice such deception.

The answer to this puzzle seems to lie in the word "blessing" which, as Nahum Sarna points out, is used no fewer than "seven times and its verbal form exactly twenty-one times" in this episode (*The JPS Torah Commentary: Genesis* [Philadelphia: Jewish Publication Society of America, 1989] p. 189). Rebekah's concern can best be understood when we recall that during her difficult pregnancy she inquired of the Lord and received a divine answer: "Two nations are in your womb, two separate people shall issue from your body; one people shall be mightier than the other, and the older shall serve the younger" (Genesis 25:23).

Since the text does not say that she told Isaac of this oracle, we may assume that she kept this knowledge to herself. Thus the decades pass, the children grow up, she sees their nature — Jacob "a mild man who dwelt in tents" and Esau "a skillful hunter, a man of the outdoors" (Genesis 25:27). This may sound like a neutral description, but it is not. Hunting carries a negative image in Israelite culture. Esau reveals himself to be a man of unbridled physical appetites and then, when he is forty years old, marries two Hittite women who are "a source of bitterness" to his parents (Genesis 26:34). The oracle seems to be playing itself out when suddenly Isaac announces that he is going to give his deathbed blessing to Esau (Genesis 27:4). To Rebekah this may well seem to be a dangerous action that will impede the oracle. This blessing will mean that Esau and not Jacob will be the chosen heir to Isaac's patriarchal position. Therefore she decides to intervene and Jacob — too much under her influence and too weak-willed to resist — obeys her even though he has his doubts (Genesis 27:11–13).

That Rebekah and Jacob were morally wrong is clear. But was she correct in her assessment of Isaac's intent? Was Isaac really so blind that he could not see that Esau was not fit to inherit the mantle of Abraham and the blessing that God had bestowed on both Abraham and Isaac? True, "his eyes were too dim to see," but was his judgment also impaired? Perhaps and perhaps not. The text tells us that Isaac favored his son Esau "because he had a taste for game" (Genesis 25:28). This seems so completely out of character for Isaac — especially when we note that when Jacob brings him a stew of kid meat he accepts it as if it were game! Perhaps this is the pathetic excuse of a father who would rather not see the truth, rather not acknowledge that one of his children — his firstborn at that — is not worthy. How often we see parents making excuses for their children's faults or looking for some trait that they can single out for praise. This too is human.

Isaac may have been too fond of Esau and may have wanted to give him more of a blessing than he deserved, but he was not so blind as to intend to grant him *the* blessing, the special blessing conferred by God that Abraham's children would multiply, would inherit the land and would become a blessing to all (see Genesis 22:17–18; 26:3–4). This promise made to Abraham would continue and be passed on through Jacob who — though not perfect — was by far the more suited of the two to become the ancestor of God's covenanted people.

When Isaac blesses Jacob, thinking that he is Esau, he bestows a very different blessing, one of prosperity and power, but not *the* blessing of Abraham (Genesis 27:28–29), while later, knowing full well what Jacob has done, he sends him off with these words: "May *El Shaddai* bless you, make you fertile and numerous, so that you become an assembly of peoples. May He grant *the blessing of Abraham* to you and your offspring, that you may possess the land where you are sojourning, which God assigned to Abraham" (Genesis 28:3–4). Isaac knew all along to whom the Abrahamic blessing belonged, and it was not Esau.

Had Rebekah known his true intent, perhaps she would not have practiced that deception. Unfortunately, she did not realize the distinction between *a* blessing and *the* blessing. Even more unfortunately, she did not trust her husband's judgment enough to discuss this with him.

Maurice Samuels, in his book *Certain People of the Book* (New York: Alfred A. Knopf, 1955, p. 168ff), puts a different spin on this. Regardless of which blessing it was to be, Rebekah saw the danger in the very fact that Isaac would be blessing Esau before blessing Jacob, thus causing Esau to believe that he was receiving the mantle of leadership and enabling him and his descendants to claim that Jacob was the rejected one. In that case, Rebekah was justified in what she did. Yet somehow the idea of the deception seems wrong. She still could have gone to Isaac and told him that his act would have disastrous consequences. As it is, her action brought upon Jacob a life of trouble and distress. How careful we must be in our relationships with others — especially with those closest to us.

God, in search of someone who could be an example to the world and father a nation that could demonstrate God's ways on earth, found Abraham and entrusted this task to his offspring. Isaac was the one most likely to continue it and now the task falls to Jacob, for all his imperfections.

Vayetze   ויצא

Genesis 28:10–32:3 | בראשית כח:י-לב:ג

1. Jacob in Exile

The active part of Jacob's life story can be divided into three parts, each of which is found in one Torah portion. The first — *Toldot* — depicts his youth, the time of his immaturity and his devious behavior. The second — *Vayetze* — is the tale of his maturing years, when the deceiver is deceived and undergoes a change of character. The third — *Vayishlaḥ* — depicts Jacob the victor, who overcomes himself and his opponents.

This middle section is devoted to his years in exile, living with his uncle Laban and struggling to establish his family and to earn a living. However, the story begins and ends with angels and the erection of sacred pillars, both before he reaches Laban and when he leaves him (Genesis 28:10-21; 31:51-32:3). These serve as parentheses marking off this period of his life. Before it he is part of his parents' household, under his mother's influence. After it he is entangled in the intrigues of his children. Here, for a brief period at least, he is his own person, responsible for his own actions. It is not accidental that the opening verses (Genesis 28:10-21) depict Jacob totally alone and that the closing episode (both at the end of this section and the beginning of the next) again finds him alone (Genesis 32:2-32).

The opening story, the vision at Beth-el, is both awe inspiring and strange. We can feel Jacob's plight and his fear in the description of his spending the night out in the open with a stone for a pillow (Genesis 28:11). Remember this is a man who was "a mild man who dwelt in tents" (Genesis 25:27), not someone — like Esau — who was used to the rough outdoors life. He was pampered by his mother and is now suddenly on his own, away from the

41

safety and comfort of home, in the dark, with only a stone — of all things — for a pillow.

And then, at this least likely of moments, he has a dream in which he sees not only angels but also "the Lord standing beside" or possibly "upon" a grandiose stairway to heaven. As Nahum Sarna points out, this imagery may be taken from the huge Babylonian ziggurat, "the temple tower...equipped with an external stairway or ramp" (*The JPS Torah Commentary: Genesis*, p. 198). And in this dream the Lord speaks to him, grants him the promise made to Abraham and Isaac and promises to protect him and bring him home safely.

This is not the first time that God speaks to someone. He spoke to Adam and Eve, to Noah, to Abraham many times. Concerning Abraham it is even written that the Lord "appeared to him" (Genesis 12:7 and 17:1) — that is, in addition to hearing God, he had a visual experience of Him as well. God also spoke to Isaac, in a similar situation, but with a different message — warning him *not* to leave the land and promising that He would be with him and grant him the blessing of Abraham (Genesis 26:2-5). At no time before this, however, do we find such an elaborate and overwhelming visual experience — even though it is only a dream. The appearance of God to Isaiah (6:1-13), which became the basis for the Kedushah prayer, is a close parallel to Jacob's experience and also causes Isaiah to be overwhelmed and to feel, as did Jacob, that he had experienced something totally outside the realm of the normal.

Why this elaborate manifestation of God's Presence? Although the story may serve to explain why Beth-el (the House of God) was called Beth-el, it has a deeper purpose. The verbal content of the vision concentrates on the fact that Jacob is to be the recipient of the blessing of Abraham and receive God's protection on his journey so that he will return in peace. Since Jacob had already received this blessing from his father (Genesis 28:4) it seems redundant for it to be repeated here, but it is not. First of all, the blessing must come from the divine source. A human being cannot really bestow it. Secondly, Jacob received it after having deceived his father. His father may have forgiven him, but how was Jacob to know that he really deserved the blessing and that God was willing for him to have it after all he had done? Perhaps he was no longer worthy. This dream assures him that regardless of his misdeeds, he — and not Esau — is the carrier of the blessing.

The dream also serves to calm his fears. Jacob has reason to be afraid. His brother has sworn to kill him, in addition to which he is setting out on a difficult journey to a place he has never been. How can he feel secure and know that he will even return home? For this reason God assures him of protection in a way that will make an impression upon him. Freudians, who view dreams as wish fulfillment, would see here a manifestation of Jacob's unconscious mind bringing him peace on the two subjects that trouble him the most — his crooked way of attaining a blessing and the danger presented by his brother.

One would think that Jacob would then feel reassured, but the text seems to indicate that, although relieved, he is still not convinced. This is implied by his vow, "*If* God remains with me, *if* He protects me...the Lord shall be my God" (Genesis 28:20-21). This seems very strange since these are the very things God has just promised him. No wonder various midrashim try to interpret this differently, some even saying that the order is wrong and the vow came before the dream, which was an answer to it (see, for example, *Genesis Rabbah* 70:4).

Yet let us not judge Jacob too harshly. He is in a difficult situation and faces great danger. His mind will not be totally relieved until he actually returns safely home. He is on the path to maturity, but not quite there.

We may be critical of Jacob, indeed we should be, but if we are honest with ourselves we will see much of him in ourselves. Few of us are heroic figures like Abraham. Many of us are like Jacob — flawed, taking bad advice, sometimes callous of others, thinking of ourselves first, slightly skeptical, waiting to be convinced. But if we are fortunate, we will mature. The first sign of being on the way to maturity is the realization that Jacob has, "Surely the Lord is present in this place, and I did not know it. How awesome is this place" (Genesis 28:16-17). After that realization there will still be ups and downs, but we — like Jacob — will never be same.

2. Rachel: A Love Story

Jacob's great adventure begins as he journeys alone from his home and makes his way to the dwelling of his uncle Laban. It is there that the Torah relates the only love story in these five books — that of Jacob and Rachel. This does not mean that other couples in the Torah did not love one another — we can assume that they did and in the case of Isaac and Rebecca we are explicitly told so, but it is mentioned after the arranged marriage, not before (Genesis 24:67). In the story of Jacob and Rachel we find all the classical elements of a love story: the woman is charming and beautiful, the suitor has to overcome tremendous obstacles to obtain her but to him they are as nothing because of his love for her. And then there is the tragic end — her early death in childbirth.

What is strange is that we actually know so little of Rachel and yet we identify so strongly with her on an emotional level. Most of her story is confined to the tale of her barrenness and the fervent desire to have children. "Give me children, or I shall die," she says to her husband (Genesis 30:1), and proceeds to find ways to compete with her fecund sister Leah, of whom she is bitterly jealous. Following Sarah's example, she gives her husband her maid as a concubine so that the resulting children can be counted as hers (Genesis 30:3). Again like Sarah she finally does conceive and bear a son — Joseph (Genesis 30:22–24). The other action she takes is to steal her father's household gods (Genesis 31:19), an act she hides from Jacob. We are unsure of the significance of this act, but we see that Laban is infuriated by it. Is it a symbol of his authority? An act of revenge and spite? It is unlikely that Rachel took them to worship them, although later on Jacob insists that everyone in his entourage dispose of the "alien gods" in their midst (Genesis 35:2).

Thus we know less about Rachel than we know of Sarah, whose character is clearly delineated in the stories told about her. We know less than we know about Rebekah, whose dominant nature is spelled out in the story of her involvement in the deception of her husband. And yet Rachel is strangely appealing, the Matriarch with whom we can most clearly empathize. She is the most sympathetic of the four. We may feel sorry for Leah, but we do not love her. The reason for our sympathy for Rachel may be her premature death in childbirth which resulted in her burial in a lonely grave, rather than in the ancestral tomb of Makhpelah where the other Matriarchs and Patriarchs are buried. The Torah narrative goes out of its way to make us empathize with her by describing the event so vividly:

> When they were still some distance short of Ephrath, Rachel was in childbirth, and she had hard labor. When her labor was at the hardest, the midwife said to her, "Have no fear, for it is another boy for you." But as she breathed her last — for she was dying — she named

him Ben-oni [son of my suffering]; but his father called him
Benjamin [son of the right hand]. Thus Rachel died. She was buried
on the road to Ephrath — now Bethlehem. Over her grave Jacob set
up a pillar; it is the pillar at Rachel's grave to this day. (Genesis
35:16–20)

Thus there hovers about her the aura of a tragic love and an unsatisfied spirit,
separated from her beloved throughout all eternity.

Much later, Jacob, now an old man, recounts the story of Rachel's death to
Joseph and says, "When I was returning from Padan, Rachel died, to my
sorrow, while I was journeying in the land of Canaan, when still some
distance short of Ephrath; and I buried her there on the road to Ephrath"
(Genesis 48:7). The Hebrew is even more poignant and impossible to trans-
late — "*meita alai Rahel*," (Rachel died upon me), which the Sages understood
to mean that the death of a wife is felt most strongly by her husband (*Sanhedrin* 22b). In this verse we can feel Jacob's grief, which was not lessened by the
passing of so much time.

Jeremiah later used this image when he wanted to speak of the tragedy of
the exile that was to come upon the people of Judah:

A cry is heard upon a height — wailing, bitter weeping — Rachel
weeping for her children. She refuses to be comforted for her children, who are gone. Thus said the Lord: restrain your voice from
weeping, your eyes from shedding tears; for there is a reward for your
labor — declares the Lord: they shall return from the enemy's land.
And there is hope for the future — declares the Lord: your children
shall return to their country. (Jeremiah 31:15–17)

Thus it is Rachel, and not Sarah, Rebekah or Leah, who becomes the
symbolic mother of Israel, pleading for her children and being comforted by
God.

The prophet was most insightful in seizing upon the idea of children who
are gone, who are no more, as the essence of Rachel's being. Bearing children
was what mattered most to her. It was in that act that she lost her life. The
story of the "contest" — as it were — between the two sisters seems almost
comical, but it was not. It was deadly serious. Taken in context we can view it
as an important part of the saga of the creation of the Jewish people. Before

this each Matriarch gave birth once, hardly enough to fulfill God's promise of becoming a great nation. Here, because of the multiplicity of births, we have the true beginnings of a people, a nation. This is the reason that we are called "Israel"(Jacob's other name) and not "Isaac" or "Abraham." We are indeed part of a people and when we read this portion we read the story of human beings with deep human emotions, human beings who were the parents of us all.

Vayishlaḥ

וישלח

Genesis 32:4–36:43 | בראשית לב:ד-לו:מג

1. Men and Angels

As Jacob anxiously awaits his first meeting with his estranged brother Esau, he wrestles with a divine being at the river Jabok (Genesis 32:25). Although this being is called "a man" in the text, when Hosea retells the story he says, "He strove with an angel and prevailed" (Hosea 12:5). In this portion, the "man" says, "you have striven with beings divine and human and have prevailed" (Genesis 32:29). Jacob calls the place "Peniel, meaning 'I have seen a divine being face to face, yet my life has been preserved'" (Genesis 32:31).

In the Torah, angels usually serve as messengers of God, or as partial manifestations of God. They have no independent powers. This angel, however, is somewhat different. Although he is not God, he has the power of blessing and changing Jacob's name (though later, in Genesis 35:10, God Himself reiterates the change). Furthermore this angel comes into physical contact with Jacob in a way unprecedented in the other Biblical stories. Rather than coming with good news or good intent, this angel comes to wrestle with Jacob. To what purpose? To stop him from returning to his home? To defeat him? Although in the end he blesses Jacob, it is a blessing that Jacob forces upon him, as if, although the "man" came with malevolent intent, that intent was turned into a positive one — like the story of the seer Balaam (Numbers 22).

Many different interpretations have been offered concerning the identity of this "man." Some have assumed that this reflects ancient belief that each stream was ruled by a spirit. Jacob here encounters the spirit of the brook Jabok (Sarra, *Understanding Genesis*, p. 204). The Sages identify the "man" with Esau's protector, his guardian angel. They believed that each nation was assigned a heavenly being (*Yalkut Shimoni Genesis* 133). The struggle was a foreshadowing of the meeting with Esau and an assurance that in the struggle with his brother, Jacob would emerge victorious.

There is symbolic meaning to the fact that although he triumphs, Jacob is wounded and limps for the rest of his life. Is this a symbol of the future of Israel, the people that carries his name? Israel will prevail — that is the good news — but the cost of the struggle will not be small and we will always carry the scars. That seems to have been our fate.

There is another peculiarity about this story. First it states, "Jacob was left alone" but then it continues "and a man wrestled with him" (Genesis 32:25). If he was alone, how could there have been a man there? Is this a hint that the man with whom he wrestled was none other than himself?

Perhaps Jacob had to overcome not only his brother, but himself and his tendency to deceive. As we have previously noted, even the prophet Hosea saw him that way: "The Lord once indicted Judah and punished Jacob for his conduct, requited him for his deeds. In the womb he tried to supplant his brother; grown to manhood, ...he strove with an angel and prevailed" (Hosea 12:3–5). Jacob struggles with his baser instincts. Which will prevail — *Ya'akov*, the crooked one, or *Yisrael*, another name for Yeshurun, the root of which is *yashar*, straight? This man has tricked his way through life, sometimes on the right side of the thin line between deception and cleverness, sometimes on the wrong side. Now is the time for decision.

All of us appreciate Jacob's struggle. It is one that takes place within each of us. We are left alone, we struggle alone, we wrestle with ourselves and, if we are fortunate, we emerge limping but better than we were before, bearing a blessing.

2. Another Encounter of Two Brothers

Two incidents in this *parashah* deal with the problem of how one confronts an enemy. The first concerns Jacob and his brother Esau. Jacob has good reason to consider Esau an enemy. Esau's anger, which the Sages said was justified, has reached such proportions that he is ready to kill Jacob (Genesis 27:41).

This encounter is a great human drama. Jacob wishes to return to the land of Canaan, to go home, but this will require that he place himself in danger. Does Esau still intend to kill him or has his anger cooled with the passage of time? Jacob has no way of knowing the answer to that question. There is always the possibility that Esau has changed.

Perhaps Jacob has changed as well. His experiences, the experience of exile, of homelessness, of having to live under the tyranny of his father-in-law Laban, may have caused him to mature as well. From a quiet, home-loving boy who listened to his mother's advice too readily, he has become an experienced man of the world. He traveled with nothing but his walking stick and learned to live by his wits, in constant tension with a man who could and did exploit him at every turn. He found the woman he loved, contended with another he did not love, fathered a dozen children and became prosperous.

There is little reason, if any, to think that Esau has mellowed with the years. On the contrary, it would be most likely that he has nursed his grudge over the years and is more ready than ever to greet Jacob with a sword and not with a kiss. Jacob's anxiety is increased when his first message of reconciliation is met with the news that Esau is approaching with four hundred men (Genesis 32:7) — an entire army! The only possible explanation is that Esau intends to wipe out not only Jacob but also his entire family.

As for Jacob, it is clear that his character has changed. In the prayer he utters prior to his meeting with Esau we hear none of the deviousness of before, none of the doubt or self-pleading that was in his oath at Beth-el (Genesis 28:20-22). Instead he speaks as a man of humility and contrition, a man who is concerned with his family, his wives and his children, a man willing to put himself in harm's way for their sake (Genesis 33:1-3), a man who throws himself on the mercy of God and prepares well to meet his brother (Genesis 32:10-14).

Jacob's response to this situation is very logical. He takes some specific tactical steps to save at least part of the family by dividing it into two camps (Genesis 32:8). He humbly invokes God's help, reminding Him of His promise to deal kindly with him and to multiply his progeny (Genesis 32:10-13). He then attempts to placate Esau with lavish gifts (Genesis 32:15-21). Thus Jacob takes three steps. He attempts to make peace, he prepares to defend himself and his family and he prays. He hopes to achieve peace and reconciliation and is prepared to pay a significant price for it, but if he has no choice he will fight, asking for God's help.

The wisdom of Jacob's actions is seen in the result. Esau greets him warmly, embracing him and kissing him (Genesis 33:4–5). The Hebrew word for "he kissed him" is marked in the Torah text with diacritical dots, which usually indicate that there is a problem with the word. This caused the Sages to question the sincerity of the kiss. Some thought that the marks meant that the kiss was not sincere and was only intended to put Jacob off his guard. Other contended that — on the contrary — we would have naturally thought that Esau's kiss was deceptive. Therefore the marks indicate the opposite: it was genuine (*Avot d'Rabbi Natan A* 34).

According to this interpretation, when Esau saw Jacob's family, he felt true compassion. Jacob's subsequent words leave no doubt that even if at that moment Esau's affection was genuine, he did not expect it to last. Therefore he refuses Esau's invitations and separates himself from his brother as expeditiously as he can, rapidly putting space between them (Genesis 33:12–17). Esau is an emotional, impulsive man and Jacob knows that while he may have succeeded in pacifying him momentarily, Esau can turn against him just as easily and just as quickly.

All in all, Jacob demonstrates maturity, clarity of thought and good strategic thinking in his meeting with Esau, the enemy.

The sensitivity of our tradition to moral dilemmas is revealed here when the Sages comment upon the verse "Jacob was very afraid and troubled" (Genesis 32:8). Why, they ask, the two different words for "fear"? Would not one suffice? Because he was fearful and troubled by two things: lest Esau kill him — but also lest he be forced to kill Esau (*Genesis Rabbah* 76:2).

The dilemma of having to defend oneself, of arming oneself and having to seriously consider killing others — even in justified self-defense — is a serious one. How do you do this and remain human and sensitive? How do you avoid turning into a brutal person? This lies at the very heart of our lives today and is a real challenge to our society. To have power and use it in accord with morality and sensitivity is extremely difficult. Of course the hardest challenge is to do what Jacob set out to do — to turn an enemy into a friend.

Like most of us, Jacob was imperfect, but he struggled, and through his struggles he overcame not only his enemies but also his baser self. And in the

end he faced the most difficult situation — reconciliation with his brother —
and was successful, setting a pattern and an example for all of us.

The second instance of dealing with an enemy recorded in this section
concerns the encounter with Shechem, the son of Hamor, who rapes and
kidnaps Jacob's daughter, Dina, and then offers to marry her and pay Jacob a
high price for her (Genesis 34:1-12). The section is puzzling for several
reasons. We can understand that Jacob keeps silent at first because his sons,
who could fight to free their sister, are not present (Genesis 34:5). But why
does he say nothing when they do return? It is also clear that Jacob — and the
Torah — denounce the violent and deceitful action subsequently taken by his
sons. But why? Jacob says that by their action they have endangered the tribe,
possibly bringing an attack from all the inhabitants of the land (Genesis
34:30). Yet certainly they were obligated to do something to rescue their sister
and to avenge her dishonor. As they say so pungently, "Should our sister be
treated like a whore?" (Genesis 34:31). And even though they acted deceitfully, with guile (Genesis 34:13), were they not justified under the circumstances since they were heavily outnumbered?

We may have a clue to this mystery when we look at Jacob's deathbed
denunciation of Simeon and Levi:

> Their weapons are tools of lawlessness.... For when angry they slew
> men, and when pleased they maimed oxen. Cursed be their anger so
> fierce, and their wrath so relentless. (Genesis 49:5-7)

Thus the problem with their actions is not that they rescued their sister and
killed her rapist, but that they "slew all the males," "plundered the town,"
taking all the wealth, all the children and women as "captives and booty"
(Genesis 34:27-28). This must be seen in contrast to Abraham, who made
war to rescue his nephew Lot and, when it was all over, refused to take "so
much as a thread or a sandal strap" (Genesis 14:23).

Even in war, there are honorable and dishonorable ways of conduct.
Jacob's children, led by Simeon and Levi, have acted dishonorably and
inflicted disproportionate injury. They have slain those who were not
involved in the crime, when it was not necessary. The men were already
disabled and incapable of fighting. There was no need to kill them. There was
no excuse for spoil and plunder.

Similar problems occur today as well. The code of ethical conduct of the

Israel Defense Forces is an attempt to instill honorable conduct in our soldiers, even in times of war. It indicates things that may be done and things that must be avoided. For example it states:

> The IDF servicemen's purity of arms is their self-control in use of armed force. They will use their arms only for the purpose of achiev-ing their mission, without inflicting unnecessary injury to human life or limb, dignity or property, of both soldiers and civilians, with special consideration for the defenseless.

If Israeli soldiers act differently, they are violating this code of conduct and may be prosecuted and punished.

Jacob's sons had no restraint, and are therefore condemned even if the cause for which they fought was justified.

The lessons from these two instances are clear. Every effort should be made to follow the example of Jacob — to avoid conflict but to prepare for self-defense when it is unavoidable. When forced to fight, honorable ways should be found to confront the enemy. "All's fair in love and war" is not a Jewish concept and we should be proud that it is not. Jacob's condemnation of his own children was a moral act of significance that echoes down to our own days.

Vayeshev

וישב

Genesis 37:1–40:23 | בראשית לז:א-מ:כג

1. The Joseph Saga

Now that the simple patriarchal family has been transformed into a complex unit of brothers, each of whom will become the head of a tribe, the Torah no longer concerns itself with the question of which brother will carry the blessing of Abraham — all of them will. All of their descendants will merge into one people, which will be dedicated to God and receive God's blessings. Instead, the narrative concentrates on the life of one of them and tells the epic story of Joseph, which is the key to the history of the tribes. Because of him, they will descend into Egypt, the true smelting furnace that forges them into a people.

Previously we have read about Jacob's sons and some of their exploits. Now we come to the main saga, the story of Joseph and his relations with his brothers. This tale, which will occupy us until the end of the book of Genesis, is a much more fully developed story of one man's life than we have read before. It is truly a compelling novella that ranks with the great creations of world literature. On one level it is a stirring adventure; on another it demonstrates God's hand in the history of our people, providing a way for the family to survive in time of famine and bringing them to a place where they will develop from a family to a people and will experience God's hand in bringing them from slavery to freedom.

We read of Joseph's descent into the depths of slavery and imprisonment, just as the tribes later will be enslaved in Egypt. When we first meet Joseph, he is the darling favorite son of a doting father (Genesis 37:3). When we leave him at the end of this portion he is a prisoner in an Egyptian jail —

"forgotten" by all (Genesis 40:23). With great artistry the Torah depicts his descent — first "they took him and cast him into the pit" (Genesis 37:24), then he goes "down into Egypt" (Genesis 39:1) as a slave and then further down to prison (Genesis 39:20), alone and seemingly abandoned.

Although it is clear that Joseph is the hero of the story, he is by no means blameless. At best one could say that he was naïve; at worst, insensitive and proud. This was pointed out long ago by our Sages who said of him that the phrase in verse 37:2, "*v'hu na'ar*" (he was a youth), actually indicates that he acted in a foolish and immature way, "coloring his eyes, curling his hair, walking with a mincing step" (*Genesis Rabbah* 84:7). He is, after all, seventeen years old, hardly a child, and he brings his father "bad reports" of his brothers. Bad enough that his father favors him above the others because he is the eldest child of his beloved wife Rachel and gives him the infamous many-colored coat as a sign of his distinction. Now Joseph makes himself the tattle-tale. And when he has dreams indicating that he will rule over all of them, he foolishly does not hesitate to tell them the details. No wonder that when his father sends him to see what his brothers are doing, they have already moved elsewhere, no doubt hoping to escape his prying eyes (Genesis 37:17). He blithely continues until he tracks them down, which brings about his narrow escape from being slaughtered by them and his being sold into slavery instead. Physically he began at the top, but spiritually he was at the bottom.

It is no surprise, then, that they hate him. Of course that is no excuse for their attempt to kill him. If he is callous and overweening, most of them are simply cruel and vicious, with no thought of the value of a human life and no care for their father. The trial that the brothers have to go through to atone for this takes place in the next Torah portion, as does the resolution of the conflict with Joseph.

Of them all, only two brothers are credited with any human feeling — Reuben, the firstborn, and Judah, who is to become the ancestor of the most important tribe from which kings will spring. Reuben and Judah each give somewhat different advice, but their intent is clear: to save Joseph's life. Reuben suggests casting him into a pit (Genesis 37:22); Judah talks of selling him to the Ishmaelites (Genesis 37:27). One wonders, incidentally, why Benjamin, Joseph's only full brother, does not speak up. Being the youngest, was he afraid? Or was he even there? Perhaps Jacob kept him at home, coddling another child of his beloved Rachel.

Yet once Joseph begins his descent, he also changes. In Egypt, for the first time, he begins to act in a moral and responsible fashion. He is able to care well for the household of his master (Genesis 39:6). As Joseph's story continues, it is an artful narrative of ups and downs — or, better, downs and ups. He descends into the pit and is lifted up from it (Genesis 37:28). He descends into Egypt as a slave and is lifted up to the position of being in charge of Potiphar's household (Genesis 39:1–4). He is put into prison, but soon is put in charge of all of the prisoners (Genesis 29:22). And of course, eventually he is taken from prison to become the vizier of all Egypt. Obviously, you can't keep a good man down.

But this is also the story of the way in which the hero overcomes all obstacles, including perfecting his own character. Joseph is learning humility and self-control. He resists the temptation of Potiphar's wife. He proves worthy of trust and demonstrates his morality, explaining that he owes his master his trust and that this act would be contrary to the morality demanded by God (Genesis 39:9). Paradoxically, this moral action leads him into further descent — to jail — where once again he demonstrates his talents, attempts to help others by interpreting their dreams and again acknowledges his dependence upon God, saying, "Surely God can interpret" (Genesis 40:8). Once again, as with Jacob, we see hardship becoming the training ground for character.

2. The Temptation of Judah

Only once is this narrative of Joseph interrupted, and that is in chapter 38 when a totally independent story concerning Judah is told, the story of his relation with his daughter-in-law Tamar, with whom he inadvertently fathers twins, Perez and Zerah, the first of whom will be the ancestor of King David. Dramatically, the story serves as a pause between Joseph's sale and his arrival in Egypt. It also is intended to serve as a contrast between Joseph's conduct and that of Judah. Judah consorts with a harlot, while Joseph refuses to lie with his master's wife. This later earned him the title in rabbinic literature of "Joseph the righteous [*tzadik*]." On the other hand, we also see Judah in a positive light in that he acknowledges his wrongdoing when he says of Tamar, "She is more right than I" (Genesis 38:26).

The placement of the unsavory story of Judah's sexual misconduct just before the story of Joseph resisting temptation is surely a deliberate way of emphasizing the morality of Joseph's conduct.

Our portion ends with Joseph still in jail, having pleaded with the chief cupbearer to remember him after being freed. Unfortunately, the cupbearer "forgot him" (Genesis 40:23). This is the low point in his life, the ultimate descent. Two years will pass, but after that he will fulfill his destiny and become not only the savior of Egypt, but also the savior of his family. The despised — and in some ways rightly disliked — boy will fulfill his ultimate destiny.

Notice the role that clothing has played in Joseph's story. Twice he has been stripped of his garments — once by his brothers who take his beautiful coat from him (Genesis 37:23) and once by Potiphar's wife who grabs his garment and uses it to accuse him of attempted rape (Genesis 39:12). To be stripped of clothing is to be humiliated and shamed before all. What can remain of Joseph's pride after these incidents? The beautifully garbed boy, the spoiled darling of his father, is reduced to a naked slave, totally dependent upon others for survival. Garments will appear in the next portion in a positive way when his fortunes are restored.

The Torah is teaching us a very clear truth: physical well-being is not always parallel to moral strength and character development. On the contrary: too much ease and luxury can lead to moral laxity. Joseph begins well off physically, but morally he is in deep trouble. Only when he is in physical trouble, down in the depths, when he has lost the wonderful toys of his immaturity and been stripped of his coat of many colors — only then does he develop the moral strength which will eventually make him a great leader, a great human being and the salvation of his brothers and his father.

Viktor Frankl, the well-known psychiatrist, often points out that while we cannot control the physical circumstances of our lives, we can control our reactions to these circumstances. Adversity can become the occasion for growth and renewed strength if we try to meet it not as a punishment from God but as a challenge.

Miketz   מקץ

Genesis 41:1-44:17 | בראשית מא:א-מד:יז

1. Joseph: The Rise to Power

Having descended to the depths of prison and degradation, Joseph now rises in one fell swoop to the heights of power and glory. Has there ever been such a swift transformation? We catch a glimmering of it in the fact that before being brought to Pharaoh Joseph receives a clean garment. Remember that his glorious garment had been torn from him and later bloodied by his brothers and another garment of his had been left in the hands of Potiphar's wife. Another transformation is hinted at here as well, for he has his beard and his head shaved, thus conforming to the custom of Egyptians, as opposed to that of the Hebrews. Indeed the ambivalence of Joseph's life — is he a Hebrew or an Egyptian or both? — is a major motif in this story. Joseph's new maturity blossoms forth in his dialogue with Pharaoh. When he first interpreted dreams in prison he ascribed this ability to God. Now he repeats that assertion in an even stronger way. He mentions God specifically four times. And as a result Pharaoh also speaks of God, calling Joseph a man "in whom is the spirit of God" (Genesis 41:38) and ascribing wisdom to Joseph "since God has made all this known to you" (Genesis 41:39). The modern Biblical commentator E. A. Speiser has pointed out that these references to God are strange for an Egyptian court since the Pharaohs considered themselves to be gods (*Genesis*, Anchor Bible Series [New York: Doubleday and Co., 1964], p. 316). The assumption, therefore, is that this story took place at a time when the non-Egyptian Hyksos Dynasty has assumed the rulership of Egypt (ca.1730-1570 BCE). These references are also important to the story because they emphasize the divine force behind these events while defining Joseph's newfound humility and piety.

But Joseph is not only pious. He is also possessed of great practical wisdom. God may have helped him interpret the dreams — which were, after all, messages from God — but it is Joseph who independently devises a plan to permit Egypt to overcome the famine and supply life-giving food to the entire region. No wonder, then, that Pharaoh immediately appoints Joseph as his second-in-command, giving this foreign youth complete control of mighty Egypt (Genesis 41:40).

Joseph undergoes a total transformation. He is given new garments "of fine linen" (Genesis 41:42). He need no longer miss his many-colored robe. He is given a chariot and runners to proclaim his greatness. He is also given a new, Egyptian, name, Zaphenath-paneah ("God speaks; he lives" or "the creator/sustainer of life," as translated by Sarna), as well as an Egyptian wife, the daughter of the priest of On, a city that was the center of the worship of the sun-god Re.

How much of his Hebrew identity did Joseph retain during his years in Egypt? When his brothers encounter him they obviously have no idea that he is Joseph, a Hebrew. He looks, speaks and acts as an Egyptian. They have no clue as to his Hebrew identity. Although the story indicates that Pharaoh himself continued to refer to him as "Joseph" and not as "Zaphenath-paneah" (see Genesis 41:55), obviously he is not so called publicly or else his brothers would have known immediately who he is. The brothers describe him simply as "the man who is lord of the land" (Genesis 42:30, 33); they have no inkling that he understands Hebrew.

On the other hand, his father-in-law's religion seems to have had no impact upon him. Consider the names Joseph gives his new sons. He calls one Manasseh, meaning, "God has made me completely forget the hardship of my parental home" (Genesis 41:51) and the other Ephraim, meaning, "God has made me fertile in the land of my affliction" (Genesis 41:52). The first thing to notice is that he gives them Hebrew names, not Egyptian ones. Secondly, once again he speaks of God and of what God has done for him, erasing his past suffering both at the hands of his brothers in his homeland and in Egypt where for years he was afflicted and enslaved. Thus he continues to consider himself a part of the family of Jacob. He may look like an Egyptian, dress like one and speak like one, but he sees his future as a Hebrew. One wonders if Joseph espoused the philosophy that became popular so much later in Europe: be a Jew at home and a man in the street.

If Joseph still thinks of himself as a Hebrew and as part of Jacob's tribe, why is it that he has made no attempt at communicating with his father during all these years? Surely the vizier of Egypt would have had no problem sending a message back to Canaan. Also, where is his consideration for his father? We are aware that Jacob has been suffering all these years, mourning the death of his favorite son. Did that never occur to Joseph? And yet Joseph has made no attempt to inform Jacob that he is alive and well and living in Egypt. Even when he meets his brothers, he does not take that opportunity to immediately reconnect with his father but plays a game with them that delays his reunion with Jacob.

Perhaps the experience he had with his brothers has made him want to have no further contact with them, even if this means keeping him from his beloved father. Or perhaps his exalted position has made him cold and distant. He finally begins to demonstrate emotion, indeed to break down, only when he sees his brother Benjamin (Genesis 43:30). Even then, he does not reveal himself and delays the reunion with his father. He has a plan to test his brothers, to make them relive their experience, to make them confess their regret and to demonstrate that they have learned their lesson. In Joseph's mind, this is more important than anything else.

Indeed the truly tragic figure in this story is poor Jacob. Far away from the scene of action, back in Canaan, he waits and is even confronted with the need to send yet another son of his beloved Rachel, Benjamin, into danger. Granted, the brothers deserve to be psychologically tested and tortured, but does Jacob? How sad that Joseph cannot accomplish his ends without causing Jacob so much pain, yet Joseph is so haunted by the past that he seems unable to help himself.

Joseph is indeed a complex individual, a man of contradictions, but also a man of great talent and wisdom who saves not only Egypt, but also his family, the house of Israel.

2. Joseph's Brothers: A Second Chance

As the story of Joseph continues, the focus returns once again to the actions of Joseph's brothers and especially to the two — Reuben and Judah — who had attempted to stop the murderous plan of the other brothers. It is no coincidence that those two brothers, who took leadership positions before, again play the leading roles in this drama.

It was Reuben, Jacob's firstborn, who had counseled the brothers not to kill Joseph when they captured him. Instead he suggested that they cast him into the pit, secretly hoping that he would be able to take him out and return him safely to Jacob (Genesis 37:22). Joseph, testing his brothers, has brought about a situation in which one brother, Simeon, is a prisoner in Egypt who will not be released unless Benjamin is brought to him (Genesis 42:20). Jacob does not want to do this, fearing, with good reason, that this would not result in the freeing of Simeon, but in the loss of Benjamin as well.

Reuben takes the initiative in trying to persuade Jacob to agree to this and says, "You may kill my two sons if I do not bring him back to you. Put him in my care, and I will return him to you" (Genesis 42:37). As the midrash points out, this offer makes little sense since obviously Jacob would never consider killing his two grandsons. "Are not your sons my sons?" Jacob responds (*Genesis Rabbah* 91:37). Nevertheless the offer is an indication of the seriousness with which Reuben takes the responsibility of caring for the life of Benjamin. In the case of Joseph, Reuben had taken a timid approach. He did not suggest to his brothers that what they had in mind was unthinkable and they should let Joseph go, rather he sought a way out that would avoid a confrontation with his brothers. His approach was halfhearted and in the end, although it saved Joseph's life, it resulted in Joseph's enslavement. Now Reuben realizes that timidity will not succeed and he takes a much bolder approach to the task before him. As the firstborn he has not only position but also responsibility, which should have made him bolder in his earlier attempt to save Joseph. Now he has a second chance to demonstrate his ability to lead.

Judah had also tried to save Joseph's life, but his solution then was even weaker than that of Reuben. Reuben had at least hoped to use a delaying tactic that would enable him to save Joseph and return him safely to his father. Judah had simply suggested, "Come let us sell him to the Ishmaelites" (Genesis 37:27). True, that is better than killing him, but it is still not an action to be praised. One wonders what Judah's true motivation was. Did he make that suggestion rather than taking an action to free Joseph out of weakness, or was he secretly happy to be rid of the troublesome lad? He too is given a second chance to show his true character and, going Reuben one better, he offers himself to Jacob: "I myself will be surety for him; you may hold me responsible: if I do not bring him back to you and set him before you, I shall stand guilty before you forever" (Genesis 43:9).

Having little choice, since the famine is so terrible, Jacob sends them off — with Benjamin. In the climactic section of the story, in the following portion, when Joseph threatens to keep Benjamin a prisoner, Judah makes good on his word to Jacob by offering to remain as a prisoner in Egypt in place of Benjamin (Genesis 44:33).

Why is it that these two brothers, the only ones who did not want Joseph to be killed, are the ones who are once again involved in expiating this crime? They seem to act more responsibly than the others. Perhaps it is because they are the leaders, and as such have greater responsibility than the other brothers, yet they had failed to use their full authority to save Joseph. Out of fear, weakness or lack of sufficient concern, they had both offered halfway measures rather than taking a firm position to free Joseph and send him back home.

The weakness of leadership that fears to lead, the failure of the leader who can stop wrongdoing but prefers not to risk himself, is exposed here. Both Reuben and Judah had taken halfhearted measures when they should have stood firm against the evil their brothers planned. A leader must speak the truth and take risks, even if this means being unpopular. Politics is no excuse for moral compromise and fear of the popular reaction is no reason to refrain from combating evil. Evil occurs in this world not only because there are evil men and evil leaders, but also because there are weak men who compromise with it, who temper moral concern with political expediency. In our story the two leaders of the family are given a second chance to prove themselves. Unfortunately in the history of the world that seldom happens and we all pay the consequences.

Vayigash

ויגש

Genesis 44:18–47:27 | בראשית מד:יח-מז:כז

1. The Reconciliation

The dramatic climax to the story of Joseph and his brothers begins with Judah's impassioned speech to the grand vizier of Egypt whom he does not recognize as his brother Joseph. Judah, who had saved Joseph from death by proposing to sell him into slavery, now offers himself as a slave in place of Benjamin. The dramatic irony is clear — the brother who caused Joseph to become a slave and go into exile is now poised to remain in exile as a slave himself.

Obviously this is what Joseph wanted to see. Are his brothers different? Will they show more concern for Benjamin than they had shown for him? Yet there is also something more that causes him to finally lose his composure, weep and shout out, "I am Joseph" (Genesis 45:3). It is the constant repetition of the word "father" in Judah's speech. In a speech that lasts for only sixteen verses, some form of the word is used fourteen times (Genesis 44:18–34). The word resounds like a heartbeat throughout Judah's tale of how much Jacob has suffered because of Joseph's supposed death.

No wonder Joseph can no longer hold himself back. As the midrash puts it, "Because [Judah] mentioned his father's suffering, he [Joseph] could no longer contain himself" (*Genesis Rabbah* 93:29).

What kind of a person was Joseph that he was able to play this game for such a prolonged period of time? Was he really so cold and calculating that he could keep up this pretense in order to test them? What about his father? Did he not think that every day he kept himself hidden he was causing additional

63

unnecessary anguish for Jacob? Was he not concerned that if he waited too long, Jacob would be dead before Joseph could see him again?

The truth seems to be that, like most of us, Joseph acted not from one motive but from a mixture of emotions that were really in conflict with one another. He wanted to be sure that his brothers had changed before he decided how he should relate to them. Certainly he also planned to arrange for a reunion with his father, but the test seemed to take precedence. Perhaps there was even a tinge of revenge in his actions, causing him to put aside his concern for his father until Judah so masterfully — although unknowingly — brought it home to him. It is interesting to speculate on what he would have done had they not responded as they did. Had they been willing to sacrifice Benjamin he might have truly taken revenge on them. He had it in his power. Fortunately for all of us the story has a happy end.

The reconciliation comes about first with a rush of words in which Joseph reveals not only himself but the entire situation and makes certain that they understand that he is not angry with them because they were only pawns in God's hand "to ensure your survival on earth, and to save your lives" by Joseph's providing food for the family during the famine (Genesis 45:7). They are so astonished, and perhaps still so suspicious, that they cannot say a word until Joseph kisses them (Genesis 45:15). We are reminded of the kiss between Esau and Jacob when they met again, a kiss that was open to more than one interpretation. Here too, Joseph's brothers may still have feared that, kiss or no kiss, Joseph could not possibly have forgiven them completely.

There is more than a hint of that in a later incident after the death of Jacob. Years have passed, but the brothers are still afraid that Joseph bears a grudge against them (Genesis 50:15). They suspect that he treated them well only because of Jacob and that now that Jacob is dead, he will show his true feelings. Perhaps they recall that it was only the thought of his father that caused Joseph to reveal himself. Therefore they make up a story, telling Joseph that Jacob had asked them to instruct Joseph to forgive them.

The "happy end" has a tinge of sadness about it. His play-acting so many years before when they encountered Joseph in Egypt had left an impression on his brothers that could not be completely eradicated, an impression of coldness and calculation that they feared could yet arise once again. The breach between them could never be completely repaired. No wonder that

Joseph cries when he hears this (Genesis 50:17). After all that he had done and all that he had said, they still did not completely trust him!

The Sages put a more positive spin upon the lie that the brothers told: "Rabban Shimon ben Gamliel said, 'Great is peace, for the brothers went so far as to tell a lie in order to bring about peace between Joseph and themselves'" (*Genesis Rabbah* 100:16).

The sad thing is that they had to resort to such a stratagem at all. Human relations are very delicate. Once broken, they can seldom be completely healed. Relationships are like fragile china. Once it has been cracked, it can be glued together, but the break will always show. Joseph's brothers could not believe that after all they had done to him, he could ever be completely reconciled to them again. Whatever his true intent, Joseph's actions confirmed this suspicion and caused his brothers to always feel that a distance remained between them, a gap that could not be bridged.

Perhaps that is what causes Jacob to say to Pharaoh, "Few and hard have been the years of my life" (Genesis 47:9). Many were his trials. His years with Laban, the deception concerning Leah, the death of Rachel, the "death" of Joseph and now, when all are reunited, there remains the breach between Joseph and his brothers, a breach which Jacob began when he gave him a coat of many colors and allowed jealousy to corrupt his family.

2. Jacob's Descent into Egypt

The climax of the Joseph saga is reached when Joseph, finally convinced that his brothers have really repented of their deed and would not repeat it if given the opportunity, reveals himself to them by emotionally crying out — in Hebrew — "I am Joseph. Is my father yet alive?" (Genesis 45:3). The tie between father and son has remained strong all of those years of separation. And this feeling is matched by Jacob who, when told that Joseph is alive, says, "Enough! My son Joseph is still alive! I must go and see him before I die" (Genesis 45:28). When Jacob meets him, after the long journey into Egypt, he repeats this thought: "Now I can die, having seen for myself that you are still alive" (Genesis 46:30).

In view of this, it is certainly strange that at the critical moment of leaving Canaan for the journey to Egypt, Jacob does not rush impulsively to reach

Joseph but takes time to pause in Beersheba and sacrifice to God at an altar that his father Isaac had prepared. What is the purpose of this action? Since God immediately assures him of His protection and tells him not to be afraid, "Fear not to go down to Egypt, for I will make you there into a great nation. I Myself will go down with you to Egypt, and I Myself will also bring you back; and Joseph's hand shall close your eyes" (Genesis 46:3-4), we may assume that — even though the text does not say it — Jacob (or Israel as he is called here) has some fear, some hesitation.

When Jacob left his home for the first time so many years before, fleeing from the wrath of his brother Esau, he also left from Beersheba and also had a revelation in which God promised Jacob that he would be the father of many descendants: "I will protect you wherever you go and will bring you back to this land" (Genesis 28:15). It is that promise that is repeated here. For all his anxiety to see his son, Jacob cannot forget that the future of his family lies here, in Canaan. He seeks reassurance from God that descending into Egypt will not endanger that. After all, his father Isaac was once told by God when there was a similar famine, "Do not go down to Egypt; stay in the land" (Genesis 26:2). Perhaps he too should remain in Canaan, but, on the contrary, he is told by God that it is important for him to go to Egypt. It is there that the promise of making his descendants into a great nation will be fulfilled.

The promise made to Jacob is not merely a personal promise — after all, Jacob's return to Canaan will be after his death! Therefore the promise, "I Myself will also bring you back," is really intended for the people of Israel and not the individual known as Israel. It is at this juncture that the history of a family really begins to be the history of a nation.

The question of why the period of Egyptian slavery was critical to the formation of the people of Israel is a difficult one. Certainly the Torah does not take it simply as something that happened, but rather sees it as part of a divine plan. Abraham was informed in the mysterious vision described in Genesis 15, in which he too was told "Fear not," that "your offspring shall be strangers in a land not theirs, and they shall be enslaved and oppressed four hundred years...and they shall return here in the fourth generation" (Genesis 15:13-16). It is almost as if without the Egyptian experience we could never have become a people. Was it the suffering that was crucial? Was it needed in order to make us, as the Sages said, "merciful children of merciful fathers"?

Thus we would become sensitive to suffering and be taught not to do to others what was done to us. Certainly the Torah frequently enough repeats the refrain: "You shall not oppress a stranger, for you know the feelings of the stranger, having yourselves been strangers in the land of Egypt" (Exodus 23:9). Or was it the redemption that was crucial to forging a readiness to become God's people? That too is repeated over and over: "You have seen what I did to the Egyptians, how I bore you on eagles' wings and brought you to Me. Now, then, if you will obey Me faithfully" (Exodus 19:4-5).

Sforno (Obadiah ben Jacob, 1470-1550, Italy) offers an entirely different explanation:

> If your children were to dwell in Canaan, they would intermarry with the Canaanites and assimilate to them. But that will not happen in Egypt because the Egyptians will not break bread with Hebrews. Therefore they will become a separate nation there, as the Sages said [in the Hagaddah]: They were distinguished there from others. (Sforno, Genesis 46:1)

His point is that the only way in which this small group — seventy souls — could ever become a separate nation with different ways of living and of belief would be for them to be in an environment in which they would not be influenced by the overwhelming majority in whose midst they would live, but be able to keep separate.

Whatever the reason, Jacob is reassured that the promise will be fulfilled and goes eagerly to meet his beloved son, knowing that his personal life will be complete and that the future of his family will be assured.

Vayeḥi

וַיְחִי

Genesis 47:28–50:26 | בראשית מז:כח-נ:כו

1. The Blessing of Jacob

We come now to the end of the book of Genesis, which is also the end of the saga of the Patriarchs and the beginning of the story of *Am Yisrael* — the people of Israel. Twice in our portion the word *Yisrael* — Israel — appears in its new meaning (Genesis 48:20 and 49:28). It is no longer simply another name of Jacob, but the name of the tribes descended from Jacob-Israel.

Appropriately enough (and sadly enough) the last word of the book is *b'Mitzrayim* (in Egypt), which describes not only the place where Joseph was entombed, but the place where Israel was to be entombed for four hundred years. This could almost be a play on words since *b'meitzarim* — a slight variation — means "in a narrow place," i.e., a place of trouble and suffering.

The sons of Jacob represent the tribes of Israel that were to descend from them. The blessings that Jacob confers upon his children, or, better, the predictions that he makes concerning their future, are predicated upon the fate of the tribes, as is obvious from the text (Genesis 49:1–28) and has been recognized by commentators early and late. This is true as well in another curious episode related here, the penultimate scene in the life of Jacob — consistently called Israel in these sections — when Joseph brings his two sons, Manasseh and Ephraim, to their dying grandfather's bed so that they should receive a blessing from him. Here too the two lads stand for the tribes to be descended from them and the preference given the younger (Ephraim) over the elder (Manasseh) stems from the fact that in later days that tribe came to be of much greater importance than the other. To quote Nahum Sarna:

The texts that record Manasseh as being the natural first-born must reflect an exceedingly early and authentic phase in the history of the Israelite tribal relationships, a phase in which Manasseh enjoyed hegemony over Ephraim. There would be no reason to invent such a tradition, given subsequent developments. The present episode provides an explanation for the reversal, with Ephraim becoming the more powerful and more influential of the two tribes, even to the extent that its name eventually became synonymous with the kingdom of Israel. This phenomenon is now traced to Jacob's blessing. (*The JPS Torah Commentary: Genesis*, p. 328)

Nevertheless this story must also be seen as a reflection of the life of Jacob and a way of bringing together many of the threads of his life. Jacob wants to somehow rectify the tragedy of Rachel's death by conferring an extra blessing upon her son Joseph. That he has this in mind is evident from his recalling of Rachel's death at this moment: "Rachel died, to my sorrow, while I was journeying in the land of Canaan" (Genesis 48:7). He accomplishes this by making her grandsons into full sons, granting them an extra portion in the land of Canaan.

This incident is also a replay and an echo of the story of what happened when Isaac wanted to confer a blessing as he thought he lay dying (Genesis 27:1–29). Note the many similarities:

- In both cases the father is on the brink of death. "I am old now and do not know how soon I may die," (Genesis 27:2) says Isaac. Of Jacob, Joseph is told "Your father is ill" (Genesis 48:1).

- In both cases the father's sight is poor: "When Isaac was old and his eyes were too dim to see" (Genesis 27:1); "Now Israel's eyes were dim with age; he could not see" (Genesis 48:10).

- In both cases a blessing is to be conferred. Isaac says, "So that I may give you my innermost blessing before I die" (Genesis 27:4). Israel says, "Bring them up to me that I may bless them" (Genesis 48:9).

- When Esau comes to get his blessing, Isaac says to him, "Who are you?" (Genesis 27:32), and here Israel asks, "Who are these?" (Genesis 48:8).

- And of course — in both cases it is the younger who receives the favored blessing.

The difference is that here the blessing is conferred willingly and knowingly — "I know, my son, I know" (Genesis 48:19) — whereas there it came about deceitfully, against Isaac's will.

There is one other major difference. In this case neither son is to be denied the blessing of Abraham. Unlike the stories of Jacob and Esau and Isaac and Ishmael before them, there is no longer to be a division of the progeny of the Patriarch into inheritors of the Abrahamic blessing and those denied it. *All* of Israel's descendants are to be part of that blessing and here he even confers it directly upon two grandsons who will become equal to his sons.

The story of a deathbed blessing which was, in an earlier generation, the beginning of a saga of enmity and hatred, has been transformed here into a positive event with no deceit and no tragic consequences. It becomes the story of a blessing in which there is nothing but good and beneficence. Jacob must have wished that history could be so easily revised and his steps retraced. Perhaps symbolically that has happened.

2. The End of the Beginning

The concluding section of the book of Genesis seems at first to be an anticlimax. There is nothing here to rival the great drama of Joseph and his brothers that we witnessed. Everything is a winding down, a preparation for death — first of Jacob and then of Joseph.

The death of Jacob is spelled out in extraordinary detail, both in his preparations to make certain that he will be buried in the land of Canaan together with his ancestors, and then in his granting of a blessing to Joseph's two sons and his deathbed confrontation with his twelve sons.

The death of Joseph is also given considerable attention, especially when we note that there is no specific record of the deaths of the other brothers. In a sense this is fitting since the story of Joseph is so central to the book. He is the only one of the brothers whose life is recorded in such detail. He deserves treatment similar to that of Abraham, Isaac and Jacob, even though it is clear that he is not to be accorded the same status as they had. There are only three Patriarchs, not four.

The unique status of the three Patriarchs is acknowledged by Joseph, who lays no claim to it, when at the end of his life he assures the Israelites that "God will surely take notice of you and bring you up from this land to the land that He promised on oath to Abraham, to Isaac and to Jacob" (Genesis 50:24).

The contrast between the burials of Jacob and Joseph is remarkable and is undoubtedly elaborated upon out in order to make us aware of the changes in the status of the Israelites in Egypt. Whereas Jacob is accorded official Egyptian burial rites and is taken to Canaan for burial (Genesis 50:7-13), Joseph can only ask the Israelites to promise that when they leave Egypt hundreds of years hence, they will take his bones with them. When he dies, he is "placed in a coffin *in Egypt*" (Genesis 50:26). The fact that the last two Hebrew words in Genesis are "a coffin in Egypt" is neither accidental nor meaningless. On the contrary, it signifies that which has happened to Jacob's descendants. They are all trapped in the coffin that is Egypt. Even if official slavery has not yet begun, the power and influence that Joseph wielded in his heyday no longer exists. The future is foreboding.

Indeed that is one of two parallel themes developed in this section that serves as a coda to Genesis. It may be anticlimactic dramatically, but not in importance. For it is informing us of two important developments. One is the beginning of enslavement; the other is the emergence of Israel as a nation, as a political entity.

For the first time we begin to hear of the tribes of Israel, and not merely of the sons of Jacob. The verse says, "And these were the tribes of Israel, twelve in number, and this is what their father said to them as he bade them farewell" (Genesis 49:28), yet Jacob is not speaking to tribes but to his sons. The individual brothers have become symbols of the tribes that are to bear their names.

This marks, then, the new phase. An entire people, a group of twelve tribes, is now coming into existence, a group that will realize this ancient promise: to make them a great multitude, to give them the land of Canaan and to make them a universal blessing. First conferred upon Abraham (Genesis 12:2-3), this blessing was transmitted to Isaac (Genesis 26:4-5), to Jacob (Genesis 28:14) and now to all his descendants. The tragedy of the divided family is at an end, and although one tribe may be larger, richer, more powerful than another, none will be excluded from the Abrahamic blessing.

The story of the Patriarchs and their trials and triumphs is concluded. The story of Israel now begins.

This emergence of the nation has a positive meaning. It is the light of hope that dispels the darkness of the enslavement that has begun. Jacob's words themselves assure us that these tribes will develop and that they will dwell not in Egypt but in their own land as a free people. For example, "The scepter shall not depart from Judah" (Genesis 49:10) or "Zebulun shall dwell by the seashore" (Genesis 49:13).

Even later, Joseph's words to his brethren (not his brothers, but their descendants) contain the promise that eventually they will leave the land of Egypt. "God will surely take notice of you and bring you up from this land to the land that He promised on oath to Abraham, to Isaac and to Jacob" (Genesis 50:24). The statement is emphatic. Joseph does not say that "*if* God takes notice of you" they should take his bones with them, but "*when* God takes notice" (Genesis 50:25). The Hebrew makes very clear that *this will happen!*

This final portion of Genesis, then, serves not only to close one section of our history, the patriarchal period, but also to open and anticipate the next stage — the story of the emergence of Israel as a people, its enslavement and its eventual emergence from the darkness of the tomb of Egypt into the light of liberation and dedication to the service of God.

EXODUS

Sh'mot

Sh'mot   שמות

Exodus 1:1–6:1 | שמות א:א-ו:א

1. Into Slavery

The fulfillment of the divine plan for Israel as revealed in the promise made to Abraham is at the core of this opening section of the book of Exodus. That promise included both the fact that the descendants of Abraham would become a great multitude and that they would inherit the land of Canaan.

Immediately we are told that although the sons of Israel were only seventy persons when they came to Egypt, "the Israelites were fertile and prolific; they multiplied and increased very greatly, so that the land was filled with them" (Exodus 1:7). The midrash imaginatively elaborated on this, saying that "Each woman gave birth to sextuplets...some say: sixty at each birth" (*Exodus Rabbah* 16:7). Although God is not specifically invoked at this point, it is obvious that the divine power is understood to be at work here.

This theme is further elaborated in the words of the new ruler of Egypt, who has conveniently forgotten Joseph, when for the first time he uses the term *am* — "a people" — to refer to the Israelites, thus indicating their new enlarged status. "Look, the Israelite people are much too numerous for us" (Exodus 1:9), he says, and attempts to find a way to keep them from increasing (Exodus 1:10). But he does not succeed because "the more they were oppressed, the more they increased and spread out" (Exodus 1:12).

The power of Pharaoh is pitted against the power of God. God wants them to increase; Pharaoh fears their numbers and wants to limit them. This is the beginning of the contest between them, a clash of titans, the One God versus the one who thinks he is god. The struggle will continue until Pharaoh's final defeat at the Sea of Reeds (Exodus 14:28). Pharaoh constantly

invokes ever-harsher methods to attain his goal. First he enslaves the Israelites and puts them to hard labor on massive building projects (Exodus 1:11).
Then he attempts to have the midwives kill the males at birth (Exodus 1:16).
This too fails and "the people multiplied and increased greatly" (Exodus
1:20). Finally he commands his entire people to stop the proliferation of the
Israelites by casting every male into the river (Exodus 1:22). The failure of
this plan is described in chapter 2: the birth and saving of the infant Moses
who will bring about Pharaoh's utter defeat. Incidentally, after this we hear no
more about plans to kill any infants and limit the multiplying of the people.
Can we assume that this genocide plan simply continued and is not
mentioned? Or did it fail, perhaps because the Egyptians did not cooperate?
After all, if Pharaoh's own daughter did not go along with it, why should we
assume that others did? On this question the Torah is silent.

The second feature of the promise to Abraham is that his descendants will
inherit the land of Canaan. For that to happen, they must be able to leave
Egypt. That theme is also featured here. Pharaoh mentions it immediately. He
is afraid that if they multiply, they will be able to join enemies of Egypt in a
revolt and thus secure the ability "to go up from of the land" (Exodus 1:10).

A careful reading of the end of the book of Genesis shows that already
during the lifetime of Joseph the tribes were not able to leave Egypt. Even
Joseph had to obtain permission to leave in order to bury his father in Canaan
(Genesis 50:5) and when Joseph himself died, he could not be taken out of
Egypt for burial. Instead he had to exact an oath from his brothers that in the
future, when God's promise would be fulfilled, "you shall carry up my bones
from here" (Genesis 50:25). As Prof. Moshe Greenberg wrote, "Our story
assumes that Pharaoh claimed absolute authority over all in his domain. For
the Israelites to win their freedom to 'go up from the land' would not have
been so much a loss to Egypt's economy — for the people were not yet
enslaved, whatever Genesis 47:6 implies — as a blow to that authority"
(*Understanding Exodus* [New York: Behrman House, 1969], p. 22).

Now, however, Pharaoh has gone one step further. Not only are they
forbidden to leave Egypt, they are enslaved in Egypt. Thus unknowingly
Pharaoh is attempting to thwart both of God's promises — the increase of the
people, which has already taken place, and their inheritance of Canaan,
which awaits the Exodus from Egypt. The attaining of that Exodus is to be the
subject of the first fifteen chapters of the book of Exodus, and the fulfillment

of the promise of inheriting Canaan will occupy the rest of the Torah and the book of Joshua as well.

It is only long after all of these preliminary steps have been taken, and only after Moses has grown, identified himself actively with the plight of his people and fled to Midian, that God steps into the picture openly, hearing their cry, remembering the covenant with Abraham and taking notice of the Israelites and their plight (Exodus 2:23-25). He turns to Moses and makes him the instrument of redemption. When God identifies Himself to Moses, He returns to the promise of Abraham, first by identifying Himself as "the God of your father, the God of Abraham, the God of Isaac and the God of Jacob" (Exodus 3:6) and then by announcing that "I have come down to rescue them from the Egyptians and to bring them out of that land to a good and spacious land, a land flowing with milk and honey, the region of the Canaanites..." (Exodus 3:8).

The Exodus from Egypt may have taken place only once, but the attempt to cancel the divine promise in the same way that Pharaoh did — by genocide and pogroms and/or by preventing our people from living freely in its own land — has been an ever-recurring feature of Jewish life. But as Pharaoh's conflict with God ended in Pharaoh's defeat, so too have all other attempts. Our losses have been devastating, but as a people we have survived. As the Haggadah puts it, "That is what has stood by us and our ancestors — that not only did one [Pharaoh] attempt to destroy us, but in every generation there are those who have sought to destroy us and the Holy One, blessed be He has rescued us from their hands."

2. The Bravery of Women

Why are some people ready to risk their lives for the sake of others? Is there any way that we can identify the personality of such brave individuals and duplicate it? These questions become pertinent to us when we consider the events of the Shoah. There were righteous Gentiles — even more than those who have been identified and honored — who were willing to save Jews, to shelter them, to hide them, knowing that by so doing they were in danger of being executed themselves.

I have met a few such people in Eastern Europe. I remember vividly one elderly woman, a simple peasant-farmer in Riga, who, together with her husband, hid Jews in her farm and helped them to escape to the forest where they could join the partisans. I doubt if she was literate, but she was devout, a devout Christian. Her only explanation was that she believed in God and that all human beings — including Jews — were God's creatures and deserving of life.

This swiftly moving Torah portion, which takes us from the beginnings of slavery in Egypt through the beginning of the mission of Moses to Pharaoh, is replete with instances of such bravery. All are performed by women. No wonder that Rabbi Akiba said, "Because of the merit of righteous women Israel was redeemed from Egypt in that generation" (*Exodus Rabbah* 1:12). Akiba was referring specifically to the desire of the Israelite women to continue to bear children even after Pharaoh had decreed that the males were to be slain, while their husbands had decided that they wanted to father no more children under such circumstances. Thus all the women of Israel were heroic, according to the midrash, in undertaking to bring life into the world when there was so much danger connected to it.

Rabbinic legend aside, the Torah narrative gives us other instances of women's heroism. The first is that of the two midwives, Shiphrah and Puah, who are in charge of birthing the Israelite women. They defy a specific order from the almighty Pharaoh to kill all of the male children, preferring to obey the Almighty instead. As the text puts it, "The midwives, *fearing God*, did not do as the king of Egypt had told them; they let the boys live" (Exodus 1:17). Nahum Sarna remarks, "Their defiance of tyranny constitutes history's first recorded act of civil disobedience in defense of a moral imperative" (*The JPS Torah Commentary: Exodus* [Philadelphia: Jewish Publication Society of America, 1991], p. 7).

Who were these two women? The Hebrew text is unclear. It could mean that they were themselves Hebrews, the term used constantly here to refer to the Israelites. That is also the interpretation of many midrashim which fancifully identify them as Yoheved and Miriam (*Exodus Rabbah* 1:13). If they were indeed Hebrews, that would still be an act of heroism. During the Shoah there were times when Jews were faced with terrible choices regarding obeying Nazi orders or defying them. Not always did they make the heroic choice.

The other possibility is that the text could mean not that they were "Hebrew midwives" but that they were the non-Israelite midwives assigned to the Hebrews. (Such is the opinion of Josephus, the Septuagint and Abravanel. See the JPS Commentary to Exodus, p. 7.) Non-Israelites thus defied Pharaoh to save these infants. Their reason — like that of the woman in Riga — was that they feared God. In the Bible that phrase is frequently used regarding non-Jews, both positively and negatively. Thus Abraham says that he was forced to hide the fact that Sarah was his wife because he feared that there was no "fear of God" among the people he was visiting (Genesis 20:11). And in the Book of Jonah, the non-Jewish sailors are praised as people who "feared the Lord greatly" (Jonah 1:16). The Bible recognized, as we all do, that there can be moral actions performed by righteous Gentiles. These midwives are the first example.

The second example of courage is that of Moses' mother, as yet not known by name, but later identified as Yoheved. "She saw that the child was *tov*" (Exodus 2:2) — which could be translated as "good" or as "beautiful"- and therefore she hides him as long as possible and then puts him into the river in a basket. The midrash explains that *tov* means that she saw that he was some-how special, perhaps that he would be the salvation of the people (*Exodus Rabbah* 1:20). It is hard to think that any mother would not want to save her child, no matter what his potential. Perhaps it means that she saw that the child was healthy and thus could survive. Whatever the reason, she bravely hides the child from those who would kill him and then embarks upon a program that has the possibility of saving his life. One is reminded of the stories of parents throwing their children over ghetto walls, or from moving trains or trucks, in the hope that someone would help them to live.

But Yoheved and Miriam have conspired to do more than that. Miriam too shows bravery as she waits for an opportunity to help the infant and to see to it that he is brought up in such a way that he will know that he is a Hebrew (Exodus 2:4). Exactly how long Moses stayed with his mother is unclear, but it seems reasonable to assume that it was long enough for him to have learned who he was and to have been told the story of his people and his ancestors. When God reveals Himself to Moses He does not do so as some unknown entity but as the God of Moses' fathers (Exodus 3:6).

Under the most difficult circumstances Moses' mother raised her son to be a loyal member of his people. She inspired him to be courageous. She gave him the feeling that he was part of a historical chain, connected to his ancient ancestors and their beliefs.

The last of the brave women is Pharaoh's daughter. She certainly knows of the decree to kill the Hebrews; she also is completely aware of the identity of the child that she finds, and yet she decides to save him and to adopt him (Exodus 2:6–10). The story is not explicit, but the assumption is that she is opposed to her father's policies. How does she explain this child to her father? She must have hidden his identity; otherwise her father would not have permitted him to exist. An Israelite boy in the palace! Impossible. We must assume that this was dangerous for her as well. This was treason.

We owe a great debt to all of these brave women, Hebrew and Egyptian, who risked their own safety for the sake of Israelite children. To paraphrase Rabbi Akiba, only because of them did our redemption come about. Nor should it be forgotten that Moses himself subsequently showed heroism in his actions to defend the weak and helpless (see Exodus 2:11–19). He had learned from his own experience that defending the weak, even when it was dangerous, was a moral imperative. He had to flee for his life, but, as a result, he was judged worthy to lead Israel to freedom.

What causes people to act so courageously? The only answer the Torah gives us is "fear of God" — meaning not fear in the sense of terror, but in the sense of reverence, belief in the importance of righteousness, in the sacredness of human life. It is this that we must inculcate in our own children so that civilization and humanity will survive.

Va'era   וארא

Exodus 6:2-9:35 | שמות ו:ב-ט:לה

1. The Beginning of Redemption

The process of redemption now begins. How will Israel be freed from Egypt? Given the oppressive nature of the Egyptian regime, with a Pharaoh who was invested with absolute power and ruled as an incarnation of a god, the task would not be simple. The reluctance that Moses evinced when first called by God (Exodus 3:11-4:17) was based upon a realistic assessment of the situation. This was only reinforced by the initial failure of his mission, which resulted in worsened conditions for the Israelites (Exodus 5:6-23). Therefore it is important that God both reiterate His determination to see them free and strengthen Moses by reassuring him that "I place you in the role of God to Pharaoh, with your brother Aaron as your prophet" (Exodus 7:1). Only a "god" can fight a Pharaoh, who thinks he is a god, and only the harshest of measures will succeed.

It is also important that in the process of attaining their freedom the Israelites recognize that this freedom is not of their own making, nor is it a gracious gift granted by a willing Pharaoh, but that it comes directly from God. And at the same time it is imperative that the Israelites, steeped for some four hundred years in Egyptian culture, recognize that the gods of Egypt are false and come to recognize the one true God — the God of Israel. Furthermore, the Egyptians themselves must be brought to recognize "that I am the Lord" (Exodus 7:5). In this context the Torah for the first time expresses a specific anti-pagan declaration — "I will mete out punishments to all the gods of Egypt, I the Lord" (Exodus 12:12). Bringing about the freedom of the Israelites was not only difficult; it was also complicated because it was intended to accomplish all of these other goals as well.

This explains the necessity of bringing the plagues upon Egypt. Only by means of these drastic, harsh measures, would the Israelites receive their freedom and understand that it came from God, thus coming to revere the Lord. Only by attacking the gods of Egypt, such as the Nile River, would the Egyptians be brought to recognize that the God of Israel alone had power and that their gods were false. Only thus would Pharaoh, who considered himself a god and was seen as such by his people, be brought to recognize the true divinity, the God of Israel.

Nevertheless there is one aspect of the plagues that has always been puzzling. In Exodus 7:3 we read, "But I will harden Pharaoh's heart, that I may multiply my signs and marvels in the land of Egypt." This is a repetition of the idea expressed before in God's initial call to Moses: "I, however, will stiffen his heart so that he will not let the people go" (Exodus 4:21). What has happened to the idea of free will? If God hardens Pharaoh's heart, preventing him from taking the proper action, in what way is Pharaoh to be held responsible for his deed? This question was asked long ago by the medieval Spanish commentator Abraham ibn Ezra: "One might ask, 'If God hardened his heart, what was his sin, what was his transgression?'" (comment to Exodus 7:3).

Various answers have been offered to this. Sforno, for example, in commenting on Exodus 7:3, says that the plagues were sent in order to bring the Egyptians to repentance, something that would not have happened had God not been able to bring so many wonders and marvels to pass. Furthermore, had Pharaoh let them go too quickly simply because he found the first plagues too annoying, he would never have come to acknowledge the role of God in these events.

The midrash (Exodus *Rabbah* 13:3) wisely notes that all during the first five plagues, the sole expression used is that Pharaoh's heart was hardened (see Exodus 7:13, 22; 8:11, 15, 28; 9:7). Only beginning with the sixth plague do we find the expression "*the Lord* stiffened the heart of Pharaoh" (Exodus 9:12), which is then repeated in 10:20 and 10:27. In the words of the midrash, "The Holy One, Blessed be He, warns an individual once, twice, thrice, but if he does not repent, He closes his heart against repentance in order to exact punishment from him for his sin.... Thus God said, 'You have chosen to stiffen your neck and harden your heart, now I will add to your guilt.'"

Hardening Pharaoh's heart was thus a well-deserved punishment, rather than the cause of his stubbornness.

Pharaoh was not an innocent person forced by God to be a tyrant against his will. He was an absolute tyrant, a man who wanted to recognize no power but himself. Benno Jacob saw this expression as meaning, "the Lord let Pharaoh remain unaffected," a shorthand way of saying that this was his God-given temperament. This may be an apologetic approach; it may be better to say that just as God helps one who wishes to repent to do so, so He punishes the wicked by making it harder for them to do so. This seems to be ibn Ezra's thought and may be what Maimonides meant when he wrote, "Sometimes a man's offence is so grave that he forecloses the possibility of repentance. At first he sinned repeatedly of his own free will, until he forfeited the capacity to repent" (*Commentary to the Mishnah*: Introduction to *Avot*, Chapter 8).

As Yehezkel Kaufmann, the brilliant Israeli Biblical scholar, wrote:

> The Bible never represents God as causing man to sin in the first instance; he hardens the heart of the voluntary sinner to prevent him from repenting. Pharaoh, the sons of Eli, the Israelites in the time of Isaiah, all began to sin of their own volition. By way of punishment God stiffens their hearts so they cannot repent. Thus the demand for justice is served and the sinner must suffer the full measure of his guilt. (*The Religion of Israel* [Chicago: University of Chicago Press, 1960], p. 76)

However we explain it, it is clear that free will remains a basic doctrine of Judaism, for without it there is no responsibility. Even if God utilizes our actions for His own purposes, as the Torah often indicates, ultimately we bear the responsibility for what we do. Pharaoh's stubbornness becomes a tool in God's hands, but Pharaoh and all of the Egyptians cannot escape the responsibility for their refusal to acknowledge the evil of their ways.

2. Overcoming Despair

The Hebrew saying, "All beginnings are difficult," seems to fit well into the story of the Exodus. This portion finds Moses discouraged by the fact that his first encounter with Pharaoh not only failed to accomplish its mission of liberating the Israelites, but resulted in a worsening of their situation so that the Israelites actually invoked God's punishment upon Moses and Aaron for their part in this catastrophe (Exodus 5:21). After that, when Moses repeats God's promise to redeem them, they refuse to listen, "their spirits crushed by cruel bondage" (Exodus 6:9). No wonder Moses feels justified in saying, "The Israelites would not listen to me; how then should Pharaoh heed me, a man of impeded speech!" (Exodus 6:12). The mention of his speech problem serves to remind us that Moses had never wanted this task in the first place, and his reluctance seems eminently justified in view of these negative developments.

History, however, is replete with enterprises that began with great difficulty only to triumph in the end. The position of the Allies in the Second World War is an easy example. The American Revolution and the Union's position in the Civil War also come to mind. To these we may add Israel's War of Independence and the Yom Kippur War as well. There are times when it is indeed difficult to believe that things will go well, they seem to be going so badly. It requires a great deal of faith and courage, qualities the Israelites seem to have lacked. It was actually not until the final triumph at the Sea of Reeds that they expressed their belief and confidence in God and God's servant Moses (Exodus 14:31). For them, seeing was believing.

Actually, the Israelites themselves played no role in their liberation. We hear nothing of them until the end of the process. Everything is conducted by Moses and Aaron, who follow God's commands time and time again and appear before Pharaoh to deliver the divine message. They too may have their doubts or at least an understandable reluctance, but they do as they were commanded and eventually succeed. What is it that gives them the confidence to continue against all odds?

Twice — once in the previous portion (Exodus 3:13–15) and once in this one — God reveals His name to Moses (Exodus 6:2–3) as part of His attempt to convince Moses that He will be able to bring about this liberation: "I appeared to Abraham, Isaac, and Jacob as *El Shaddai*, but I did not make Myself known to them by My name YHVH" (6:3). The commentators, old and new, are divided as to whether or not these passages mean that the Name of God, the four letters YHVH which we no longer pronounce but read instead as *Adonai* (usually translated as "Lord") was unknown before the time of Moses or was known but not fully understood until that time.

In either case the message conveyed by that name must have been a powerful one that impressed Moses and made him believe that he should follow the commands of this God. The only "explanation" the Torah gives of the name is "*Eheyeh-Asher-Eheyeh*" (Exodus 3:14). This has been translated as "I Am That I Am," "I Am Who I Am" and "I Will Be What I Will Be." Martin Buber translated it as "I Will Be Present When I Will Be Present" (*Moses*, [New York: Harper & Brothers, 1958] p. 52). The only thing that is certain is that it is based upon the Hebrew verb meaning "to be."

In a sense, then, it is not a name at all but a verb. This is significant because in pre-Israelite religions the name of a god was always used not only to invoke but also to control that god. Gods too were subject to fate and controllable by magic. Knowing the god's name was important because it gave one control. Thus the God of Israel announced immediately that no one can control Him. He has no "name" that can be used in magical invocations. God is what God is. His "name" indicates His actions, His Presence, and tells us that God is the essence of all being, that He causes all else to be, that no force has power outside of Him.

Yehezkel Kaufmann summed up the essence of the difference between the God of Israel and pagan deities in this way:

> The basic idea of Israelite religion is that God is supreme over all. There is no realm above or beside Him to limit His absolute sovereignty. He is utterly distinct from, and other than, the world. He is subject to no laws, no compulsions, or powers that transcend Him.... Israelite religion conceived a radically new idea: It did not proclaim a new chief god, a god who ruled among or over his fellows. It conceived, for the first time, of a god independent of a primordial realm, who was the source of all. (*The Religion of Israel*, pp. 60–61)

Moses believed in "*Eheyeh*" — the God of all being, the God always present, the God who was the sole power of the universe. The magicians of Egypt could have no control over such a God. This overwhelming awareness of a power unlike that of any other and unlike any previously known became the foundation for all of Moses' actions and enabled him to triumph even over the might of Egypt.

One of the rabbinic interpretations of the verse telling that the Israelites would not heed Moses, "their spirits crushed by cruel bondage" (Exodus 6:9), is based upon the fact that the word "bondage" (*avodah* in Hebrew) is found

in the phrase *avodah zarah*, or "idol worship" (*Exodus Rabbah* 6:5). The Israelites would not listen, said the rabbis, because they were so entranced by idol
worship in Egypt, with all of its magnificent statues, temples and impressive
rites, which they did not want to give up for the worship of the non-represen-
tational, non-magical God described by Moses. Idols were much easier to
comprehend and much more impressive.

Even today, it is very easy to slip from belief in God into superstition,
from the purity of Mosaic belief into the magical realm of blessings, curses
and charms, from the God whose name is a verb to the God who has magical
names that can be used for all kinds of dubious purposes. This happens all
too often within Judaism, and requires us to be constantly on our guard to
keep Judaism as pure as it was when Moses taught it.

It was this purity of belief that inspired Moses and the prophets after him
and bequeathed to us the world's first truly monotheistic religion, a religion
that has inspired other religions to follow in its path. It is this purity that can,
even today, provide the basis for a worthy system of belief and action.

Bo נא

Exodus 10:1–13:16 | שמות י:א–יג:טז

1. The End of Slavery

In no other section of the Torah is there such a perfect blending of history, theology and practice. This portion first describes the last plagues and then tells of the preparations the Israelites made to leave Egypt and the laws for commemorating the event in future generations. It rightly emphasizes the tenth plague, the death of the firstborn, which totally shattered Pharaoh's will. A broken man — no longer a god incarnate — mourning his dead son summons Moses and Aaron in the middle of the night and tells them to leave and take everything they have with them. His parting words are filled with pathos: "Bless me as well!" (Exodus 12:32). The defiant Pharaoh who "knew not Joseph" and "knew not the Lord" begs a blessing from the leaders of the despised Hebrew slaves! The narrative then describes in terse language the Exodus itself (Exodus 12:33–39). Four hundred thirty years of dwelling in Egypt come to an end in these seven brief verses.

Many more words are used to emphasize the meaning of these events. No other event in Jewish or world history plays such a central role in Jewish consciousness and in our theology. Every major Biblical festival, including Shabbat, is termed "a remembrance of the Exodus from Egypt." The Ten Commandments begin with the proclamation that "I the Lord am your God who brought you out of the land of Egypt, the house of bondage" (Exodus 20:2). The Sh'ma concludes with the words "I the Lord am your God who brought you out of the land of Egypt to be your God" (Numbers 15:41). This section itself begins with God saying that He is performing all of these signs in Egypt "that you may recount in the hearing of your sons and of your sons'

sons how I made a mockery of the Egyptians and how I displayed My signs among them — in order that you may know that I am the Lord" (Exodus 10:2).

The festival of Matzot that is to be celebrated throughout the ages is explained as being observed because "on this very day I brought your ranks out of the land of Egypt" (Exodus 12:17). The eating of the lamb, the Pesah, is interpreted as a remembrance of the fact that "He protected the houses of the Israelites in Egypt when He smote the Egyptians, but saved our houses" (Exodus 12:26). This is repeated in Exodus 13:8, 9 and 16. These festivals, as has often been pointed out, seem to have been known to the Israelites from ancient days (Martin Buber, *Moses*, p. 70). Our Passover is really an amalgam of two ancient holidays — Pesah, the shepherds' feast celebrating the birth of new lambs, and Matzot, the farmers' feast of the new crop. These are given new meaning and assigned the task of signifying the new unity of the people and interpreting the events they are living through. Similarly the dedication of the firstborn to God is to be connected to the fact that "When Pharaoh stubbornly refused to let us go, the Lord slew every firstborn in the land of Egypt, the firstborn of both man and beast" (Exodus 13:15).

Ancient pagan religions were based upon events in the lives of the gods — births, battles, triumphs, loves, deaths, resurrections. Some religions center themselves upon the lives of specific individuals. Judaism bases itself upon the interaction between God — the one God — and the people of Israel. The central event in that history is the Exodus from Egypt. Even God's creation of the world, as important and central as that is, takes second place to the Exodus. The Exodus demonstrates God's care for Israel, God's fulfillment of the promise made to the Patriarchs. Without it the covenant of Sinai could never have taken place. Without it the settlement in Canaan could not have happened.

Jewish practice is the expression of our theology and belief. It is the way in which we perpetuate these beliefs and make our children and ourselves conscious of them. That is why so much space is devoted in this section to the specifics of celebrating the Exodus through the offering of the Paschal Lamb, the eating of *matzot*, and the consecration of the firstborn (Exodus 13:1-2, 14-16). All of these practices are meant to concretize and perpetuate the memory of the story of the Exodus, from the slaying of the firstborn through the night of watching and protection (Pesah) and the hasty Exodus itself

(Matzot). The importance that the Torah places upon these observances can be seen from the fact that they are not only given and described in detail and at length in chapter 12:1-27, before the events take place, but are repeated again in Exodus 12:43-13:10 after the Exodus.

As Martin Buber has written:

> By celebrating the memory of their liberation they glorify the unfettering power whose activity in Nature manifests itself every year in the likeness of the spring. Yet since the night of the Exodus it has become a history feast, and indeed *the* history feast par excellence of the world; not a feast of pious remembrance, but of the ever-recurrent contemporaneousness of that which once befell. Every celebrating generation becomes united with the first generation and with all those who have followed. As in that night the families united into the living people, so in the Passover night the generations of the people unite together, year after year. (*Moses*, pp. 72-73)

Thus history, belief and practice are intertwined in this section as they are intertwined in Judaism and Jewish life. It is this triangle that constitutes the basis of traditional Judaism.

2. *Mitzvot* with Meaning

As a prelude to the last and most terrible plague, that which will break Pharaoh's hard-hearted refusal, twenty-eight verses are devoted to instructions to the Israelites concerning how they are to observe that first Passover and subsequent ones. After the plague itself, the killing of the firstborn and the subsequent Exodus are described (Exodus 12:29-42), the Torah continues with further instructions concerning the laws of Passover and the laws of the firstborn (Exodus 12:43-13:16). Thus the story of the actual Exodus from Egypt is surrounded by a series of observances, termed in the Hebrew *ḥukot* (laws). We would refer to them as *mitzvot*. This would seem to be a strange literary structure and it is worth asking why it was done that way.

Rashi, the famous medieval commentator, quoting Rabbi Yitzhak, begins his commentary to the Torah with the question, "Should not the Torah have begun with 'This month shall mark for you the beginning of the months'

(Exodus 12:2) since that is the first *mitzvah* in the Torah?" His answer is that
the Torah begins with Genesis in order to establish that God created the
entire earth and therefore has the right to distribute sections of it to whom-
ever He pleases, thus establishing our right to the land of Israel.

Whatever the answer, Rashi's question is a fundamental one. Is the Torah
a book of *mitzvot* alone — in which case we could do without Genesis as well
as much of Exodus, Leviticus, Numbers and Deuteronomy — or is it broader
than that, a book of doctrines, beliefs, ideas, philosophy and theology?
Rashi's answer is obviously the latter. Laws and regulations by themselves are
not sufficient. Judaism also wishes to influence our beliefs and our thinking.
It does not want blind obedience, nor does it believe that the observance of
mitzvot is enough. It is necessary, but not adequate. Observance alone can
breed a kind of blind religious adherence. All too often we see that happen,
resulting in a reduction of Judaism that omits the true riches of the tradition.

On the other hand, ideas and beliefs without deeds lead to an amorphous
"spirituality" that has no spine and no staying power. Judaism is a combination of both. One might term it a system of "*mitzvot* with meaning."

The sudden appearance of *mitzvot* in chapter 12 of Exodus, then, is a
matter of great significance. For the first time the Torah introduces this basic
concept that is so important in Judaism. It is truly a foreshadowing of the
revelation at Sinai when a covenant was made between God and Israel, the
terms of which included our observance of *mitzvot*. Throughout the Torah
narrative, stories and *mitzvot* exist side by side. There is no one book of regulations separated from the stories and ideas because the two are and must be
interwoven into one fabric. This portion illustrates that well.

There are three different sets of *mitzvot* found here, sometimes intertwined. Two come before the recounting of the Exodus and one follows it. All
three have the same general purpose: to memorialize for us aspects of the
Exodus from Egypt, the central event in the formation of our people. Yet each
one is also distinct.

The first set of regulations concerns the lamb, known as the Pesah. These
verses (Exodus 12:1–13, 21–28, 43–49) are addressed to the Israelites in Egypt
and tell them specifically what they are to do. They also indicate what must be
done thereafter throughout all generations. The Israelites in Egypt must take
a lamb and then slaughter it, smearing the blood on their doorposts so that
"when I see the blood I will pass over you, so that no plague will destroy you

when I strike the land of Egypt" (Exodus 12:13). The Sages emphasized time and time again that God did not need this sign in order to know where the Israelites lived. As Rashi puts it, "Everything is revealed to Him. Said the Holy One, Blessed be He, 'I will look to see if you are busying yourselves with *mitzvot* — and then I will protect you (Rashi, Exodus 12:13)!'" As a matter of fact the usual meaning of *Pesah* according to the rabbis is not "pass over" but "protect."

The purpose of these observances is stated explicitly in 12:26-27. In the future, children will ask why this is being done and will be told that it is because when the Egyptians were killed, the Israelites were spared.

The second set of regulations, Exodus 12:14-21 and 13:3-10, concerns the unleavened bread, *matzah*. It was to be eaten for seven days and no leaven was to be found in their dwellings. Later rabbinic interpretation taught that it need be eaten only on the first night. Here too the meaning and purpose is specified. It was to serve as a reminder of the fact that on that day Israel left Egypt: "And you shall explain to your son on that day, 'It is because of what the Lord did for me when I went free from Egypt'" (Exodus 13:8).

The third set of *mitzvot* (Exodus 13:1-2, 11-16), related after the Exodus itself takes place, concerns the laws of the firstborn. All of the firstborn belong to God and the reason, once again to be explained to children in future generations, is that "It was with a mighty hand that the Lord brought us out from Egypt, the house of bondage. When Pharaoh stubbornly refused to let us go, the Lord slew every firstborn of Egypt" (Exodus 13:14-15).

The pattern set in this portion is continued throughout the Torah and throughout the history of Judaism. It is a pattern in which we mix law and legend, *halakhah* and *aggadah*, practice and belief, so that deeds are not dry and automatic and so that ideas and beliefs are not mere words without practical consequences. It is this combination that makes Judaism so powerful and so meaningful.

B'shalaḥ   בשלח

Exodus 13:17-17:16 | שמות יג:יז-יז:טז

1. The Transformation at the Sea

The story of the Exodus is not over until the army of Pharaoh is defeated so that Israel need fear no more. This happens at *Yam Suf*, the Sea of Reeds, identified by most scholars today as Lake Sirbonis, a marshy area in the north of Egypt near the Mediterranean Sea. The events at the sea are narrated in a prose account in Exodus 14:10-31 and then celebrated in poetry in the magnificent Song at the Sea (Exodus 15:1-18), a poem which has served ever since as the expression *par excellence* of thanksgiving for God's salvation. In reality the Exodus is not over until the people sing.

The prose narrative is framed by the Hebrew word *yirah* (fear) that appears before the destruction of the Egyptians and again after it. The first time is in the verse "the Israelites were greatly frightened [*vayir'u*] and cried out to the Lord" (Exodus 14:10). The second time, after the Egyptians have drowned and the Israelites have passed over in safety, the verse states, "the people feared [*vayir'u*] the Lord and had faith in the Lord and in His servant Moses" (Exodus 14:31). The fear of the Egyptians has changed to fear of God.

A great transformation has taken place. At first the Israelites fear the Egyptians, they fear for their lives and they complain to Moses that they never should have left Egypt in the first place! "Let us be, and we will serve the Egyptians, for it is better for us to serve the Egyptians than to die in the wilderness" (Exodus 14:12). To this Moses replies (using that same Hebrew word) "Have no fear!" and assures them that God will fight for them and deliver them (Exodus 14:13-14). This is exactly what happens, and the result is that they now fear — or better, "revere" — God and put their trust in the Lord and in Moses.

Whatever it is that transpired in those marshy waters was an event that transformed them, an event that we can never exactly describe, for all we have is the impression that it made upon the Israelites. In a sense, that is what is important. Although the word "miracle" is not used in the description, it is obvious that what happened was perceived as a direct intervention of God. Martin Buber wrote of it:

> It is irrelevant whether "much" or "little", unusual things or usual, tremendous or trifling events happened; what is vital is only that what happened was experienced, while it happened, as the act of God…we have found that the permissible concept of miracle from the historical approach means, to begin with, nothing but an abiding astonishment…. The real miracle means that in the astonishing experience of the event the current system of cause and effect becomes, as it were, transparent and permits a glimpse of the sphere in which a sole power, not restricted by any other, is at work. (*Moses*, p. 77)

There were two such transforming events in the creation of our people and our faith. This was the first. The second was the event at Sinai recorded in the following Torah portion. It is not accidental that the general custom in synagogues is to stand when hearing the readings of both of these events. At the sea we experienced "the hand of God" in our salvation. At Sinai we heard "the voice of God" speaking the terms of the covenant that made us God's people. At the sea we experienced God in our history. At Sinai, we experienced God in our moral and spiritual development.

It is disappointing that after reaching this pinnacle of faith, revering God and trusting Him and His servant Moses, within a short time the people begin again to complain and to doubt. They grumble about water (Exodus 15:24), about food (Exodus 16:3) and yet once again about water (Exodus 17:2).

The question that arises, then, is: did the "miracle" at the sea have any lasting effect or did it only generate a momentary trust and banish fear temporarily? As Buber wrote, "To live with the miracle means to recognize this power on every given occasion as the effecting one" (*Moses*, p. 77). But it is difficult to do that and there are moments when the miracle is forgotten.

Yet it seems to me that the final event recorded in this portion, the battle against Amalek, demonstrates that something *has* happened to the people of Israel. They *have* changed — and for the better. For the first time the Israelites take arms against an enemy. Moses commands Joshua to "pick some men for us, and go out and do battle with Amalek" (Exodus 17:9). Joshua complies, and they defeat the forces of Amalek.

Contrast this with the events at the sea, when the Israelites were told, "The Lord will battle for you; you hold your peace!" (Exodus 14:14). Granted that the Amalekites were not as powerful as Pharaoh's army, there is nevertheless a startling contrast between "hold your peace" and "go out and do battle!" And note too that here there is not a word of complaint. They go to battle with no mumbling and no grumbling. Something has taken place after all. The fear they had at the beginning has somehow been mitigated and they enter their first battle with courage.

As we know, the generation of the Exodus, better known as the generation of the wilderness, will never totally overcome its slave mentality and is doomed to perish before coming to the land of promise, but nevertheless, having experienced salvation at the sea, they will never again be the same. Something of the miracle abides. Such moments can never be erased, even if at times they are submerged. So too it is with our lives. There are times when we achieve moments of transcendence, moments when we feel touched by the Divine, when life seems to have great meaning and purpose. And even if we cannot sustain that peak of belief, it never completely disappears. It is like a small ember that continues to glow and that can once again become a great flame if we nurture it properly.

2. The Return to Normalcy

As we have seen, the magnificent Song at the Sea stands as the high point of this portion. It commemorates an event that was the climax of the Exodus. Only with the utter defeat of the Egyptian army can Israel be said to be truly free, with no further danger of enslavement. Tradition, taking its cue from the words "they had faith in the Lord and in His servant Moses" (Exodus 14:31), went so far as to say that every Israelite, even the lowliest handmaiden, "saw" — i.e., experienced — God in a way that even the greatest prophets were unable to do (*Mekhilta Shirata* 3). No wonder the Sages decreed that this song had to be quoted and referred to daily in our prayers as part of the last blessing of the Sh'ma, just prior to the recitation of the Amidah. Only when we feel that we have experienced God's salvation can we truly sing or pray to God wholeheartedly.

And yet the story does not end there. The sections which follow this moment of triumph and of supreme faith and belief, as we saw, tell a story of a people not yet ready to follow God and His servant Moses into freedom.

Only three verses later they have come to an oasis and found the water bitter: "And the people grumbled against Moses, saying, 'What shall we drink?'" (Exodus 15:24). Patiently, God arranges to sweeten the water for them. A few verses later, only one month after their departure from Egypt, they say, "If only we had died by the hand of the Lord in the land of Egypt, when we sat by the fleshpots, when we ate our fill of bread! For you have brought us out into this wilderness to starve this whole congregation to death" (Exodus 16:3). Hardly the words of people who have seen God and attained perfect faith. Furthermore one wonders just how good and plentiful the food of slave-laborers really was. What short memories people have!

In each instance the reaction of God is very mild. He does not rebuke the people but answers their requests and gives them water, manna and meat. It is as if God realizes that it is too much to expect them to undergo the difficulties of a wilderness journey without complaint and so He indulges them as a parent would indulge a child whose immediate needs require gratification. Moses is less patient with them.

They are told not to gather the manna on Shabbat, yet some of them do (Exodus 16:27). By now God Himself is grumbling: "How long will you men refuse to obey My commandments and My teachings?" (Exodus 16:28). Yet again they complain about the lack of water: "Why did you bring us up from Egypt, to kill us and our children and livestock with thirst?" (Exodus 17:3). Moses strikes a rock and gets water for them in a place called "Massah [trial] and Meribah [quarrel], because the Israelites quarreled and because they tried the Lord, saying, 'Is the Lord present among us or not?'"(Exodus 17:7). So there we have it — four incidents of complaint between the Sea of Reeds and the theophany at Sinai that took place less than two months after the

Exodus. Since their first complaint took place one month after the Exodus, that makes one complaint a week.

Of course if we look back at the actions of the Israelites before the Exodus, we find that then too they complained and grumbled. See Exodus 6:21 where they complain that Moses' actions have made them loathsome to Pharaoh and Exodus 14:11 where they say, "Was it for want of graves in Egypt that you brought us forth to die in the wilderness?"

Evidently the exalted moment of the rescue at the sea made no lasting difference in their temperament. Perhaps this is human nature. We can exult for a moment after a particularly inspiring experience. We can even make all kinds of resolutions about what we will do or not do, but a little while later we go back to our old habits, our old patterns. Yet God is willing to enter into a covenant with the Israelites at Sinai even after seeing their continuously quarrelsome nature. As the midrash puts it, "The Israelites were like sheep…just as the owner of sheep does not complain even when his sheep do damage and gnaw away at trees, so even when Israel sinned, God treated them as His sheep" (*Exodus Rabbah* 24:3). The Torah seems to be telling us something about God. Even when the Israelites have sinned, He will be merciful toward them. He is willing to forgive these very human foibles. They want creature comforts — water, food. They are just emerging from slavery and cannot yet be expected to have fully matured into independent people with mature judgment. Later on, in the story of the golden calf and then again in the incident of the spies, we will see that God too has His limits and will call on the Israelites to account for certain things. Concerning food and water, however, He is willing to forgive them and will not let their actions interfere with the plan that He has in mind.

From the very first, God intended to solemnize a new covenant with the people of Israel, a covenant that would go far beyond the promises made to the Patriarchs. Without spelling this out, the Torah has given us two hints. The first was when God said of Abraham, "For I have singled him out, that *he may instruct his children and his posterity to keep the way of the Lord by doing what is just and right*" (Genesis 18:19). The second was when, in the first revelation to Moses that took place at Mount Sinai, Moses was told, "When you have freed the people from Egypt, you shall worship God *at this mountain*" (Exodus 3:12). Something of great importance is to take place "at this mountain," at Sinai. It is here that Israel will be instructed "to keep the way of the Lord by doing what is just and right" through the commandments that will be given to them. It is here that they will become God's holy people.

They are not a perfect people and they never will be. They will grumble and complain, but they will also strive to achieve holiness.

Yitro יתרו

Exodus 18:1–20:23 | שמות יח:א-כ:כג

1. The Mystery at the Mountain

What happened at Mount Sinai? That is the question that stands at the heart of this Torah portion. It also stands at the heart of Judaism and of our understanding of our history and the meaning of our existence. It is curious that such an important event as revelation is virtually ignored in Jewish liturgy.

The noted German Jewish philosopher Franz Rosenzweig posited three major themes in Judaism: Creation, Revelation and Redemption. Two of these are spoken of often. Time and time again we recall the Exodus or the Creation in our prayers. The phrases "in remembrance of the Exodus from Egypt" or "in remembrance of the Creation" are often on our lips. Not so "in remembrance of Mount Sinai." Revelation is thus ignored. In the Torah itself there is no holiday devoted to it. Shavuot, which in rabbinic times came to be "the time of the giving of our Torah," is not so designated in the Torah and one wonders why. It is only much later that the Pharisees determined that Shavuot was the commemoration of the Sinai theophany.

If one seeks a detailed description of the event and its chronology, it may be impossible to find. It is difficult to discern what actually happened. A careful reading of the account in the Torah makes it quite clear that there is no attempt to give us a logical, rational, explanation of this event. On the contrary, it seems as if the Torah is deliberately shrouding it in clouds just as the mountain itself was covered by a "dense cloud" (Exodus 19:16). The event itself, as described in the Torah, is an enigma wrapped in a mystery. Moses ascends and descends the mountain many times, often seemingly without purpose. Where exactly was Moses when God spoke? (See especially Exodus

19:21–25.) When exactly does God speak and what does God say? What do the people hear? All of the so-called Ten Commandments (the Hebrew *aseret hadevarim* means "the ten utterances")? Some of them? A few words? Or — as one tradition has it — only the first letter, which, of course, is the unutterable *aleph*?

This mysteriousness can be encapsulated in the way in which the event is described: the people saw the thunder and lightening, the sound of the shofar and the mountain smoking (Exodus 20:15). As Rabbi Akiba put it, "They see *and hear* what can be seen" (*Mekhilta Baḥodesh* 9). In other words, they hear things that can usually only be seen. Thus this is an event that cannot be described, that cannot be put into human language.

Even the exact location of Sinai remains unknown. Mount Sinai did not retain any sacredness once the revelation was over. We do not even have any Jewish tradition concerning its location. The place visited today, commonly known as Jebel Musa, received its designation in Christian tradition, as is evident from the fact that a monastery is located there. It is a wonderful place to visit, but it is most unlikely that it is the real location of the mountain that Moses climbed and from which God spoke to the entire people of Israel. That remains unknown. Mount Sinai itself, where this tremendous event took place, played no part in our tradition. With one exception — the story of Elijah related in 1 Kings 19:8–18 — no one ever went back there in pilgrimage, and when Elijah did so the revelation of God he experienced was exactly the opposite of that in our account. Instead of thunder and lightning, he experienced God in "a still, small voice." Perhaps the message is that the event was an encounter that cannot be described in the terms we usually use for historical events, a direct encounter with the Divine that can never be captured in human language.

Maurice Samuel wrote of it thus:

> At Sinai He revealed Himself. At Sinai, wherever it is located, at a certain point in time, whenever we date it, a people saw God; or, rather, as the record itself says, a people became overwhelmingly aware of Him — He is not to be seen. And this flash of awareness became an everlasting fixation. In this fixation the people has endured when all its early contemporaries, as well as other peoples who came upon the world scene subsequently, have disappeared.

(*The Ten Commandments* [Chicago: University of Chicago Press, 1956], pp.xii-xiii)

The narrative cannot be understood because the event was unique. It could not simply be reproduced in any way because we have no way of understanding it. The account in the Torah is deliberately ambiguous. Like an impressionist painting, it cannot be understood literally. The Exodus, the wandering, even if seen as the work of the hand of God, nevertheless took place within the realm of history and human experience. Therefore it could be retold and relived at Pesah and Sukkot. Sinai was outside of that realm and would only be cheapened by any attempt to capture or relive it. Thus the reluctance to commemorate it or to refer to it in commonplace terms. To paraphrase the title of a mysterious film, Sinai was "a close encounter of the third kind."

2. The Covenant

We may not be able to say exactly what happened at Sinai, but we know its effect and we may be certain that the purpose of the encounter was to create a covenanted people. As the text puts it, "Indeed, all the earth is Mine, but you shall be to Me a kingdom of priests and a holy nation" (Exodus 19:5-6). But this covenant is conditional upon obedience to God (see Exodus 19:5). One might say that the rest of Jewish history is the unfolding attempt to discover exactly what that obedience entails. The first stage of that discovery is found in the writings of the Torah, the second in the Prophets, followed by the interpretations and applications of the Sages and the religious leaders of Israel throughout the generations. It is a task that is no less relevant today than in ages past.

The Decalogue (the "ten words") — as the Ten Commandments are more correctly called — represents the basic terms of the covenantal relationship, but by no means exhausts what is required of us. If it did, the rest of the Torah would be irrelevant. Even according to the Torah itself and to the Sages (much less according to theories of modern Biblical scholars) the Torah was not complete until forty years later when Moses either wrote or compiled all of the instructions conveyed to him by God during those years of wandering.

As we read in the Talmud, some Sages teach that the Torah was given "scroll by scroll," which Rashi interprets as meaning that "When a section was spoken to Moses, he would write it down, and at the end of forty years when all the sections were complete, he gathered them together and sewed them together with sinews." Others teach that the Torah was given "sealed" and Rashi explains that as meaning that Moses received sections from God year by year orally "but only wrote them down all together at the end of the forty years" (*Gittin* 60a).

And yet it is obvious that there is something special, even unique, about the Decalogue itself. It is the only part of the Torah to have been spoken directly by God in a public way, rather than being conveyed through Moses and Aaron. It is the only part that was written in stone "inscribed with the finger of God" (Exodus 31:18; see also 32:16). Ironically the tablets that survived whole were only the second set that was carved and written by Moses, not by God (Exodus 34:27–28).

Although, as scholars such as Nahum Sarna have pointed out, the prohibitions of murder, adultery, theft, etc. found in the Decalogue are not unique and formed part of the legal codes of many ancient nations, in no other place in the ancient world are they presented as the unconditional demands of God, absolute moral imperatives, rather than the legislation of a human ruler, enforceable only by human punishment. In addition to these moral demands, which are equally applicable to all humanity, parts of the Decalogue apply exclusively to Israel. Absolute moral laws form the basis of our relationship to God, but in addition, as God's "particular treasure" (Exodus 19:5) we must also obey two "ritual" imperatives — the imageless worship of the Lord alone as outlined in the first three commandments, prohibiting idols and idolatry (Exodus 20:2–7), and the observance of the Sabbath delineated in the fourth commandment (Exodus 20:8–11), the sign of belief in God, the Creator of all.

Rabbinic tradition wisely saw the terms of the Decalogue and its acceptance by Israel as the acceptance of two "yokes" — i.e., obligations. First came the acceptance of the "yoke of God's sovereignty" (*kabbalat ol malkhut shamayim*), unconditional acceptance of God as our sole ruler. This was followed by the "yoke of the *mitzvot*" (*kabbalat ol mitzvot*), the acceptance of whatever rules God wished to place upon us (*Mekhilta Baḥodesh* 5 and 6). When reciting the Sh'ma twice daily we repeat this act of acceptance of these two "yokes" and thus carry the meaning of Sinai into our own lives continually.

The importance of those "ten utterances" or "declarations" is to be found not only in their content, but also in the claim that they are God's utterances and express the divine, moral underpinnings of human civilization. Exactly how they were transmitted to us remains a matter of faith, the mystery at the heart of Jewish belief.

Abraham Joshua Heschel once commented on the question of the sanctity of the Bible as follows:

> How these words were written down is not the fundamental problem. That is why the theme of Biblical criticism is not the theme of faith, just as the question of whether the lightning and thunder at Sinai were a natural phenomenon or not is irrelevant to our faith in revelation. The act of revelation is a mystery, while the record of revelation is a literary fact, phrased in the language of man. (*God In Search of Man* [Philadelphia: Jewish Publication Society of America, 1956], p. 258)

Judaism's reluctance to explain and describe clearly what happened at Sinai should not detract from our emphasis on the importance of the event. Just as Creation seems inexplicable to us, no matter how science describes it, so too the communication of the divine will remains inexplicable. But just as we can believe in the one without grasping all the details, so too can we accept the other. A God great enough to create this magnificent, unbounded universe is also great enough to communicate with human beings. That is what happened at Sinai, in a way no one can truly describe, and the echoes of that event reverberate through history and inspire us to moral living today as they did then.

It was this event that sealed Israel in a great covenant with God that had been foretold in God's first encounter with Moses, "And I will take you to be My people, and I will be your God" (Exodus 6:7), and which has sustained us ever since. The Exodus was the event that made us a people. The experience of Sinai made us a holy people, committed to the worship of God alone and to the discovery and observance of God's ways. The Exodus is the paradigm of all acts of redemption and can be replicated in events small and large. Sinai occurred only once and can never be repeated — because it has never ceased.

It is the seed from which all of Judaism has grown and continues to grow as we devote ourselves to the application of this covenant and its teachings to the needs of each and every age.

Mishpatim   משפטים

Exodus 21:1–24:18 | שמות כא:א-כד:יח

1. The Laws of Daily Life

The revelation at Sinai was not confined to the Ten Commandments but continued with the entire series of laws that are contained in this portion. This section of the Torah, commonly referred to as the "Covenant Code," is a mixture of specific laws governing cases of civil law and general statements explaining the religious and moral motivations behind this code. Throughout the centuries these laws have served as the basis for *Nezikin*, laws of damages that are discussed at great length in the Mishnah, the Talmud and all the codes of Jewish law. The way of life prescribed in the Torah was not confined to relations between God and human beings, nor to general principles, but sought to bring the Torah's concepts of righteousness and justice into the everyday affairs of society.

Until the time of the emancipation, a few hundred years ago, and in some locations far beyond that, Jews lived in self-governing communities, so that these laws were the actual code by which Jews governed themselves and were judged when they came before their own courts. One of the most drastic changes that has come about in modern Jewish life is that these laws are no longer operative, even in the State of Israel, but have been superseded by the civil laws of the countries in which Jews live. Nevertheless they still deserve study and understanding because they have valuable lessons to teach us that can help guide us in the ethical choices we make. In Israel, they can also serve to influence judicial decisions and legislative initiatives of the Knesset.

When we begin to read this portion, however, we are puzzled by the fact that the very first laws set down for the fledgling people Israel after their liberation from Egyptian bondage are laws of slavery: "When you acquire a Hebrew slave" (Exodus 21:2). Is there not something ironic in the fact that just after attaining their own freedom, the Hebrews are given a code that includes the possibility of enslaving others — in this case, their fellow Israelites?

Especially troubling is the verse that states that if a slave dies after being beaten by his owner, if he has survived even for a day "he is not to be avenged, since he is the other's property" (Exodus 21:21). How does one square this with the principle that "Whoever sheds the blood of a human being, by a human being shall his blood be shed, for God created the human being [Adam] in His image" (Genesis 9:6)? Of course we could also ask how the United States squared slavery with its declaration that "all men are created equal". It often takes some time before great principles are completely understood and translated into proper norms.

In other words, some of the precepts of the Torah do not necessarily represent the final word of God, but rather the beginning of a gradual change leading toward that which would be the ultimate goal. Laws of slavery, then, do not mean that God desires slavery to be a part of human existence, but that given the fact that slavery existed everywhere and could not suddenly be eradicated, it must at least be controlled and modified. It is not accidental that the first thing we are told about slavery is that "in the seventh year he shall go free, without payment" (Exodus 21:2). We are not told to acquire a slave, but we are commanded that after six years we must let that slave go free. Nahum Sarna has pointed out that the laws of slavery found in Exodus 21:2–11 deal specifically with "the imposition of legal restraints on the power of a master over his Hebrew male and female slaves, and the establishment of the legal rights of slaves" (*Exploring Exodus*, [New York: Schocken, 1996], p. 159). The emphasis of the Torah is not on the fact that we should have slaves, but on the way in which slaves must be treated as human beings, rather than chattel, and the legal limitations put upon the rights of the "owner."

All of this stands in stark contrast to laws of slavery in other ancient Near Eastern codes, such as the famous code of Hammurabi. Again, as Sarna points out, "the laws mitigate the harshness that accompanies the status of chattel, and they enhance the recognition of the slave as a human being" (p. 181). Exodus 21:26 grants the slave freedom if the master injures him seriously. The Ten Commandments specify that "your male or female slave" shall not work on the Sabbath (Exodus 20:10) and, in total contradiction to all other codes at that time, and indeed to laws of slavery in the United States in the 1800s, Deuteronomy 23:16–17 decrees that a runaway slave is not to be returned to his master. Slavery was not abolished, which would be the desired goal, but it was modified.

The later development of rabbinic law certainly recognized this trend, as we can see from such statements as that in *Tosefta Baba Kama* 7:5, which interprets the verse in Exodus 21:6 that if a slave decides not to go free after six years as is his right, "his master shall pierce his ear with an awl; and he shall then remain his slave for life": The ear, which heard at Sinai "You are My slaves" (Leviticus 25:42) but nevertheless preferred subjection to men rather than to God, deserves to be pierced!

This tendency in Jewish law can be seen even more clearly in the rabbinic enactments, which, in effect, made slavery inoperative. For example, Jewish law prohibits the Hebrew slave from washing his master's feet, putting on his shoes, carrying his things before him to the bathhouse, supporting him by the hips when going up stairs, carrying him in a litter (a vehicle designed to be carried by people or animals), a chair or a sedan chair. Nor may his master put him to work in anything where he has to serve the public, force him to change his trade or work at night (*Mekhilta Nezikin* 1)! It could be said that if one acquires a slave, one acquires a master.

2. Law Into Life

Mishpatim is undoubtedly one of the most important sections of the Torah because it indicates that religious belief cannot remain in the realm of sweeping principles, but must be translated into specific norms and laws for individuals and societies. We have seen that it is sometimes troubling because it contains laws that are far from our current concepts of righteousness, laws that none of us would want to have as part of our modern way of life.

Equally disturbing is the notion that a father can sell his daughter into servitude (Exodus 21:7). As well, the wholesale usage of the death penalty also seems at variance with our values. Fortunately we know that many of these laws were modified and reinterpreted by our Sages. Modern Biblical studies have also demonstrated that many of these laws were forward looking for their time and were not instituted to be severe but, on the contrary, to modify what was then the existing practice among the peoples of the Near East.

In the words of Maimonides:

> Many precepts in our Law [Torah] are the result of a similar course adopted by the same Supreme Being. It is, namely, impossible to go suddenly from one extreme to the other. It is therefore according to the nature of man impossible for him suddenly to discontinue every-thing to which he has been accustomed. (*Guide for the Perplexed*, trans. M. Friedlander [New York: Dover, 1956], 3:32)

When looked upon in this way, as a concession to human nature and in context against the background of their time and place, rather than absolute norms, they are better understood and less problematic.

Maimonides was quite right and far ahead of his time in teaching that the Torah must be understood within historical context. With our current knowledge of the writings, laws and culture of other nations during the formative years of the creation of the people Israel, we can understand the laws of the Torah better than ever before. We can appreciate the tremendous strides that the Torah took in advancing humankind toward justice and decency in human relationships and in actualizing the ideals inherent in the Torah's fundamental principle that humans are created in the image of God.

On the other hand we must not forget that this section also contains laws that are so exalted as to take one's breath away. We have, for example, a whole series that deals with the treatment of the weaker elements of society: "You shall not wrong a stranger or oppress him, for you were strangers in the land of Egypt. You shall not ill-treat any widow or orphan" (Exodus 22:20-21). It is not accidental that these concepts are repeated over and over, both in our portion (Exodus 23:9) and elsewhere in the Torah.

Perhaps even more astonishing and sensitive are the laws concerning one's enemies: we are instructed to return their stray animals and help them when their beasts fall down (Exodus 23:4-5). And as for the poor, not only are we forbidden from taking interest when we loan to them, but if we take a garment as pledge we must return it "before the sun sets; it is his only clothing, the sole covering for his skin. In what else shall he sleep? Therefore, if he cries out to Me, I will pay heed, for I am compassionate" (Exodus 22:25-26). If ever verses could make one believe in the divinity of the Torah, surely these can.

Yet another main feature of these laws is the emphasis on justice. There are two dangers: that the rich and powerful will receive special treatment and that the poor will be given deference. Both are forbidden (Exodus 23:2, 6). We are warned against false testimony (Exodus 23:1-2) and we are forbidden to take bribes (Exodus 23:8). There is nothing more basic to society than a just system of courts so that both rich and poor can expect an impartial hearing. Throughout the ages Jewish communities have been renowned for honest courts. This is a tradition that is proudly upheld today as well and any hint of corruption is and must be ferreted out immediately.

All of these laws are intimately connected to the Sinai revelation. As a matter of fact the story of the events at Sinai did not conclude with the Ten Commandments but continues in this portion as well. When all of the various statutes have been enumerated, the narrative portion of the story of Sinai is resumed in chapter 24 with the description of Moses once more ascending the mountain together with Aaron, Nadab, Abihu and seventy elders. It is only then that Moses tells the people all that has been commanded and Israel accepts these laws saying, "All the things that the Lord has commanded we will do" (Exodus 24:3).

The Sages further emphasized this connection by telling us that the letter *vav* (meaning "and") — with which this section begins — is there in order to connect these laws with what came before, so that just as the Ten Commandments came from God at Sinai, so did these laws. They are not less important or less holy. This teaching was undoubtedly intended to refute those heretical groups in ancient times who taught that only the Ten Commandments were holy, while all the rest was man-made. That is also the reason the Ten Commandments, which had originally been included in the recitation of the Sh'ma, were removed and have no place in our daily prayers.

No, the Torah, the divine word, is not simply a set of general principles. It must include matters of daily life, of commerce, of agriculture, of human relations. To be a holy people, as we are commanded here (Exodus 22:30), means fashioning an entire way of life, an entire society in which these principles are put into practice. The development of Jewish Law (*halakhah*) through the ages has been the search for the way to encompass our understanding of God's will in our way of life. It is a process that began at Sinai and has never ceased. It is that search which makes us worthy of God's revelation.

Terumah   תרומה

Exodus 25:1–27:19 | שמות כה:א-כז:יט

1. The Sanctuary: The House of God

The instructions given to Moses while he remained at the top of Mount Sinai
contained not only the specific laws that were to be conveyed to the people of
Israel so that they could create their own society, but also instructions
concerning the building of a sanctuary, the *Mishkan*. They were not to leave
Sinai without having constructed a tent-like structure that would provide —
as it were — a dwelling place for God, a home for the Tablets of Testimony
and a place where Israel could worship God. Sinai was known as "the mountain of God" and now this tabernacle would replace it as the "dwelling of
God."

Of course, none of this should be taken too literally. Centuries later, when
this tent was replaced by a magnificent permanent structure, Solomon, the
Temple-builder, clearly stated, "even the heavens and the heavens of heavens
cannot contain You, much less this house that I have built!" (1 Kings 8:27).
Yet some way had to be found to bring the Presence of God closer to human
beings. There was a need to build a structure that would foster the feeling of
holiness so that God would not be simply an abstraction, but a living Presence.

This was especially important in the case of the religion of Israel that
taught an imageless God. Pagans could see their gods, or at least representations of them. Israelites could not. It is true that here and there we find scat-
tered hints that perhaps some visible manifestation of God was seen — as
when Moses sees not God's face but God's back (Exodus 33:23) or when the
elders "saw the God of Israel…. They beheld God, and they ate and drank"

(Exodus 24:10-11). On the other hand, the book of Deuteronomy makes it quite clear in its polemic against idol worship that "you heard the sound of words but perceived no shape — nothing but a voice" (Deuteronomy 4:12). To emphasize the point, Deuteronomy repeats it — "you saw no shape when the Lord your God spoke to you at Horeb out of the fire" (Deuteronomy 4:15) — and therefore we are forbidden to make any images for worship.

Yet human beings are the sum of their senses and need something to concretize their thoughts, beliefs and feelings. The incident of the golden calf proves that point. Some of the Sages even indicated that the command to make the Sanctuary was a reaction to that incident. Lacking images and statues, the Tabernacle was to serve that purpose. It provided a locus for the Divine — here is where one can go to worship. Within the Sanctuary, holiness increased as one approached the Holy of Holies, since that is where the Ark was found — the Ark that was both the throne of God and the repository of God's word.

The midrash comments on the words "And let them make Me a sanctuary that I may dwell among them" (Exodus 25:8):

> When the Holy One, blessed be He said this to Moses, Moses was amazed and replied, "The glory of the Holy One, blessed be He fills the high and low places — yet He says to me "Make Me a sanctuary!" But the Holy One, blessed be He said to him, "It's not what you think, rather take this piece of wood, and that piece of wood..." (*Exodus Rabbah* 24:1)

In other words, you are not asked to create a supernatural building that can truly contain the Divine. Just follow the instructions and that will be sufficient. It should also be noted that the words are very explicit. The verse does not say, "that I may dwell *in it*" but "that I may dwell *among them.*"

Certainly the Tabernacle served its function well during the days of wandering and even beyond. Interestingly enough, for all its holiness, when David came to place the Ark in Jerusalem it seems that he erected a tent of his own devising and did not use this structure which was so specifically and divinely ordained (2 Samuel 6:17).

Later there were two almost contradictory developments concerning the Sanctuary. The first was that once the kingdom was established, a portable tent seemed no longer appropriate and a much more pretentious structure, the Temple, was built even though God expressed His reservations to it, saying, "From the day that I brought the people of Israel out of Egypt to this day I have not dwelt in a house, but have moved about in Tent and Tabernacle…. Did I ever reproach any of the tribal leaders whom I appointed…saying: why have you not built Me a house of cedar?" (2 Samuel 7:6-7). Nevertheless, He gave permission for Solomon to build it — more as a concession to the new times than as an answer to any need God may have had.

The second development, which seems to have taken place later during the Second Temple period, and went in the opposite direction, was the development of synagogues that existed side-by-side with that Temple prior to its destruction. The synagogue too was and is a place in which God's Presence can be found — but in a very different way. The Temple was a one-of-a-kind building. It was not to be duplicated wherever Israelites — later Jews — lived. Its structure and placement were very specific and it was the domain of one hereditary group of people, the kohanim. The formal worship therein was sacrificial. As such it could not meet all the needs of the people. Physically it was too far away from most of them. Spiritually it lacked the element of personal verbal worship and the ability of every Jew to be an active participant. Nor did it provide a place for learning and instruction. Therefore the creation of synagogues was a religious imperative. How much poorer our lives today would be had we never developed the synagogue. The synagogue is not a temple, but it is a place that plays for us the role that the Tabernacle must have played for our ancestors — a focus for holiness and the experience of the presence of the Divine.

The creation of the *Mishkan* — a physical structure in which God's Presence could rest but which was not God's literal house and in which there could be no physical representation of God — was a revolutionary event in the history of religion. The creation of the synagogue — a place that could be erected anywhere, in which one could hear and study the Torah and worship without sacrifice — was no less revolutionary. We are the beneficiaries of both revolutions.

2. Sacred Space

I once visited the magnificent Neolog synagogue in Szeged, Hungary, a fantasy in blue, white and gold. It is one of the — if not *the* — most beautiful synagogues in the world. I was awestruck at the efforts Jews have made wherever they lived to create a physical structure that would mirror the beauty of holiness. This tradition begins with the description in this portion of the *Mishkan* — the sanctuary — and its appurtenances.

The civil laws came first — a clear sign that the relationship of one human being to another, justice, righteousness and merciful acts are the most important foundations of a religious life. But establishing a relationship to God was critical to the new society that Moses was forming and that is done through the erection of a physical structure that concretizes this relationship. That is the meaning of the words "And let them make Me a sanctuary that I may dwell among them" (Exodus 25:8).

As Nahum Sarna points out:

> The literal meaning of *shakhan* is 'to rest,' not 'to dwell.' The sanctuary is not meant to be taken as God's abode... [it] makes tangible the concept of the indwelling of the divine Presence, God's immanence, in the camp of Israel, a presence to which the people may direct their hearts and minds." (*Etz Hayim* [Philadelphia: Jewish Publication Society of America, 2001], p. 487)

In creating this structure and its furnishings, ancient Israelite religion adopted many of the outward forms of pagan worship, but with a profound difference. In paganism, the temples were literally the houses of the gods; the altars were places where food was offered to them. In our religion all of this became symbolic because of the fundamental difference in our understanding of the nature of God, who has no physical needs.

Furthermore it created a sacred space, so that the Israelites would be constantly aware of God and God's protecting care. In a profound sense this building was a representation of Mount Sinai, "the Mountain of God," where the Lord had first manifested Himself to Moses at the burning bush and then to all Israel. They could neither take the mountain with them nor stay there, but they could make a representation of it, the Sanctuary, which would accompany them wherever they went and which would later be erected permanently in Jerusalem on another holy mountain, Moriah.

The danger in creating such a place is that people may come to regard it as pagans regarded their temples, a place so imbued with the presence of the gods that it has the potency to protect the people regardless of their conduct. That was exactly the belief that Jeremiah railed against centuries later. He saw a generation that had abandoned God's commands, that had violated the restrictions against theft, oppression of the poor and the shedding of blood. Nevertheless at a time of danger they came to the Temple in Jerusalem, proclaiming, "The Temple of the Lord, the Temple of the Lord are these!" (Jeremiah 7:4). Jeremiah told them that the building meant nothing, that such trust was an illusion. They had turned the Temple into a den of thieves and it would not protect them. God has no need of such a building when those who worship within it do not heed God's word.

There is always the danger that structure will become more important than substance. When anything, be it a building or a ritual, becomes more important than obedience to God's ethical commands, we are in trouble.

It is important to remember the verse that specifies that the Sanctuary is to be created from free will offerings: "Tell the Israelite people to bring Me gifts; you shall accept gifts for Me from every person whose heart so moves him" (Exodus 25:2). There is a profound message in this. God could and did command the people to observe many laws and ordinances. But when it came to building the *Mishkan*, which truly symbolized the close relationship between God and the people, He did not command it. Either it would come willingly, from their hearts, or it would not be worth building. Belief, religion, cannot be forced. Coercion only corrupts religion and creates resentment. We can build sanctuaries for God, both physical structures and spiritual structures within our own lives, but to be meaningful they must come from within, from our own free will, from our desire to express love of God and appreciation of the life and the world that God has given us. Then and only then will God truly dwell in our midst.

Titzaveh   תצוה

Exodus 27:20–30:10 | שמות כז:כ-ל:י

1. The Role of the Priest

The previous Torah portion dealt with the physical structure that was to be erected to symbolize God's presence among the people of Israel, the Tabernacle or *Mishkan*. This section is devoted to those who are to serve God within that structure and the garments they are to wear.

Knowing what we know, we take it for granted that this task will be given to the descendants of Aaron. They will be the priests (*kohanim*) consecrated to God's service. But that choice was not inevitable nor was it mentioned before. As a matter of fact, the midrash indicates that Moses thought that this task was to be given to him and may even have been disappointed that it was not. He was pacified, however, in that at least it went to his own tribe and his own brother, Aaron (*Exodus Rabbah* 37:1).

One could argue that Aaron's position was better than that of Moses because it was hereditary. This honor was bestowed not only upon him but upon his descendants, whereas Moses' children had no role of importance to play. Moses was a prophet, and prophecy is not inherited; it is bestowed by God upon individuals.

As a matter of fact there is no particular reason indicated as to why Aaron and his family received this honor. In the case of Moses, the Torah tells us several incidents that indicate his merit: his concern for his people and for justice are named and various midrashim expand upon this as well. Aaron is simply "the brother" who is to serve as Moses' spokesman. As the Torah puts it, "Thus he shall serve as your mouth" (Exodus 4:16). Perhaps it is this closeness to Moses and his role in working with him under divine guidance that makes him the natural choice.

It may be that Aaron's very anonymity makes him fit for the position. Unlike the prophet, the priest does not have to take the initiative, only to follow instructions. In Judaism, in opposition to other religions, the priest does not speak to God nor does he convey messages from God. He is not God's spokesman. That is the role of the prophet. He is not the ruler of the people. That is the role of the judge (*shofet*) and later of the king. He does not cast spells or work magic. He does not heal or cure.

What exactly, then, was the role of the priest? It seems to have been rather confined and proscribed. The basic role of the priest was to be the representative of the people in serving God in the Sanctuary. This representational role is emphasized in the vestments that the high priest wore. Two lazuli stones were worn on his shoulders and on each were engraved the names of six of the tribes of Israel "as stones for remembrance of the Israelite people, whose names Aaron shall carry upon his two shoulder-pieces for remembrance before the Lord" (Exodus 28:12).

He also had a breastplate with twelve precious stones, each of which had engraved upon it the name of one of the tribes: "Aaron shall carry the names of the sons of Israel on the breastplate of decision over his heart, when he enters the Sanctuary, for remembrance before the Lord at all times" (Exodus 28:29). Thus he is a symbol of the entire people. Whatever he does, whatever ceremonies he conducts, he performs as the living embodiment of all the tribes of Israel. Similarly when the priests offered sacrifices in the Sanctuary, it was not on their own behalf, but as representatives of the people.

There is very little importance ascribed to the priest as a person, as an individual. His significance was in his representation of the people. In contrast to priests in other groups, his position implied no particular superiority, and certainly no magical powers, but rather emphasized the importance of the entire people Israel. Judaism is not and never has been a priestly religion. The priests were there to serve the people and not the other way around. It is Israel, the people, that stands at the center of Judaism.

A second task that the priests had, which is not mentioned here but appears later in Numbers 6:22, was to recite God's blessing upon the people, the so-called "Priestly Benediction": "Thus they shall link My name with the people of Israel, and I will bless them" (Numbers 6:27). Here too the priest as an individual was merely a conduit. The blessing came from God. And the words of the blessing were fixed and had to be recited exactly as recorded.

The third task of the priests was that of judgment. The Torah sees them as teachers and deciders. As Moses says in his blessing, "They shall teach Your laws to Jacob and Your instructions to Israel" (Deuteronomy 33:10). The priests were those who conveyed "Torah" — instruction — to the people. Here too, the instruction was fixed. And since we learn later that other judges were to be appointed to judge the people (Deuteronomy 16:18), it may be that the role of the priests was limited largely to ritual and ceremonial matters. So the priest, for all his importance, remained a ceremonial figure, a conduit.

In later times a new group of leaders arose who supplanted the priest in regard to the teaching and interpretation of Torah, although not in the task of serving in the Temple and offering the sacrifices on behalf of the people. That group, the Sages, was the genesis of the rabbis — the teachers — that formed and continue to form Judaism as we know it.

Like the development of the synagogue, which supplemented the Temple, the Sages supplemented the priests. And just as the synagogue was a new development which permitted worship anywhere and which created a service without sacrifice, so the Sages brought about an important change. Unlike priests, there is nothing hereditary about being a sage or later a rabbi. It is open to all, dependent only upon knowledge and ability. This development was crucial for the development of Judaism as we know it.

The description in our portion completes the basic institutions that the newly freed Israelites needed to form a society. They had the basic civil laws by which they were to live, as well as ritual laws. They had the Sanctuary representing God's Presence and the priests who were to serve within it. Now they could embark on their journey toward the land of promise, a journey that was intended to be brief but that in truth was to last for forty years. Only the new generation would ever see the dream fulfilled.

2. Sacred Garments

Much of this section is devoted to what may seem a very prosaic topic, hardly worthy of so many verses: the clothing of the priests, with special emphasis upon the garments of the high priest.

In the modern world we tend to place less importance on clothing as a symbol of status and authority than in previous times. The elaborate garments that signify special status are mostly relics of the past, although Hassidic groups are very careful to identify themselves through their garments and there is a tendency for "official" Orthodox rabbis and chief rabbis to wear a certain style of garment to indicate their status. If one wishes to see clothing that resembles that described in today's portion, however, the closest would be the garments of the Catholic hierarchy, which were influenced by the Torah's description.

The importance that the Torah attaches to the high priest's garments and those of the other priests can be seen in the fact that twice it warns that they must wear this specific clothing lest they die (Exodus 28:35, 43). Since it cannot possibly matter to God, it must be that this is in order to impress both the people and the priests themselves with the sanctity and the importance of their service. This is not to be taken lightly. Service in the Sanctuary must be prepared for; the outer garments are a reflection of the inner preparation and also of the dedication of the priests to the service of God. It is a further way of distinguishing them from others, just as later we learn that each Israelite was to wear a special garment — the *tzitzit* — to indicate the special status of Israel as a "a kingdom of priests and a holy nation" (Exodus 19:6).

It is surely not accidental that the color *techeilet* — blue — that is to be put into the *tzitzit* of all Israelites (Numbers 15:38) also features prominently in the garments of the high priest: "You shall make the robe of the ephod of pure blue" (Exodus 28:31). The frontlet inscribed with God's name was suspended "on a cord of blue" (Exodus 28:37). Blue, as the Sages recognized, represents the Divine since it is the color of the sky and represents "the divine throne" (*Genesis Rabbah* 17:5). (See also Numbers 4, where it is specified that blue cloths be used to cover the various components of the Tabernacle when it is dismantled for traveling.) All human beings are God's creations and God's children, but Israel has been designated to serve God in a special way and is distinguished by a special garment. All Israelites are dedicated to God, but the kohanim have been designated to serve God in a special way and are therefore distinguished by special garments.

The garments also have symbolic meaning, much of which is unknown to us today. Some aspects, however, are clear. The significance of blue has already been mentioned. In addition to wearing a color that signifies the

Divine, the high priest, as we noted, carries upon himself the names of the tribes of Israel. In other words, the high priest as an individual is of little or no importance. He serves God as a representative of the twelve tribes of Israel, of the entire people. His very being thus adorned is a way of asking God to "remember" Israel, that is, to grant Israel's requests and fulfill the promises made to Israel.

The frontlet of pure gold worn on the Priest's forehead has written upon it the words "Holy to the Lord" (Exodus 28:36). It is not clear if this refers to the priest himself or to the entire people of Israel that he represents. There is no question, however, that this too is reminiscent of the fact that the ordinary Israelite also wears something on his forehead — "frontlets" (Deuteronomy 6:8), symbolic of the fact that he belongs to God. The *tefillin* are the fulfillment of this command.

All the priests are instructed to wear linen breeches "to cover their nakedness" (Exodus 28:42). It hardly seems necessary to mention this, but it takes on greater importance when we remember that in many instances pagan priests and priestesses officiated at fertility rites as an integral part of their religious worship. This abhorrent practice is obviously forbidden in Israel and therefore priestly modesty becomes a vital part of their very garments.

One item of clothing is conspicuous by its absence — footwear. The priests officiated barefooted in the Sanctuary, a practice reflected today in the fact that when pronouncing the Priestly Blessing in synagogues, kohanim do so without shoes, as well as in the prohibition of shoes on Yom Kippur (later modified to not wearing leather). We encounter this for the first time in the story of Moses at the burning bush, when he is told, "Remove your sandals from your feet, for the place on which you stand is holy ground" (Exodus 3:5). Stepping on ground with shoes was considered an act of claiming that ground. Holy ground belongs only to God and therefore we tread on it lightly, with bare feet (Buber, *Moses*, p. 42). Because of this Moslems to this day take off their shoes before entering mosques.

The priests were the religious leaders of ancient Israel. These special garments made them aware of the importance of their position, of the fact that they were representative of the entire people and not individuals of special importance in and of themselves. Their importance was in serving the people and in serving God. It was a given that they were to follow the Torah's laws of decency, justice and mercy and that they were to think of how best to serve God and how best to represent Israel at all times and to place their own interests far behind. Unfortunately we know that throughout history not all priests lived up to this, regardless of the garments they wore. Hillel's advice to the priests of his time would be well heeded by all religious leaders: "Love peace and pursue peace, love human beings and bring them close to Torah" (*Pirkei Avot* 1:12).

Ki Tissa

כי תשא

Exodus 30:11-34:35 | שמות ל:יא-לד:לה

1. The Calf of Gold

After three Torah portions devoted to specific laws and commandments, we return to the narrative of the events at Mount Sinai. The exalted story of a people imbued with love and reverence of God, ready to accept whatever God commands them and to enter into the covenant, takes an unexpected twist and turns from triumph to tragedy. Forgetting their pledge, losing their trust and faith, they turn to pagan ways and seek to build an image, a golden calf. Moses is gone for less than forty days and that is enough to cause them to panic: "Come, make us a god who shall go before us, for that man Moses, who brought us from the land of Egypt — we do not know what has happened to him"(Exodus 32:1). Their first mistake was in forgetting the very beginning of the Ten Commandments: "I the Lord am your God *who brought you out of the land of Egypt*" (Exodus 20:2). It was God, not Moses, who freed them. Forgetting God and ascribing their salvation to a human being, they lost confidence.

The fascinating narrative turns around three "personalities" — Aaron, Moses and God — and their interaction. The character of Moses is the easiest to understand. He is both angry and loving. He is angry with Aaron for misleading the people (Exodus 32:21) and angry with the people for their apostasy (Exodus 32:19). At the same time his love for the people is so great that he becomes their advocate, pleading with God for forgiveness. As a matter of fact it is this sympathy for Israel that he expresses even before anger. Moses' very first utterance when confronted with this terrible sin is "Let not Your anger, O Lord, blaze forth against Your people, whom You delivered from the land of Egypt" (Exodus 32:11). The people may have forgotten who brought them from Egypt; Moses has not. And throughout the story, he continues his defense of Israel, imploring God time and time again to be with them and to reestablish the loving relationship that existed before this rupture.

The nature of Aaron and his actions is more difficult to fathom and has been open to multiple interpretations by commentators, ancient and modern. On a simple level he seems to have been weak and to have given in to the demands of the mob. Yet one could make a case for saying that he was only trying to delay the people and keep them from getting out of hand. Certainly he did not believe in their actions. He says to them "Tomorrow shall be a festival *to the Lord*" (Exodus 32:5), not to the calf, whereas they bow down to it and say, "This is your god, O Israel, who brought you out of the land of Egypt!" (Exodus 32:8) — clear blasphemy. Some commentators have said that Aaron even feared for his life.

It is most interesting to try and understand the "personality" (if you will) of God. Before doing so, a word about this very controversial phrase. Does God have a personality? On the one hand, Maimonides depicted a God so far above such things that we cannot even speak about His traits except in negative terms. On the other hand, both the Torah and the rabbinic writings never hesitate to ascribe "human" emotions and feelings to God. From the very earliest moment, Judaism never described God in mythological terms or as having human physical needs. But it did not hesitate to ascribe emotions to Him. Abraham Joshua Heschel has written:

> To the prophet…God does not reveal himself in an abstract absoluteness, but in a personal and intimate relation to the world. He does not simply command and expect obedience: He is also moved and affected by what happens in the world, and reacts accordingly. Events and human actions arouse in Him joy or sorrow, pleasure or wrath…. This notion that God can be intimately affected, that He possesses not merely intelligence and will, but also pathos, basically defines the prophetic consciousness of God…God is concerned about the world…. Indeed, this is the essence of God's moral nature: His willingness to be intimately involved in the history of man. (*The Prophets* [Philadelphia: Jewish Publication Society of America, 1962], p. 224)

Certainly that is the Biblical view of God. Nevertheless we must be careful today not to be too literal. Rather, like Maimonides, we must realize that words used in relation to God only hint at reality and cannot describe God fully. Having said that, we can talk about God's "reactions."

At first, God reacts to the deeds of the Israelites with anger. He goes so far as to threaten their annihilation and to say to Moses that He will "make of *you* a great nation" (Exodus 32:10). It is to the everlasting credit of Moses that he refuses this offer and pleads instead for Israel. But if God's anger is manifest, so is His forgiveness. The midrash (*Exodus Rabbah* 42:9) cleverly comments on the words "Now, let Me be, that My anger may blaze forth against them" (Exodus 32:10), asking, what does God mean by this? "Was Moses holding on to Him that God said 'let Me be'?" The rabbis answer that this was God's way of hinting to Moses that if he would only plead for the people — and *not* "let God be" — God would forgive them, as indeed He did (Exodus 32:14).

But His forgiveness is not complete. God distances Himself from the people, as if to say "I forgive you because of Moses' pleas and because of the covenant I made with the ancestors, but I cannot reestablish the relationship of closeness that existed before." But when Moses pleads with Him again, God relents completely and reveals to Moses His essential nature — "a God compassionate and gracious, slow to anger, abounding in kindness and faithfulness" (Exodus 34:6).

And so it is that Moses, the man of anger but the man who loves his people, reprimands Aaron, the leader who out of weakness, or out of fear, or in an attempt to keep them from committing even worse transgressions, let the people sin. And this same Moses holds back his anger in order to appease God, while God reacts with anger at this betrayal, but is gradually persuaded — as it were — to reestablish His relationship with Israel and bring them to the land of Canaan as He had promised.

2. Achieving Forgiveness

This portion is both frightening and enlightening. It is frightening because it describes the dark side of the people of Israel, their rapid descent from the heights of accepting God and the covenant — "All the things that the Lord has commanded we will do!" (Exodus 24:3) — to the worship of a golden calf and the debauchery that accompanied it (Exodus 32:6). It is enlightening, because in the end it reveals the nature of God and stresses God's merciful and forgiving qualities.

This was a pivotal moment in the history of our people. We stood on the brink of disaster, of complete destruction. For a moment it seemed as if the experiment of choosing the descendants of Abraham as the vehicle for God's will on earth had failed and the choice would be narrowed even further to the children of Moses alone.

In the words of the psalmist: "Thus they exchanged their glory for the likeness of an ox that eats grass.... Therefore He decided that He would destroy them, had not Moses His chosen one confronted Him in the breach, to avert His wrath, lest He should destroy them" (Psalm 106:20, 23).

In a long and complicated series of arguments described above, Moses "persuades" God — as it were — to change His mind and to forgive the people of Israel. Moses follows in the footsteps of Abraham who did not hesitate to dispute with God regarding Sodom and Gomorrah (Genesis 18:23–32). Abraham's plea was for justice. Moses pleads for forgiveness. The Israelites may well deserve punishment, but Moses argues that if He destroys Israel, God's own reputation among the nations will suffer. It will cause *hillul hashem*, for the Egyptians will say that God delivered them with "evil intent," having always intended to kill them (Exodus 32:12).

Moses' most cogent argument, however, is that God had made a promise to the fathers — even more than a promise, an unalterable covenant to "make your offspring as numerous as the stars of heaven" and to give them "the whole land to possess forever" (Exodus 32:13). Remembering that Abrahamic covenant, God renounces the punishment (Exodus 32:14). But this is not the end of the story. Renouncing the punishment because of the commitment to the ancestors of Israel does not indicate forgiveness, and that is what Moses really desires to attain.

Therefore Moses continues his dialogue with God, wanting to be certain that God's Presence will be with Israel. He asks to know the very nature of God. Is He truly forgiving? Does He show mercy? That is the meaning of Moses' request, "Oh, let me behold Your Presence" (Exodus 33:18), to which God replies positively, "I will make My goodness pass before you and I will proclaim before you the name of the Lord, and I will be gracious to whom I will be gracious, and I will be compassionate to whom I will be compassionate" (Exodus 33:19).

It is worth looking at this passage closely because it is the Torah's most explicit attempt at enumerating the qualities of God. And it does so both so that we should have an understanding of the Divine and so that we should imitate the Divine in our own lives. The passage, known in rabbinic literature as "the thirteen attributes," reads:

> The Lord! The Lord! — a God compassionate and gracious, slow to anger, abounding in kindness and faithfulness, extending kindness to the thousandth generation, forgiving iniquity and transgression and sin; yet He does not remit all punishment, but visits the iniquity of the fathers upon children and children's children, upon the third and fourth generation. (Exodus 34:6-7)

Comparing these words with a similar utterance in the Ten Commandments we discover that this is a Biblical expansion of that earlier passage. The Torah is actually commenting and explaining itself. The verses in the Ten Commandments read:

> I the Lord your God am an impassioned God, visiting the guilt of the parents upon the children, upon the third and upon the fourth generations of those who reject Me, but showing kindness to the thousandth generation of those who love Me and keep My commandments. (Exodus 20:5-6)

Notice how these words have been expanded and changed in this Torah portion. Firstly the order has been reversed. Now mercy comes before justice or punishment. Kindness is emphasized before punishment is even mentioned. Secondly the description and even the number of qualities of mercy have been expanded so that we now have "compassionate and gracious, slow to anger, abounding in kindness and faithfulness, extending kindness...forgiving iniquity and transgression and sin" whereas in the Ten Commandments all that is mentioned is "showing kindness." These changes cannot be accidental.

God has not changed in the forty or so days that have passed since the Sinai revelation, but the situation has changed. Israel has sinned and needs assurance that God is forgiving, that God is merciful, that the relationship that has been established with God will continue. Moses does not even want to go further in their journey if he cannot know that God has forgiven them and will be with them every step of the way (Exodus 33:15). Thus, by expanding that earlier passage and emphasizing the positive, the merciful aspect, God gives the reassurance needed to continue the journey.

The Sages who formulated our prayers went a step further. When we read these verses as we stand before the Ark on holidays or on Yom Kippur or other such times, we do not read them in their entirety. The last section concerning punishment is omitted, as are the two Hebrew words, *lo yinakeh*. This has the effect of changing the entire meaning of the phrase. In the Torah we read *nakeh lo yinakeh*, which means, "yet He does not remit all punishment," while the elimination of those two words changes the meaning to "He *will* remit all punishment." What a bold change!

The next step, which rabbinic Judaism made explicit, was to teach that we must pattern ourselves not after God's essence — Judaism does not permit human beings to say they are divine — but after God's qualities. Thus the midrash teaches us in the name of Abba Saul: "Be like Him! Just as he is gracious and merciful, so should you be gracious and merciful!" (*Mekhilta Shirata* 3).

How ironic, then, that people should speak of Judaism as a harsh religion, a religion of justice and revenge and not of love and mercy when love, mercy and forgiveness are the fundamental teachings of this section and of later rabbinic interpretations. Shakespeare's phrase "The quality of mercy is not strain'd" (The Merchant of Venice, Act 4, Scene 1) should have belonged to Shylock and not his enemies, for those words represent the very essence of Judaism and the way in which Jews are commanded to live.

Vayak'hel

ויקהל

Exodus 35:1–38:20 | שמות לה:א-לח:כ

1. The Relationship Continues

The sin of the golden calf has been expiated. The relationship between God and the people Israel has been reestablished, even though it is cooler than before. The Lord is once again their God who will lead them through the wilderness to the Land of Promise. The text now describes in great detail the work that was done to build the Tabernacle and all of its furnishings. The place of God's dwelling which would be erected every stop along the way, this portable Mount Sinai, would be the center of their camp from now on. This was to be the visible symbol of the invisible God.

The description that we have in these chapters is very much like that which we read in Exodus 25–27, which recounts the commands given to Moses on Mount Sinai concerning the Tabernacle. There — prior to the sin of the calf — detailed instructions were given for its construction and for everything that was to be placed within it. Now we have the story of the actual work being done. Those early instructions are carried out with great fidelity. As we will read in the following portion, the conclusion of this detailed description, "Thus was completed all the work of the Tabernacle of the Tent of Meeting. The Israelites did so; *just as the Lord had commanded Moses, so they did*" (Exodus 39:32). The text goes out of its way to emphasize the fidelity with which the instructions were carried out.

The question we might ask ourselves is: why bother with this repetition? Would it not have been sufficient to simply say that now they built the Tabernacle and its furnishings "just as the Lord had commanded Moses"? In order to understand the purpose of these chapters we must remember that it was not to be taken for granted that God would permit that building to be erected after the terrible rupture caused by the sin of the calf. Perhaps they no longer deserved to have such a place of meeting with God. Yes, prior to that sin God had commanded that they erect a "sanctuary that I may dwell among them" (Exodus 25:8). But that was before the sin. After the sin, God had threatened to totally destroy them (Exodus 32:10) and, even when He relented, still threatened that "I will not go in your midst…lest I destroy you on the way" (Exodus 33:3). That would have been the complete antithesis of having the Sanctuary in which God would be present.

Just as the writing of a second set of tablets (Exodus 34:4) indicated that the covenant would continue, so now the erection of the Tabernacle indicates that the relationship symbolized by the *Mishkan* — "the dwelling place" — has not been broken but will continue. The description of its erection thus emphasizes this point. The relationship has not really changed, it tells us. The Tabernacle goes up just as planned. There will still be a Holy of Holies containing the Ark of the Covenant, the symbolic throne of the Almighty containing the Ten Commandments. Thus the holiness of the camp and of the people Israel will continue. This point needs to be emphasized and the Torah does so by this detailed repetition.

Interestingly enough some of the Sages in the midrash had a different understanding of this. They applied the principle of interpretation that there is no necessary chronological order to the stories of the Torah. Sometimes — for whatever reason — the chapters are out of order. Some of the rabbis said that that is the case here, that the commands to build the Sanctuary that we read earlier were actually only given after the golden calf, after the reconciliation, not before (*Exodus Rabbah* 51:4). What they were saying was that after the sin it became clear to God — as it were — that the people were in need of a physical structure to symbolize God's Presence, a place where they could gather regularly in order to reiterate their commitment to God and to God's commands.

2. The Festival of Giving

The relationship that is reconstituted by the building of the Tabernacle is not one-sided. The covenant is mutual, and if the relationship continues to be solid from God's point of view, so too does it continue from the point of view of the people Israel and that is also emphasized in this account.

There is a great enthusiasm and exuberance expressed here that we might not have known had this account not been given in such detail. For example we are told "And everyone who excelled in ability and everyone whose spirit moved him came, bringing to the Lord his offering" (Exodus 35:21). And immediately thereafter the text continues with a recital of their enthusiasms, specifying "men and women, all whose hearts moved them" brought offerings (Exodus 35:21). Not only that, but the text even goes so far as to list exactly what they brought: "brooches, earrings, rings, and pendants — gold objects of all kinds" (Exodus 35:22). The whole passage, which goes on and on to describe how women spun the fabrics and chieftains brought precious stones, is an exuberant depiction of an enthusiastic people willingly and lovingly putting up this structure. It gets to the point that they bring so much that Moses has to tell them to stop: "Let no man or woman make further effort toward gifts for the Sanctuary!" (Exodus 36:6). This may be the only instance in the entire history of fund-raising that the campaign was so oversubscribed that it had to be brought to a halt. Never before or after did we have to be told to stop giving.

Does guilt play a part in this festival of giving? Perhaps they are attempting to atone for their earlier enthusiasm in bringing all that gold for the building of the idol (Exodus 32:3). In the midrash there is a discussion of the relationship between the gold brought for the calf and the gold brought for the Tabernacle. One opinion, offered by Rabbi Simeon, cynically suggests that their giving meant nothing because they could not differentiate between a good cause and a bad one, and simply gave enthusiastically whenever asked: "Enough gold for the Tabernacle and enough gold for the calf!" Rabbi Benaiah, however, offers the opposite opinion. Because they had given gold to build the calf, a sin that warranted their annihilation, they are now given the opportunity to atone for it by bringing gold for the Tabernacle: "Let the gold of the Tabernacle therefore atone for the gold of the calf" (*Sifre Deuteronomy* 1). That would seem to be the thrust of the Torah's description. They want to cement their reconciliation with God by enthusiastically contributing their goods and their personal services to building the Tabernacle, the concrete expression that God dwells among them.

This portion, then, is not as superfluous as it appears at first. On the contrary, it is the much needed depiction of a people that has recovered from a terrible event and is now ready to fulfill the task it willingly undertook at Sinai to be God's "treasured possession among all the people" (Exodus 19:5).

Pekudei   פקודי

Exodus 38:21-40:38 | שמות לח:כא-מ:לח

1. Mount Sinai Recreated

This portion, as the previous one, is a wonderful tribute to architects, builders and artisans. As we have seen, things seem to continue as if nothing untoward had happened. One could wish indeed that chapters 32:1-34:9 (the golden calf) had never occurred and that the commands given to Moses to build the Sanctuary could have been followed immediately by his descending the mountain and overseeing the construction. Someone wishing to revise the Torah, to turn it into propaganda for the faithfulness of the Israelites, would have done just that, but the Torah is an honest document and tells the truth about the people Israel even when it hurts.

There is no question that continuing with the building of the Tabernacle even after that terrible sin is a further indication of God's forgiveness. Before the sin He had said that He would dwell among them — "Let them make for Me a sanctuary that I may dwell among them" (Exodus 25:8) — and at the conclusion of Exodus we have a description that indicates that that has indeed occurred:

> Moses finished the work. The cloud covered the Tent of Meeting, and the Presence of the Lord filled the Tabernacle. Moses could not enter the Tent of Meeting because the cloud had settled upon it and the Presence of the Lord filled the Tabernacle. (Exodus 40:33-35)

It is surely not accidental that in these verses we are told not once but twice that the cloud had settled there and that "the Presence of the Lord" filled the newly erected Sanctuary. That God's Presence or Glory has come to dwell among them is a certainty.

Furthermore this description is quite similar to the description of Mount Sinai found earlier when, following the revelation of the Ten Commandments, Moses was asked to come up onto the mountain:

> When Moses had ascended the mountain, the cloud covered the mountain. The Presence of the Lord abode on Mount Sinai and the cloud hid it for six days. (Exodus 24:15-16)

The very same terms are used. In both instances we have the cloud and the Presence of the Lord mentioned. It is quite clear, therefore, that the Tabernacle has now assumed the place of Sinai, "The Mountain of God" (Exodus 3:1). They had journeyed from Egypt and come to God's dwelling — Sinai. Now God's new dwelling, the Tabernacle, will journey with them wherever they go. God's Presence will never depart from them.

How far we have come! Exodus began with a small group of the children of Israel-Jacob that both multiplied and descended into slavery simultaneously. It concludes with Israel a free people that has escaped from tyranny, experienced the salvation of God at the sea, witnessed God's revelation at Sinai and now has all that is needed for the future. The people have the laws by which they are to live and they have the institutions, civil and sacred, that will govern their community. They also have the Tabernacle, the abode of God, with all the symbols within it that give meaning to their community. The one blot on this otherwise harmonious picture is the sin of the golden calf, and although it has not been obliterated or erased from memory, neither has it caused the total rupture that was feared.

It is interesting that in the description of the setting up of the Tabernacle Moses is given credit for it. "Moses set up the Tabernacle," we are told (Exodus 40:18), and all the verses thereafter say "he spread," "he took," "he placed," as if Moses did all of this himself, alone, something that is surely impossible. Even at the end it says, "When Moses had finished the work" (Exodus 40:33). The rabbis in the midrash to this verse (Tanhuma Pekudei 11) see in this a miracle — that the Tabernacle erected itself — while modern scholars understand this as a way of indicating that since Moses had been shown the divine plan for the Tabernacle (Exodus 25:9), he alone could supervise the work of setting it up.

A Hassidic rebbe once answered the question, "Where does God dwell?" by saying, "God dwells wherever we let Him in." We may no longer have a building constructed by a divine plan, but the Presence of God can be experienced by us as well when we willingly construct our lives according to God's precepts and build our society according to God's commands of righteousness and compassion. Then God dwells among us as surely as He dwelt among the Israelites when they journeyed from Sinai.

2. All Is in Place

This section concludes the record of the building of the Tabernacle that began in the previous portion, giving an account of the exact amounts of gold and other metals used in its construction (Exodus 38:21–31). This is followed by a detailed description of the garments made for the high priest. These accounts would seem to be superfluous just as the details of the sanctuary seemed unnecessary. They add nothing to the descriptions we had previously when the Israelites were commanded to make these things and when they actually fabricated them. What then is their purpose if not to help emphasize the importance of this structure and the accoutrements needed to make it function, permitting us to feel as if we could visualize it ourselves? It is almost as if by reading these detailed descriptions, we are creating a virtual Tabernacle in our own minds.

The erection of the Tabernacle took place on "the first day of the first month" (Exodus 40:2), the first of Nissan, less than a year after the Exodus and nine months after their arrival at Mount Sinai (Exodus 19:1). This day had a very special significance. It was not the anniversary of the Exodus, which took place on the fifteenth of the month, but the first of the month had been singled out while they were in Egypt when God said to them (in Everett Fox's accurate translation [*The Five Books of Moses* (New York: Schocken, 1995)]), "Let this New-Moon [*haḥodesh hazeh*] be for you the beginning of New-Moons, the beginning-one let it be for you of the New Moons of the year" (Exodus 12:2). The Hebrew word *ḥodesh*, as the Sages understood, means the New-Moon, what we would term Rosh Ḥodesh. In the midrash that verse is interpreted as indicating that God "pointed it [the New-Moon] out to him [Moses] with His finger" showing him what the New-Moon looked like so that Israel would be able to recognize when the new month was to be proclaimed (*Mekhilta Pisha* 2).

Thus from the very beginning the appearance of the New-Moon of Nissan was important. It signaled the beginning of the redemption and taught that that month was to be considered the first month of the year because of its importance. As a matter of fact, for centuries there were those who considered the first of Nissan to be the day of the Creation rather than the first of Tishrei; as is assumed today. In the second century CE there was a dispute between two Tannaim. Rabbi Eliezer taught that the world was created in Tishrei; but Rabbi Joshua said, "The world was created in Nissan" (*Rosh Hashanah* 11a).

The Torah thus connects the erection of the Tabernacle to two important events — the moment of the announcement that this was to be the month of redemption and thus the first of all months, and the anniversary of Creation. Nahum Sarna has pointed out that there is a parallel in the descriptions of the conclusion of Creation and the conclusion of the creation of the Tabernacle. In the first we read, "God saw all that He had made and found it very good" (Genesis 1:31) and in the second, "Moses saw that they had preformed all the tasks — as the Lord had commanded, so had they done" (Exodus 39:42-43). In both cases the work is concluded with a blessing: "And God blessed the seventh day" (Genesis 2:3), "Moses blessed them" (Exodus 39:43).

Based on this analogy, we can say that the Tabernacle itself came to represent two things: the world that God created and the sacred space of Mount Sinai. God created the cosmos; human beings created the Tabernacle as a symbol of Creation. Mount Sinai was the sacred space upon which Israel encountered God, "the mount of God" (Exodus 3:1). To meet with God, Moses had to enter the sacred precinct at the top — an area that was forbidden to anyone else (Exodus 20:18; 24:15-18). So too the Tabernacle contains the Holy of Holies which is restricted to the high priest alone for therein is the throne of God (Leviticus 16:3). Just as the cloud signifying the Presence of God had covered Sinai (Exodus 19:16) so now it covers the Tabernacle: "and the Presence of the Lord filled the Tabernacle. Moses could not enter the Tent of Meeting because the cloud had settled upon it and the Presence of the Lord filled the Tabernacle" (Exodus 40:34-35).

In contrast to the book of Genesis which concluded with the ominous description of the death of Joseph and his internment in Egypt — a premonition of Israel's enslavement there — the book of Exodus ends with the joyous description of the *Shekhinah* (God's Presence) resting upon the newly erected Tabernacle that would accompany the Israelites in their journey to freedom. It should be remembered that although with hindsight we know that this journey was to last for forty years and conclude only after the extinction of the generation that left Egypt, this had not yet been determined. On the contrary, Moses and Israel envisioned at most a brief journey to Canaan so that within a few years of leaving slavery, they would be established in their own land. At the moment depicted in our Torah portion, that bright prospect was still open before them.

The book of Exodus has taken us from the slavery of Egypt to the depiction of free Israelites in their encampment, in the very center of which is the portable Tabernacle in which resides the Presence of the Lord, ready to accompany and guard them on their journey toward their new-old homeland. In a sense, the redemption is almost complete. They have attained freedom; they have concluded a covenant with God and have received God's moral, ethical and ritual laws. Now they also have a sacred space, the tangible representation of God's Presence. All that is needed is to come to and occupy the Land of Promise.

It is one year less two weeks since they left Egypt and in that brief time all the foundations have been put in place for an Israelite society. What a pity that yet another sin will cause a delay of forty years before they can establish that society on their own soil.

LEVITICUS

Vayikra

Vayikra ויקרא

Leviticus 1:1–5:26 | ויקרא א:א-ה:כו

1. The Book of Holiness

The word with which this portion begins and which became the name of this entire book is an unusual one: "And He called." The Lord called to Moses before speaking to Him from the newly erected tent of meeting. Usually we read "The Lord said" or "The Lord spoke." Why "called"? The Sages explained that Moses was so overwhelmed by the way in which the Tent was filled by the cloud — the Presence of God — that in his great humility he hesitated to enter. Therefore he had to be called, i.e., summoned to come in (*Leviticus Rabbah* 1:1).

In a sense this is symbolic of the entire book. We have to be called to come in. We are either overwhelmed by the sense of holiness and mystery that is contained in it or we are unsure as to how to deal with its subject matter, so much of which has to do with laws of ritual purity and with the offering of sacrifices, subjects that are far from our everyday lives in this modern age.

In ancient days the book was known as *Torat Kohanim* (The Instruction of the Priests). If so, of what value is it for those who are not kohanim? Yet although it contains instructions for the priests, it is not intended solely for them. Rather it should be understood as a book of "Instruction *by* the Priests," i.e., the concepts that the kohanim want to impart to the people. Unlike other ancient and not-so-ancient religions in which the priests had books that were reserved for them and which no non-priest was to read, Judaism has nothing of that sort. There are no magical powers given to the kohanim, no secret rites that the priests alone can know. They are nothing

143

more than those chosen to represent the people before God and to represent God to the people in certain limited ways.

The reputation of the book of Leviticus has suffered from ups and downs in the public eye. In traditional Judaism it was considered so important that the education of little children began with the study of Leviticus. "Let those who are pure come and study the laws of purity" was the common saying (Leviticus *Rabbah* 7:3). In the nineteenth century, however, Leviticus was severely criticized by non-Jewish Biblical critics, who considered it to be a primitive book, concerned only with dry ritual, far from the high ideals of the prophets.

Fortunately the reputation of Leviticus has recently been restored by the work of two outstanding individuals: Rabbi Jacob Milgrom and the late Prof. Mary Douglas. Rabbi Milgrom has written a magnificent three-volume commentary that has revealed the religious concepts that underlie the book (*Leviticus*: Anchor Yale Biblical Commentaries [New Haven: Yale, 2007]). This has now been issued in a one-volume work for the general public as well (*Leviticus* [Minneapolis: Fortress Press, 2004]). Prof. Douglas, a devout English Christian anthropologist, viewed the book from a unique perspective. In *Leviticus As Literature* (Oxford: Oxford University Press, 1999) she explains the purpose of Leviticus as follows:

> Read in the perspective of anthropology the food laws of Moses are not expressions of squeamishness about dirty animals and invasive insects. The purity rules for sex and leprosy are not examples of priestly prurience. The religion of Leviticus turns out to be not very different from that of the prophets which demanded humble and contrite hearts, or from the psalmists' love of God.... The more closely the text is studied, the more clearly Leviticus reveals itself as a modern religion, legislating for justice between persons and persons, between God and His people, and between people and animals. (pp. 1–2)

As we shall see, Leviticus represents a concept of sacred living in which rituals and ethical elements are combined to create human beings who are aware of their duty to God and to others. The high moral standards emphasized by the prophets are not unique to them, but are incorporated into the teachings of the priests as well. Holiness is not a primitive goal but a high aspiration.

2. The Purpose of Sacrifice

This first portion concentrates solely on sacrifices (*korbanot*) outlining different types of sacrifices and the reasons for bringing them. There is the *olah*, something that "goes up" entirely — i.e., a sacrifice that is not eaten and therefore expresses the individual's desire to present a gift to God so that God will be gracious to that individual (Leviticus 1:1–17). Chapter 2 describes the *minhah*, an offering of grain rather than animals. A third type is described in chapter 3 — the *shelamim*, variously translated as "well-being" or "gift of greeting." This offering was a sacred meal, since in part it was eaten by the one who brought it and expressed gratitude to God. In chapters 4 and 5 the *hattat*, expiatory offerings brought for inadvertent transgressions, are described.

Putting aside for the moment the question of whether or not sacrifices are appropriate in the modern world, we should be able to appreciate the ancient sacrificial system described here for what it was — and for what it was not. In the first place it was an expression of the sacredness of all life. Leviticus envisions no animal slaughter except ritual slaughter. The taking of the life of an animal may be done only within a sacred context that in itself atones for and permits this action. Secondly, we see that the sacrifice is intended to create a positive relationship between the worshipper and God and to indicate the individual's desire to express thanksgiving, to be closer to God or to ask forgiveness. The guilt offering, for example, which must follow the restoration of whatever was gained through deceit, is clearly intended to assuage guilt. Guilt is a major source of emotional distress. Judaism here provides a way of ridding ourselves of unwarranted guilt. When the Temple existed, sacrifice was the way to indicate a desire to be at peace with God.

What is missing in this passage is as important as what is present. There is no indication anywhere that the sacrifice is needed by God or is of benefit to God. This is in complete contradiction to the sacrificial rites of paganism that existed prior to and during the period of the emergence of the Israelite religion. As Yehezkel Kaufmann put it so succinctly, "The fundamental idea of paganism is most strikingly set forth in the notion that the gods use the cult for their own benefit" (*The Religion of Israel*, p. 57). Because of their limited nature, their imperfection, their physical nature and their dependence on outside forces, the so-called "gods" of paganism were dependent upon sacrifices for food and, through magical efficacy, for their continued existence.

The religion of Israel, on the other hand, knows none of this because of the transcendent nature of God. For the Torah and for all of Judaism, sacrifices are for the benefit of human beings. God can do without them.

This explains the fact that the prophets could say such things as Amos's famous diatribe:

> If you offer Me burnt offerings — or your meal offerings — I will not accept them; I will pay no heed to your gifts of fatlings. Spare Me the sound of your hymns, and let Me not hear the music of your lutes. But let justice well up like water, righteousness like an unfailing stream. (Amos 5:22-24)

Since God has no need of sacrifices — or of any other cultic acts, for that matter — He can do without them. What God cannot do without is righteousness and justice. No amount of sacrifices will make up for immorality.

This also explains another missing element in the rituals described in these chapters. It is amazing that there are no prescriptions of words to be uttered during the sacrificial ceremonies, no formulas, not even prayers. It is as if the entire ritual was to be conducted in silence. We can only understand this as a rejection of the magical elements that were part of pagan ritual, the incantations which were thought to have an automatic effect upon the gods. The God of Israel is not subject to magic and the sacrifices must therefore be divorced from that completely, to the extreme of uttering no words at all during these ceremonies.

As the book of Leviticus proceeds we shall see the moral considerations of the book emphasized clearly. Yet even in this portion, which is so completely devoted to the ritual of sacrifices, a careful reading indicates that in ancient Israel as in modern Judaism, ritual was not to be divorced from morality. On the contrary, it expressed the basic moral concepts of Judaism and provided a way in which human beings could express their feelings and bring themselves closer to the Divine. After all, the Hebrew root of sacrifice — *k.r.v.* — means "close." The Torah does not provide us with a way of either bribing God or forcing God's will. It does tell us how we may come closer to God and assert the value of all life. That is the "Instruction of the Priests" that can enrich our lives.

Tzav   צו

Leviticus 6:1–8:36 | ויקרא ו:א-ח:לו

1. Priestly Tasks

This portion is concerned both with instructions concerning the daily rituals of bringing sacrifices to the Sanctuary (Leviticus 6–7) and with the ceremonies held to consecrate the Tabernacle, the altar and the priests to the sacred service of God (Leviticus 8). The daily rituals connected with the bringing of sacrifices were the major tasks of the priests. Although being a priest brought with it honor and privilege, it was also difficult and perhaps even unpleasant work. Dealing with animals, slaughtering them, offering parts on the altar, sprinkling blood, could hardly have been a matter of delight. Yet the priests did all this themselves. They did not assign the work to underlings. Even more compelling is the fact that they even had to haul away the ashes! "He shall take off his vestments and put on other vestments, and carry the ashes outside the camp to a clean place" (Leviticus 6:4).

The ancient tractate of the Mishnah known as *Tamid* records the way in which this work was actually done in the Second Temple prior to its destruction in 70 CE. According to this record, there was a daily lottery drawing to see who had the "privilege" of climbing up the ramp to the top of the altar and carrying away the ashes (*Tamid* 1:2). The Talmud relates that the institution of the lottery came about because there was such a strong competition to do this work. "Many of them would run up the ramp and whoever got there first had the privilege of doing the work. If there was a tie between two of them the person in charge told them, 'Put your fingers out' [i.e., they played a kind of odds-and-evens game to determine who would win]. Once it happened that two were running up the ramp and one pushed the other so that he broke his leg." It was then that they decided to use a lottery system in order to avoid injury (*Tamid* 28a)!

Although they may have been a trifle overenthusiastic, the ancient priests, as demonstrated by this story, nevertheless were highly dedicated to their service and did not shirk difficult and unpleasant work in order to perform it. Their high status did not cause them to avoid menial tasks. All of us, even those who have positions of honor and leadership, should follow their example and be willing to undertake whatever has to be done in order to fulfill the will of the Almighty.

The narrative in the second half of the Torah portion (chapter 8) describes the anointing of the priests by Moses. The ritual was a complicated one. It included purification by water (Leviticus 8:6), putting on the special garments (Leviticus 8:7-8), anointing with oil (Leviticus 8:12), a sacrificial offering (Leviticus 8:14-29) and the sprinkling of blood (Leviticus 8:30). Thus three liquids were used — water, oil and blood. Each of these has special significance.

Water is a symbol of purification. It signifies a new birth, a new beginning. As we find in Ezekiel 36:25, "I will sprinkle clean water upon you, and you shall be clean; I will cleanse you from all your uncleanness and from all your fetishes." Jeremiah used this concept in a clever play on words — "The Lord is the *mikveh* of Israel!" (17:13) — using a word that means both a place of immersion and hope. At the conclusion of the verse he calls God "the Fount of living waters." Water is used in this way in many of Judaism's significant rituals — washing the hands upon arising, washing before eating, the use of the mikvah and the ritual of immersion at the time of a conversion.

Oil is a symbol of joy and abundance: "You anoint my head with oil; my cup overflows" (Psalm 23:5). It was used not only in the dedication of the priests, but also in the anointing of kings. The word Messiah (*mashiaḥ*) means "the anointed one."

Blood is the very symbol of life itself. Thus we are commanded not to eat the blood of animals, even though we are permitted to eat flesh: "But make sure that you do not partake of the blood; for the blood is the life, and you must not consume the life with the flesh" (Deuteronomy 12:23). This perception of blood as life itself is also reflected in the story of Cain and Abel when God says, "Hark, your brother's blood cries out to Me from the ground!" (Genesis 4:10). Thus blood also becomes the vehicle for atonement, and the

blood of circumcision is a symbol of the covenant. When the covenant ceremony — the *brit* — is performed we quote the verse from Ezekiel, "Live in [or
through] your blood — live in your blood!" (Ezekiel 16:6). Nor is it accidental
that blood was to be placed upon the houses of the Israelites in Egypt as a sign
of protection at the time of the plague of the firstborn (Exodus 12:13).

When Ezekiel describes God's redemption of the people of Israel from
their exile and their return to their own land, he uses all three of these liquids:
"I bathed you with water, and washed the blood off you, and anointed you
with oil" (Ezekiel 16:9).

With these symbols of purity, abundance and life the priests enter their
new status and their new tasks. They must wait seven days in isolation,
however, and emerge only on the eighth day to begin their new work (Leviticus 8:33–35). The sacred number seven indicates that they are created anew
— just as the work of Creation itself took seven days and just as the *brit* of a
male child takes place only on the eighth day when seven days of life have
been completed. On the eighth day they are to begin their new work — sacred
work, important work, but also difficult and at times menial work — all for
the sake of Heaven.

2. Sacrifice and Atonement

How important are sacrifices in Judaism? Considering the fact that a large
portion of Leviticus — including this reading — is devoted to the detailed
exposition of what sacrifices to bring, when and how to offer them, and
considering that sections from the Torah describing the sacrifices are
included in the Musaf Amidah of holy days, the answer would seem to be
obvious. Their importance is emphasized by the fact that when the list of
sacrifices is completed, the Torah states specifically that these are the rituals
of the offerings "with which the Lord charged Moses on Mount Sinai, when
He commanded that the Israelites present their offerings to the Lord in the
wilderness of Sinai" (Leviticus 7:38).

Nothing could be clearer, yet how are we to explain the words of the
prophets that seem to deny not only the importance of, but even the validity
of, sacrifices? Jeremiah, for example, spoke at the Temple saying, "For when I
freed your fathers from the land of Egypt, I did not speak with them or

command them concerning offerings or sacrifice. But this is what I commanded them: Do My bidding, that I may be your God and you may be My people; walk only in the way that I enjoin upon you, that it may go well with you" (Jeremiah 7:22–23).

Jeremiah is not the only prophet to have written thus about sacrifices. Amos says something similar, "If you offer Me burnt offerings — or your meal offerings — I will not accept them…. But let justice well up like water, righteousness like an unfailing stream. Did you offer sacrifice and oblation to Me those forty years in the wilderness, O House of Israel?" (Amos 5:22–25). And Hosea made the well-known statement, "For I desire goodness, not sacrifice, obedience to God, rather than burnt offerings" (Hosea 6:6).

Furthermore those scathing words of Jeremiah were chosen by the Sages to be read in the Haftarah that usually accompanies this reading. There is something remarkable about the fact that Jeremiah's denigration of sacrifices was chosen to be chanted together with this particular Torah portion, which deals almost entirely with sacrifices. After all, Jeremiah goes so far as to deny that God commanded the Israelites to bring sacrifices when they were freed from Egypt!

The choice of this prophetic portion is similar to the choice of the reading on Yom Kippur. On the most important fast day we have, the Sages chose as the Haftarah the words of Isaiah that denigrate the importance of fasting and teach that the true fast is "to unlock fetters of wickedness and untie the cords of the yoke, to let the oppressed go free; to break off every yoke. It is to share your bread with the hungry, and to take the wretched poor into your home; when you see the naked, to clothe him" (Isaiah 58:6–7). Surely there is a message here concerning the relative importance of cult and morality.

Did these prophets totally reject the sacrifices and the cult or did they merely condemn their misuse? That is difficult to determine. Looked at closely, Jeremiah's statement may be literally true. For he is paraphrasing the words of Exodus 19:5–6 in which, preparing Israel for the experience at Sinai, God says, "But then, if you will obey Me faithfully and keep My covenant, you shall be My treasured possession among all the peoples. Indeed, all the earth is Mine, but you shall be to Me a kingdom of priests and a holy nation." Note that there is no command here concerning sacrifices. Nor are sacrifices mentioned in the Decalogue at all. They are not mentioned "when Israel was freed." Therefore at the very least one could say that sacrifices are not God's primary concern. At most they take second place to morality and obedience.

As a matter of fact, as noted previously, according to some rabbinic interpretations the commands to erect the Sanctuary and to bring sacrifices were not absolute but were a reaction to the worship of the golden calf. Seeing that Israel went astray so easily after idols and descended into a sacrificial orgy, God decided that it was impossible for them to do without some tangible form of worship, so He decided to institute the sacrificial cult. (See for example *Tanḥuma Terumah* 8.)

This is quite similar to Maimonides' well-known explanation of sacrifices in his Guide III:32, where he states that God could not expect Israel to go immediately from the sacrificial system to which they were accustomed to a worship system consisting of prayer alone. Therefore He permitted them to continue to offer sacrifices but proscribed and limited the way in which they were to be offered.

As for the attitude of the Sages themselves, we know that when the Temple was destroyed Rabban Yohanan ben Zakkai found no difficulty in teaching that even without sacrifice Israel could atone for its sins and be reconciled to God through acts of *gemilut ḥasadim* — loving kindness — toward one another. Quoting Hosea's verse, "For I desire goodness [*hesed*], not sacrifice," he assured Rabbi Yehoshua that "we have another atonement as effective as this" of the Temple ritual — *gemilut ḥasadim* (*Avot d'Rabbi Natan A* 4).

Once when teaching a group of fundamentalist Christians about Judaism's doctrine of atonement, I was confronted by them with the statement, "But there can be no atonement without blood!" Their reference was to the blood of Jesus, which in their minds was the equivalent of the blood of the sacrifices. I was unable to persuade them that in Judaism we found it perfectly possible to attain atonement without sacrifices and that we had certainly never believed that God required or desired the blood of any human being to be shed in order to atone for sins. The story of the *Akeidah* — the binding of Isaac — settled that once and for all.

By choosing to read Jeremiah together with the chapters concerning sacrifices, the Sages gave a very clear message. When you are engaged in ritual acts — be they fasting or sacrificing — do not lose sight of the great truth that ritual is only a means to an end, a way of helping us to become ethical human beings who obey God's commands to deal morally with our fellow human beings. As the rabbis taught, "The *mitzvot* were given solely in order to purify human beings" (*Genesis Rabbah* 44:1). Or as my teacher Rabbi Louis Finkelstein put it, when Hillel taught that "Love your neighbor" is the greatest and most fundamental commandment and that "all the rest is commentary," he meant that all of the *mitzvot* were intended to create a person who would act lovingly toward others. "The ritual and moral commandments, and the legal system of the Torah are dramatizations of the belief in human dignity; and the narrative portions offer a validation of the belief" (*Symbols and Values* [New York: Jewish Theological Seminary of America, 1954], p. 89).

Sacrifices may have been a way of helping people to draw closer to God and to express their feelings, be they of guilt or of thanksgiving, but they could never substitute for the acts of human goodness and love that form the basis of God's teachings. "For I desire goodness, not sacrifice." That prophetic lesson remains a profound, eternal truth.

Sh'mini

שמיני

ויקרא ט:א-יא:מז

Leviticus 9:1–11:47

1. Holiness in Daily Life

This portion can be divided into two sections. It begins with the conclusion of the story of the dedication of the priests and the altar, including the tragedy of the death of Aaron's two sons (Leviticus 9–10), and continues with a list of living creatures that are clean or unclean for purposes of eating (Leviticus 11). At first glance there seems to be very little connection, if any, between these sections. Upon closer examination, however, we note that the Hebrew word *kadosh* (holy or sacred) is invoked in both. Not only are the priests and the altar going through a process of sanctification, but when Nadab and Abihu are killed, it is because they have offered "alien fire" (Leviticus 10:1) — the opposite of sacred fire — in the Sanctuary and God says of them and their deaths: "Through those near to Me I show Myself *holy*" (Leviticus 10:3). Concerning the laws of clean and unclean creatures God says, "You shall make yourselves *holy* and be *holy*, for I am *holy*. You shall not make yourselves unclean through any swarming thing that moves upon the earth…you shall be *holy*, for I am *holy*" (Leviticus 11:44–45). Both sections, then, deal with aspects of holiness.

Holiness is a concept difficult to grasp. It indicates a connection to and dedication to God, partaking in some way of God's essential nature. Although holiness definitely has an ethical and moral dimension, as can be clearly seen in Leviticus 19, here it is being used in a narrower sense of ritual actions that connect us to the Divine. As such it usually means separation from certain things. As the Sages interpreted it: "You shall be holy — you shall be separated" (*Sifra K'doshim*, beginning). The priests had to separate themselves from impure objects and the people of Israel had to separate itself from unclean animals, thus signifying that it was indeed "a kingdom of priests and a holy nation" (Exodus 19:6).

Throughout the centuries the laws that appear here, together with the concept of not eating blood and not mixing milk and meat, have constituted the system of kashrut which has been a basic component of Jewish living. It has always served to distinguish Jews from others and as such has helped us to keep our distinctive nature. It has also been criticized from within and without. Non-Jews have referred to the laws as outmoded taboos. Some Jews have seen them as overly restrictive and as based upon a primitive system of health regulations that no longer apply to life today. Indeed, if one were to try to justify kashrut on the basis of health regulations, one would have a difficult time. Fortunately, we realize today that although at certain times it may have had health benefits, that is not its true meaning and purpose.

The late Rabbi Samuel Dresner, in his book *The Jewish Dietary Laws* (New York: Burning Bush Press, 1959), demonstrated that, among other things, kashrut was a concrete manifestation of the sacredness of all life. Animal life is not to be treated as unimportant. An animal may be killed only for purposes of eating, not for sport. An animal that is not kosher may not be killed at all except in self-defense. When killing an animal for food, it must be done in a way that inflicts the minimum amount of pain; a blessing is said which in a sense indicates that this is done only with God's permission. The blood is not eaten because it symbolizes life itself which we take only with hesitancy. And if we are so careful with animal life and prize it so, how much more so must we consider human life to be inviolable! To quote Rabbi Dresner:

> The laws of Kashrut — which forbid the eating of blood, limit the number of animals which may be eaten and provides for a humane method of slaughter and a specially trained slaughterer — have helped to attain Judaism's goal of hallowing the act of eating by reminding the Jew that the life of the animal is sacred and may be taken to provide him with food only under these fixed conditions. From this he learns reverence for life, both animal and human. (p. 38)

In her book *Leviticus As Literature*, Mary Douglas has performed an invaluable service by providing an in-depth analysis of this chapter of Leviticus. Her point of view strengthens the connection between these laws and the reverence for life and fecundity. She points out the similarity between this section and the Biblical description of Creation in which God creates all the "swarms of living creatures…and all the living creatures of every kind that creep, which the waters brought forth in swarms" (Genesis 1:20–21) and commands them to "be fertile and increase, fill the waters of the seas, and let the birds increase on earth" (Genesis 1:22). The verses that describe various living beings in Leviticus often echo those words.

The creatures that are not to be eaten, contends Douglas, are not inherently bad, otherwise God would not have created them and gloried in their creation. They are only "unclean *unto you*" (Leviticus 11:4, 5, 6, 7, 8 and so on). They include the creatures that swarm, that are abundant, as well as those who cannot defend themselves easily. As a matter of fact, the list of animals that we may not eat is far greater than those we may. They are, in a sense, "protected creatures." Those we can eat are domestic animals and birds and fish that are well protected by having scales and fins. Unlike others, these creatures are in no danger of extinction. All of this indicates even more than we may have previously thought that the basic concept here is of life's importance and sanctity. These commands signify the importance of fertility and stress God's compassion and love of life.

The priests functioned in the Sanctuary, following rules of holiness. Through the observance of kashrut each Jew makes his or her home a sanctuary, the table an altar and eating a holy act that enhances our reverence for life.

2. Sanctity and Sin

As we have seen, all too often a moment of exaltation and holiness is followed by a descent into sin and tragedy. Following the miracle at the sea, for example, Israel immediately began a series of complaints with which they sorely tried God's patience. Similarly, no sooner had the Ten Commandments been given than Israel built a golden calf, resulting in severe punishment. In this portion the glorious dedication of the priests to God's service when "fire came forth before the Lord and consumed the burnt offering" (Leviticus 9:24) is immediately followed by the sin of Aaron's sons. Nadab and Abihu offered "alien fire before the Lord, which He had not enjoined upon them" (Leviticus 10:1). Once again "fire came forth from the Lord," but this time it consumed not the offering but the priests who brought it (Leviticus 10:2). Aaron, who had been so exalted, is now plunged into mourning so deep that he cannot even speak — "And Aaron was silent" (Leviticus 10:3). Sacred fire became profane fire and resulted in the fire of punishment.

The Sages offered many fanciful yet meaningful explanations of the sin of Nadab and Abihu. Among their suggestions were:

- They were intoxicated;
- They entered the Holy of Holies without permission;
- In their enthusiasm they added practices that had not been ordained;
- They gave instruction in the law in the presence of their elders, a practice the rabbis did not permit in their houses of study;
- They did not take counsel with one another;
- They did not take counsel with Moses;
- They did not given honor to Aaron; and
- They were impatient for Moses and Aaron to die so that they could assume the leadership. (*Sifra Sh'mini*, beginning)

All of these are interesting, but the text of the Torah is actually quite clear about their sin. It states specifically that they offered strange, alien fire which God had not commanded. The Hebrew word for alien is *zarah* — the same word found in the expression *avodah zarah*, meaning idolatry or alien worship. They brought an incense offering that did not follow the rules they had been given. If the rules given to the priests are not followed, strange worship, idolatry, could easily corrupt the sacrificial ritual.

The question that begs to be asked is not "What did they do?" but "Did that offence warrant such severe punishment?" Moses' answer is "yes," because "Through those near to me I show Myself holy" (Leviticus 10:3). Those who are closest to God, those who represent God's will, must sanctify God through all their actions. The higher the office, the more is expected and demanded. What might be excusable in an ordinary person cannot be tolerated in someone in that exalted role.

The issue here is *kiddush hashem* (the sanctification of God's name). This refers to any action that brings glory and holiness to God, causing others to revere God. *Ḥillul hashem* (the desecration of God's name), bringing shame upon God or Judaism, is the opposite. The ultimate act of *kiddush hashem* is martyrdom, but everyday actions can also be acts of sanctification of God — or the opposite.

When one who is identified with the Jewish religion acts immorally this becomes a desecration of God's name. When one identified as a religious person is caught stealing, embezzling or otherwise acting deceitfully, that person brings shame upon God's name and upon Judaism.

The same rule applies to anyone who holds high office. The least infraction of the law cannot be tolerated in those who hold high office. They must be good examples for others. All elected officials must be careful to keep far away from even the appearance of dishonesty. As the saying goes, Caesar's wife must be above suspicion.

The midrash interprets the verse "In the days when the judges judged" (Ruth 1:1) as "In the days when the judges were judged" and remarks, "Woe to the generation that judges its judges and woe to the generation whose judges must be judged!" (*Ruth Rabbah* 1:1).

Since the entire Jewish people is designated "a kingdom of priests," it behooves all of us to live up to the highest standards of decency and honesty, for whenever we do wrong it brings shame upon Judaism and whatever we do right brings honor.

Tazria תזריע

Leviticus 12:1–13:59 | ויקרא יב:א-יג:נט

1. Purity and Impurity

Both this portion and the next (which are frequently read together) are concerned with one topic: ritual impurity because of bodily discharges or eruptions. They are not the most pleasant sections to read because of their detailed descriptions of these symptoms. They deal both with things that we would consider to be normal (Leviticus 12) — and in the case of childbirth even wondrous and blessed — and with those that are symptoms of illness (Leviticus 13). In all cases the Torah considers them to be matters that both render one impure — and therefore forbidden to come in contact with God's realm of holiness — and also require a ritual of "atonement" in order to conclude the period of impurity. Although a "sin offering" is required, in this case there is no implication that the person has done anything wrong. Being in a state of impurity requires something to expiate or cover over that impurity so that one can return to normal life.

What binds all of these ostensibly disparate conditions together is that all of them seem to indicate some possibility of danger or some diminishment of potential life. Thus a menstruating woman (Leviticus 15:19-24) is not capable of conceiving and the discharge of semen (Leviticus 15:16-18) is a negation of the possibility of impregnation. Although today giving birth is generally not considered dangerous, this is a fairly recent development. Death in childbirth and infant mortality were common until recently and still are in certain parts of the world.

Furthermore, it has been pointed out that in ancient Mesopotamian religion, which forms the background to the religion of Israel, all of these instances were believed to have been brought about by evil demons and dangerous spirits. To quote Mary Douglas:

> In Babylonian beliefs there was a dreaded goddess who systematically preyed on pregnant women and babies, a god of epilepsy who was also god of leprosy, and the belief that demons could be manufactured from nocturnal emissions collected in a bucket. (*Leviticus As Literature*, p. 189)

It is clear that Leviticus wants to negate these pagan beliefs. True, says the Torah, these are dangerous conditions, but they are not brought about by any demonic forces, nor can they be healed by any magical spells. Their cause is never discussed. It is true that later Jewish tradition tended to identify one of these conditions, the so-called leprosy, as a punishment for "the evil tongue" — slander. This was largely based on the fact that Miriam is punished with a kind of leprosy for her slander against Moses (Numbers 12). We may take this, however, as an instance of midrashic license intended to teach us to avoid slander, and certainly not as meant to indicate that illness is always a sign of sin! See the full discussion of this below.

As for the role of the religious leader, it is merely diagnosis and the proclamation of the end of the period of uncleanness. "The priest shall examine it. If some hair has turned white in the discoloration, which itself appears to go deeper than the skin, it is leprosy that has broken out in the burn. The priest shall pronounce him unclean…the priest shall isolate him for seven days. On the seventh day the priest shall examine him…if the discoloration has remained stationary…the priest shall pronounce him clean" (Leviticus 13:25–28). At no time does the priest do anything to bring about a cure. Never does he utter any words of incantation or even of prayer. The Torah seeks to separate itself and the religious leaders of Israel from anything even resembling the magical practices of paganism as it was then practiced.

Maimonides, who attempted to explain the reasons behind all the *mitzvot*, had difficulty in understanding some of the details of these laws of purity, but he did offer general reasons for them all:

1. They are necessary for good health. They keep us from things that are dirty and help prevent disease. This is certainly true in the case of isolating those who had leprous diseases.

2. They increase our respect for the Sanctuary. If one cannot always enter the holy place but must wait until one is in a state of purity, one gains reverence for the holy place: "Such acts of reverence for the Sanctuary lead one to humility."

3. They continued practices that the people were already accustomed to because they were done in other religions.

4. They nevertheless changed those practices to make them less burdensome (and, I would add, to make them more in accord with monotheistic belief). (See *Guide For The Perplexed*, III:47.)

Maimonides' points are well taken. There is special significance to his second point regarding the reverence for the Sanctuary. In the first law mentioned in this section, that of the woman who had given birth, the only prohibition specified is that "she shall not touch any consecrated thing, nor enter the Sanctuary until her period of purification be completed" (Leviticus 12:4). Unlike the leper, she was not isolated from the community. That was clearly done to protect others from infection. The new mother and all others who acquired ritual impurity through any means were prohibited from coming to the Sanctuary not as a punishment, but as a way of exalting the status of the Sanctuary and emphasizing its holiness. Israel was warned against "defiling My Tabernacle which is among them" (Leviticus 15:31). This explains the fact that these chapters, which form a distinct code of ritual purity, are placed right in the midst of the story of the Sanctuary's dedication. As the symbol of God's Presence, it was to be treated with reverence and respect. Restricting entrance to it added to that aura of awe.

It should be remembered, however, that ritual purity was not the only requirement for entrance to the Sanctuary. The guardians of the Sanctuary themselves, the Levites who wrote most of the psalms, clearly stated:

> Who may ascend the mountain of the Lord? Who may stand in His holy place?
> One who has clean hands and a pure heart, who has not taken a false oath by My life or sworn deceitfully.
> Such a one may carry away a blessing from the Lord, a just reward from God, one's deliverer. (Psalms 24:3-5)

Laws of ritual impurity have played an important part in Judaism and in developing our reverence for God. But their most important role is in leading us to realize that purity of deeds and purity of heart are essential for a relationship to God and for attaining worthiness to be in God's Presence.

2. Disease and Sin

Much time is spent in this portion detailing skin disease and growths on houses and on garments. As Mary Douglas puts it:

> The body, the garment, and the house are given the same diagnostic treatment and the cleaned house gets atonement as does the body. They have not cropped up by accident, and they cannot be ignored without losing the sense of the whole passage. (*Leviticus As Literature*, p. 177)

Strangely enough, nothing is done to "cure" any of these diseases. The sections are filled with diagnostic instructions to the priest, but, as mentioned above, he does not serve in any way either as a doctor or as a miracle-healer. He is told what the signs of the impurity are so that he can pronounce the person or the object as either pure or impure, but he is not told to do anything that would change the situation. Only after the condition has been cured does he perform the rituals of purification. There is nothing of the witch doctor here.

The main concern, then, is not really health — although there is little doubt that in many cases isolating a diseased person would have a good effect on preventing the spread of a contagious disease. Ritual purity is the subject and ritual impurity stems from the flow of bodily fluids that are needed for procreation, thus negating the creative nature of the Divine. It also comes from growths that distort the body and thus render it imperfect. Just as a priest who is defective cannot officiate in the Sanctuary, so an individual who is suffering from such an affliction cannot be part of the sacred community. There is great concern shown for bringing the afflicted person back into the community and into contact with the realm of the sacred.

One of the more problematic parts of this reading is the chapter concerning so-called leprosy (Leviticus 13). First of all, everyone today is in agreement that the disease described here is not true leprosy, Hansen's disease, but some other curable form of illness *(The JPS Torah Commentary: Leviticus, p. 75)*. More worrisome is the fact that all too often the simplistic identification has been made between the condition and some sin that is thought to have brought it about. Mainly because of the fact that in a later story in Numbers 12 Miriam is afflicted with this disease as a punishment for her slanderous words against Moses, the tendency has been to say that anyone who suffered from this did so as a punishment for slander (see also Deuteronomy 24:8). This tendency was strengthened by the Sages who, in *Leviticus Rabbah* 16:1, cited not only the case of Miriam but many others as well as instances in which slander caused leprosy. Even Maimonides, the great rationalist, wrote that "all agree that leprosy is a punishment for slander" (*Guide*, III:47). Rabbi S.R. Hirsch takes the same position — every instance of this affliction is "a punitive admonition for social misbehavior." (*The Pentateuch: Leviticus*, trans. Isaac Levy [London: Judaica press, 1958], p. 358)

Now it is understandable that the Sages would take this opportunity to rail against "the evil tongue" in their homilies, but to understand this as the simple meaning of the text is both to distort the text and to make the unwarranted and indeed cruel assumption that anyone who suffers this illness is being punished by God and, by extension, that any illness is a sign of sin. The text itself says nothing of that sort. It is surprising, then, that Rabbi Gunther Plaut in his commentary to the Torah states that the Torah takes this affliction as "the manifestation of extreme divine displeasure...the expression of God's anger" (*The Torah: A Modern Commentary* [New York: Union of American Hebrew Congregations, 1981], p. 829). *Etz Hayim,* on the other hand, clearly states that "It should be noted that the Torah itself presents *tzara'at* as an affliction to be cured, not as a punishment to be explained" (p. 653).

Again, to quote Mary Douglas:

> There is no attempt to identify a sin that caused the disease. This is very striking. Nowhere does Leviticus say that the disease can be attributed to the sin of the victim.... Leviticus is not at all inclined to search out causes of disasters or attribute blame. (p. 185)

Because Judaism teaches the doctrine of reward and punishment, i.e., that God is concerned with our actions and that our actions result in reward or in punishment, it is all too easy to reverse the process and say that anything bad that happens to us — and illness is certainly one such thing — is a result of sin, of something we have done wrong. Thousands of years ago the author of the book of Job, one of the greatest religious thinkers of all time, dealt with this question. The "friends" of the suffering Job come to him and "comfort" him with the message that surely he has sinned (Job 11:14), even if unintentionally, and that this explains why he has been afflicted with diseases not dissimilar from those described in Leviticus. Job, on the other hand, holds on to his integrity and refuses to agree (Job 27:5–6). He questions why God has done this to him, but he will not admit that he sinned when he did not. In the end it is Job who is vindicated by God Himself and declared innocent of sin (Job 42:7). In that one stroke the book of Job severed the cord between illness and sin. However we explain suffering — and truly we cannot explain it any more than could Job — we cannot assume that it is punishment by God for sin.

All too often we hear the terrible events of the Shoah "explained" as God's punishment for this or that sin on the part of the Jews. Such reasoning is an insult to the memory of those who perished and a grave blasphemy of God. To ascribe to God's will the slaughter of six million innocents is to make a mockery of our belief in a merciful God. Rather it is important for us to affirm the truth of that which Abraham Joshua Heschel once remarked, "History is the arena in which the will of God is defied."

By all means, let us avoid slander, but not because it brings on physical illness. Rather understand the Torah's injunction here as a means of keeping us aware of the realm of holiness, the realm of the Divine and the need to be pure and worthy of entering it.

M'tzorah

מצרע

Leviticus 14:1–15:33 | ויקרא יד:א-טו:לג

1. Being Cleansed

M'tzorah completes the manual on bodily manifestations that render a person or an object impure and call for individuals to be separated from contact with the Sanctuary. In the previous portion, *Tazria*, we read of the way in which the impurity is detected and diagnosed (Leviticus 12–13). In this portion we read of the way in which the person or object is declared pure and brought back into normal relations with the community and the Sanctuary: "This shall be the ritual for a leper at the time that he is to be cleansed" (Leviticus 14:2).

Part of the ceremony held in order to permit the person with a leprosy-like illness to be declared "clean" is the ritual offering of one bird and the freeing of another: "He shall set the live bird free in the open country" (Leviticus 14:4-7). One cannot help but reminded here of another purification ceremony — that of the scapegoat on Yom Kippur. There too one animal — in that case a goat — is sacrificed and another is set free: "Thus the goat shall carry on it all their iniquities to an inaccessible region; and the goat shall be set free in the wilderness" (Leviticus 16:22). The freeing of the bird and of the goat both have the same significance — the impurity or the sin is carried away, set free, and is no longer present in the individual or, in the case of the goat, in the community. In the eyes of the Torah all of this is purely symbolic.

But here, as in so many other cases, the Torah has taken rituals that originated previously in non-monotheistic religions and transformed them. It has retained an outer shell but changed the inner meaning. In ancient religions such ceremonies of purgation revolved around gods, demons or spirits that

were actually being expelled and sent away. In Judaism, with its strict monotheistic teaching, these superstitious beliefs are done away with and only
symbolism remains.

Another part of this portion, which can also best be understood against
its ancient background, concerns the fact that sexual intercourse renders one
impure (Leviticus 15:18), as does giving birth itself (Leviticus 12:2-6). As
Baruch Levine remarks in his commentary to Leviticus:

> As a matter of fact, the impurity of semen made it forbidden ever to
> have sex within sacred precincts, once again creating a distance
> between the process of procreation and the cult. In other ancient
> Near Eastern religions, fertility was celebrated in the cult — on
> special occasions, sexual intercourse might even be dramatized and
> myths telling of the mating of the gods were recited. Not so in the cult
> of Israelite monotheism. (*The JPS Torah Commentary: Leviticus*
> [Philadelphia: Jewish Publication Society of America, 1989], p. 96)

The religion of Israel had to take drastic steps to separate itself from the
ancient religions that surrounded it. Therefore, for Judaism, anything even
remotely connected to sexual relations and fertility made one impure and
kept one away from the Sanctuary.

Similarly, the Egyptian religion was largely focused on the dead and their
priests dealt with immortalizing the dead. Therefore, for the priests of Israel,
the exact opposite was the case — they were rendered impure by contact with
the dead (Leviticus 21:1-4)!

It is often the case that ancient forms are preserved and given new meanings. In this way continuity is preserved, but religion is constantly renewed
and made relevant to our lives.

2. The Reason for Rituals

There are many rituals described in the Torah that are difficult to explain
without some knowledge of ancient religions, rituals that seem to be simply
decrees that must be followed without any understanding. A prime example
of this would be the ritual of the red heifer whose ashes are used in ceremonies of purification while those who prepare those ashes are rendered impure

(Numbers 19:1-10). The midrash relates that a pagan once asked Rabban Yohanan ben Zakkai to explain this and said that it looked to him like magic. Ben Zakkai gave him an explanation in which he compared this ritual to the exorcizing of a spirit. His pupils then said to him, "Rabban — you put him off with a reed — but what do you say to us?" To which he replied, "By your lives! The dead body does not render impure and the water does not render pure; rather, says the Holy One, 'I have enacted a law, I have decreed a decree. You are not permitted to disobey it'" (*Numbers Rabbah* 19:8). Rabban Yohanan ben Zakkai wanted to make it very clear that there was no magic involved in this ritual or any other rituals. We might extend this to say that perhaps these same forms were used by others in magical ways, but that in Judaism they have no such meaning. New wine has been poured into old bottles. That seems to be Maimonides' point of view when he explains the pagan background to many of the *mitzvot*.

Unfortunately this story has also often been used to inculcate the idea that rituals need have no meaning, no explanation. All that is required is to do them. That was not the approach of the Sages. A glance at Yitzhak Heinemann's classic work *Ta'amei Hamitzvot* (The Reasons for the Mitzvot; Jerusalem: Zionist Confederation Press, 1942) is enough to prove the point. The midrash is full of attempts to explain and give meanings to the various rituals. Indeed, immediately following this story, for example, the same midrashic work offers an explanation of why this particular offering, the heifer, is a female while all other sacrifices are male. It is as if a mother is called upon to make up for the deed of a child — thus the cow can cleanse the sin caused by the golden calf (*Numbers Rabbah* 19:8).

There must be a golden mean between those who say, "These rituals are outmoded and can be abandoned" and those who say, "Just do them. Don't think about them." That mean can be found in the work of the Sages, of Maimonides and other Jewish thinkers and philosophers up to our own day, thinkers who want to preserve the rituals but also want them to be meaningful and rational. Sometimes meaning can be given to specifics, sometimes meaning comes from understanding ancient origins and sometimes it comes from viewing rituals as a pattern intended to bring us closer to God, to make us aware of the Divine or to connect us to our Jewish roots. One saying of the Sages is particularly meaningful in this regard: "The *mitzvot* were given solely in order to purify human beings"(*Genesis Rabbah* 44:1). Performing these acts helps us to rise above our baser selves and to direct ourselves to following God's ways. A regimen of *mitzvot* pervading all of life can help transform us into better human beings, but it does not do so automatically. Without thought and understanding, observance loses its true meaning and purpose.

Aharei Mot   אחרי מות

Leviticus 16:1–18:30 | ויקרא טז:א-יח:ל

1. Animal Life

This portion is constructed in an unusual way. It consists of three chapters, each of which begins with a verse stating that the Lord spoke to Moses and gave him laws concerning one specific subject. Each chapter is a self-contained unit giving the regulations on that topic. In chapter 16 we find the laws concerning atonement. Therefore this chapter is also read on Yom Kippur. Chapter 17 contains laws pertaining to the slaughter of animals, with particular emphasis on the prohibition of partaking of blood. Chapter 18 records sexual practices that are forbidden by the religion of Israel in contrast to the practices then current in Egypt and Canaan. All three sections may be said to outline ways in which the purity and holiness of Israel can be preserved.

Let us look at chapter 17. It begins by prohibiting the slaughter of domestic animals unless they are brought to the Tent of Meeting and offered there as a sacrifice (Leviticus 17:3–4). As Baruch Levine points out in his commentary (*The JPS Torah Commentary: Leviticus*, p. 112), this may be interpreted in two different ways and indeed was so interpreted by the Sages. It could either mean that no slaughter of animals was permitted unless it was done at the Sanctuary (this is Rabbi Ishmael's view found in the *Sifra*) or that sacrifices could be offered only at the Sanctuary but the slaughter of animals for food could be done elsewhere (so Rabbi Akiba) (*Sifra*, ed. Isaac Hirsch Weiss [New York: Om Publishing Company, 1946], 83b, 6).

The first interpretation is not as radical or impractical as it may at first appear when we remember that although there was only one Sanctuary in the wilderness, when they arrived at Canaan they had many local sanctuaries. For this reason, anyone wanting to eat meat could easily bring the animal to a local sanctuary and slaughter it there, leaving part for an offering and taking the rest for food. It became impractical only when those local sanctuaries were eliminated, as required by the book of Deuteronomy. But Deuteronomy also specifically gives permission to slaughter animals for food outside the Sanctuary (12:13-16).

What is most striking here, regardless of which interpretation one prefers, is that the Torah is most insistent on prohibiting two things: the offering of sacrifices to any being other than the Lord and the consumption of blood. The Torah explains its command that animals be offered in the Sanctuary thus:

> This is in order that the Israelites may bring the sacrifices which they have been making in the open — that they may bring them before the Lord, to the priest, at the entrance of the Tent of Meeting, and offer them as sacrifices of well-being to the Lord; that the priest may dash the blood against the altar of the Lord at the entrance of the Tent of Meeting, and turn the fat into smoke as a pleasing odor to the Lord; and that they may offer their sacrifices no more to the goat-demons after whom they stray. (Leviticus 17:5-7)

Thus it is obvious that it was the fear of idolatry that prompted this prohibition. "Goat-demons" were not necessarily gods, but the new monotheism taught by Moses could brook no worship of any being except God, nor any practice that even smacked of such worship. This may have been closer to superstition than to idolatry, but it was close enough to be perceived as a danger to pure monotheism, causing Israelites to "stray" after other beings and thus be unfaithful to the one true God. Restricting slaughter to the sacred precinct was an excellent way to fight against the easy slide into pagan worship.

Maimonides cited this prohibition as his explanation for the existence of sacrifices in Judaism. "God allowed these kind of services to continue; He transferred to His service that which had formerly served as a worship of created beings and of things imaginary and unreal" (*Guide For The Perplexed* III:32; see also III:46). Rather than sacrifice to goat-demons, sacrifice to God.

2. Blood Is Life

As for the prohibition against partaking of blood, obviously it was seen as a matter of great importance. The Torah speaks of bloodguilt in slaughter outside of the sacred place (Leviticus 17:4). It prohibits partaking of blood twice in verse 17:10 and then repeats the prohibition in 17:12 and yet again in 17:14. The explanation given for this is, "For the life of the flesh is in the blood" (Leviticus 17:11), which is then repeated again: "For the life of all flesh — its blood is its life" (Leviticus 17:14). In Deuteronomy 12:16, where slaughter for food is permitted, we are told once again: "But you must not partake of the blood; you shall pour it out on the ground like water." This must be seen against the background of Genesis 9:4 where, after the flood, humans were given permission for the first time to eat animal flesh but with the proviso that "You must not, however, eat flesh with its life-blood in it," which is followed by the prohibition of spilling human blood: "Whoever sheds the blood of a human being, by a human being shall his blood be shed; for in His image did God create the human being" (Genesis 9:6).

It is clear, then, that blood represents life and the Torah sees the taking of life — any life — as a matter of great seriousness. It goes without saying that human life is sacred and that we are forbidden to kill except in cases that warrant it — in self-defense or as a punishment for crime — and yet in those cases the laws are so strict that it becomes very difficult to execute anyone. Even in the case of animals, the Torah teaches us that we are permitted to take animal life only for purposes of eating — not because we want to take the life. Therefore we do not partake of the blood — the very essence of life. That is why hunting for sport is unthinkable in Judaism. That is why bullfighting or any other kind of cruelty to animals is out of the question for us.

Living as we do in a world in which blood is shed so easily, this chapter has special importance for us. We should never become callous about the taking of life, animal or human. If one is forced to shed blood, it should never be considered a happy choice or an easy one. There is nothing more precious than life and nothing more terrible than wantonly destroying it. All of Judaism is based on that belief.

K'doshim   קדשים

Leviticus 19:1–20:27 | ויקרא יט:א-כ:כז

1. The Holiness Code

K'doshim is one of the most significant portions of the Torah. It contains rules and regulations for living, statutes that have been called "the holiness code."

Scholars are divided over the question of exactly where this code begins and ends. Some would begin it at chapter 17, some at chapter 18 and some only at chapter 19 where the phrase "be holy" occurs for the first time (Leviticus 19:2). There is also a disagreement as to where it ends. Is it at the end of chapter 19, which resembles the Ten Commandments in reminding us that God brought us out of Egypt, or at 20:26 where the phrase "be holy" appears again? Or does this code include everything until the end of Leviticus?

I tend to see chapters 19 and 20 as a specific unit because of the way in which they are framed by the phrase "be holy." The Sages (*Leviticus Rabbah* 24:5) emphasized the uniqueness of chapter 19. They said that it was proclaimed to the entire people of Israel at a special gathering because the basic principles of the Torah are all found in it, as are the Ten Commandments.

Indeed there is an intimate connection between this chapter and the earlier covenant made at Mount Sinai. Remember that the purpose of that was spelled out in these words, "You shall be to Me a kingdom of priests and *a holy nation*" (Exodus 19:6). There are also clear echoes of the Ten Commandments in this section, especially in chapter 19. Honoring parents (Leviticus 19:3), observing Shabbat (Leviticus 19:3, 30), rejecting idol worship (Leviticus 19:4), the prohibition of stealing (Leviticus 19:11), not swearing falsely (Leviticus 19:12) — all are found here just as they are found in the Ten

173

Commandments. One might see this chapter as a kind of Levitical version or expansion of the Sinai covenant. Chapter 20 also prohibits adultery (verse 10) and expands the discussion to other prohibitions of sexual conduct. The Sages took special care to enlarge the concept of holiness to include sexual morality. They said that chapter 20 is attached to the section on holiness in order to teach that wherever there is sexual propriety there is holiness (*Leviticus Rabbah* 24:6).

So once again we find that we are directed to the question of the meaning of holiness. Indeed it is difficult to escape it in the book of Leviticus. There is something both daring and daunting in the verse with which this code begins, "You shall be holy, for I, the Lord your God, am holy" (Leviticus 19:2). Baruch Levine writes that this should be translated as "You *must* be holy!" (*The JPS Torah Commentary: Leviticus*). It is not a statement but a command.

But it is the second part of the verse that is truly troubling. It tells us that the reason we must be holy is not because God commands it, or because God wants us to become a people dedicated to Him, but because "I, the Lord your God, am holy." What does that mean? Can we, human beings, share God's holiness? Surely we cannot become divine. If there is one thing that is certain in Jewish belief and that contrasts us to other faith systems, it is that there is a clear line between God and humans. We cannot become divine and God does not become human. So if holiness is the essence of God, in what way can we become holy?

Rabbi Shimon ben Lakish was troubled by this question and he therefore interpreted the verse somewhat differently:

> "You shall be holy" — Is it possible that you can be like Me? The verse says, "*Although* I am holy" — that is: My holiness is above, higher than your holiness. (*Leviticus Rabbah* 24:9)

We can never attain the holiness that is the essence of God, but we can and we must aspire to bring a measure of godliness into our lives. This was made clear in the rabbinic interpretation of the verse "You shall follow the Lord your God" (Deuteronomy 13:5):

> Is it possible for a person to literally follow the *Shekhinah*? Rather it means that one should follow the attributes of the Holy One, blessed be He. As He clothes the naked…so should you clothe the naked. He

visited the sick...so should you visit the sick. He comforted mourners...so should you comfort mourners. He buried the dead...so
should you bury the dead. (*Sotah* 14a)

Thus we are instructed to imitate God, not to become God. God's holiness is
an attribute that is indefinable and impossible to imitate, but it includes ethical concerns as well as separation from impurity. These are what human holiness demands to whatever extent we can attain them. That is why we find in
this holiness code both rituals that separate us from impurity and thereby
help us to feel close to God (Leviticus 19:8, 19, 25–28; 20:25) and ethical
precepts that follow "the attributes of the Holy One."

It is surely no accident that the ethical commands are more numerous
than the ritual ones and that the very first imperative following the words "be
holy" is reverence for parents (Leviticus 19:3). It is in this magnificent chapter
that we find the verse that, as will be discussed below, forms the very essence
of Judaism, "Love your fellow as yourself" (Leviticus 19:18), as well as the
commands to pay laborers their wages immediately (19:13), leave food for
the poor (19:9–10) and love the stranger who dwells with you (19:34). Indeed
if — heaven forbid — all of the Torah were to disappear and only Leviticus 19
remained, we would still retain the basis for moral, ethical, religious living.

We often ask ourselves what it means to be a Jew. One answer to this question is embedded in these chapters: "be holy...imitate the ways of the Holy
One, the ways of purity, love and ethical living."

2. The Ethical Dimension of Holiness

Since seven is Judaism's sacred number, it is probably not an accident that the
seventh section of Leviticus is also the most important part of the book
containing a "holiness code." In addition to repeating major commandments
found in the Ten Commandments, this holiness code expands the idea of
holiness to include ritual commands such as those concerning the proper
offering of sacrifices (Leviticus 19:5–8) and prohibitions against mixtures of
diverse kinds (Leviticus 19:19), eating fruit before the fourth year (Leviticus
19:23–25), trimming one's beard (Leviticus 19:27) and making marks on the

body (Leviticus 19:28). All of these may be seen as attempts to distinguish Israel and cement a bond between God and the people Israel.

The main emphasis of the holiness code, however, is on a series of moral and ethical commands that show great sensitivity. As we have seen above, we are commanded to share our harvest with the poor (Leviticus 19:9–10). We are forbidden to defraud, to keep wages overnight, to insult the deaf or place an obstacle before the blind (Leviticus 19:13–14). We are commanded to give deference to the aged (Leviticus 19:32) and forbidden to wrong the stranger (Leviticus 19:33). It is impossible not to remark that the world and our own society would be very different if these rules were obeyed today. Indeed the holiness code has lost none of its relevance in the thousands of years since it was promulgated.

Perhaps the height of holiness in this section can be seen in two verses that demand loving conduct from us. The first is the well-known verse, "Love your fellow as yourself" (Leviticus 19:18). To think that this verse comes from Leviticus — the priestly code — of all places! It was this verse that was singled out both by Hillel and Akiba as the very essence of the teaching of Torah. As Hillel put it after paraphrasing that verse in Aramaic, "All the rest is commentary — now go and learn!" (*Shabbat* 31a). But this verse is supplemented by another of no less importance: "You shall love him [the stranger] as yourself, for you were strangers in the land of Egypt" (Leviticus 19:34). The reason for the importance of this verse is that "your fellow" in verse 18 could be taken to refer only to your fellow Israelite. Here we are told that loving conduct must be practiced not only toward our fellow Jews, but also toward strangers — i.e., non-Jews — who dwell with us. That is much more difficult, but no less important.

Frequently we hear it said that the prophets alone taught that morality was the highest form of religious living. Indeed many of the prophets, such as Jeremiah and Amos, denounce ritual acts when they are not accompanied by ethical conduct. Jeremiah, for example, castigates the people who come to the Temple thinking that worship will save them while they continue to ignore the Torah's moral demands. "If you execute justice between one another, if you do not oppress the stranger, the orphan, and the widow" (Jeremiah 7:5–6) — only then will God accept their worship! But while the prophets may have placed great emphasis on this, it is not true that the Torah does not contain the same thought. Jeremiah's demands are based on Leviticus and other parts of the Torah. Our chapters make the same point. To be holy one must treat others fairly, one must pay fair wages, one must be generous to the poor. No amount of outward "piety" in observance of rituals will make up for dishonesty. Leviticus, that most maligned book, the very essence of dry ritual, teaches us the most important lessons of ethical living. The prophets may have emphasized morality for us, but they did not invent it.

These chapters cause us to pause and ponder the question, "What does it mean to be holy?" Different religions give different answers to that question, and even within Judaism different groups place varied emphases on the meaning of holiness. The Torah seems to have a very clear answer. Holiness does not mean separation from society, but living within it. Holiness does not mean devoting oneself totally to ritual, but combining ritual with good deeds toward others. Although it might be possible to be moral without being holy, it is not possible to be holy without being ethical.

Emor אמר

Leviticus 21:1–24:23 | ויקרא כא:א-כד:כג

1. The Obligations of the Priest

The previous Torah portion was concerned with the holiness of the people Israel. This reading begins with instructions concerning the holiness of the religious leaders of Israel at that time, the kohanim. If the regulations for the ordinary Israelite were strict, requiring both high ritual and ethical norms, the ritual requirements for the priests were even higher — and for the high priest, higher yet.

As an example, regarding Israelites the Torah states that they are not to "round off the side-growth on your head, or destroy the side-growth of your beard. You shall not make gashes in your flesh for the dead, or any marks on yourselves" (Leviticus 19:27–28) as signs of mourning. Concerning the priests the regulations are much more extensive — they are not allowed to have any contact with a dead body except for their closest blood relatives (Leviticus 21:1–4); they are not allowed to "shave smooth any part of their heads, or cut the side-growth of their beards, or make gashes in their flesh" (Leviticus 21:5). The high priest may not come in contact with any dead body, "even for his father or mother" (Leviticus 21:11), nor is he allowed to "bear his head or rend his vestments" in mourning (Leviticus 21:10).

All of this is done in the name of holiness: "They shall be holy to their God and not profane the name of their God" (Leviticus 21:6). The Hebrew root for holy — k-d-sh — appears no less than fourteen times in chapter 21 alone. The word itself is never defined and perhaps defies definition. In a prosaic sense it means "to belong to." But more importantly it is the quality of God Himself as stated clearly in the previous Torah portion: "You shall be holy to Me, for I the Lord am holy, and I have set you apart from other peoples to be Mine" (Leviticus 20:26). This is repeated in our portion as well: "for I the Lord who sanctify you am holy" (Leviticus 21:8).

One who serves God somehow shares in God's holiness. The more intensive the service, the higher the degree of holiness and the more one must be set apart by following certain regulations. Thus all the people of Israel are holy, but the priests who specifically serve God must be still stricter and the high priest even more so.

The two specific areas in which the kohanim have special requirements are those of marriage and, as we have seen, contact with the dead. This is not accidental. Rather it reflects the way in which the Torah rejects the ways of the pagan religions that surrounded Israel in ancient times. Pagan priests were often involved in fertility rites. The priests of Israel were not allowed to marry a woman who had been divorced, which in Biblical times probably meant that she had been suspected of adultery (Leviticus 21:7). The high priest could not even marry a widow (Leviticus 21:14). It is important to note, however, that the priests were not required to be or even expected to be celibate. These regulations do not indicate that sexual relations per se were considered somehow forbidden, but that sexual purity, sex within marriage, was required. The fact that later Judaism termed marriage itself *kiddushin* — from that same root of "holiness" — speaks volumes for Judaism's attitude toward sexual relations.

The same motivation of rejection of pagan ways lies behind the regulations concerning contact with the dead and excessive rites of mourning. Many ancient religions were steeped in cults of the dead. In Egypt, in particular, concern with the afterlife, with preparing the dead for entry into the world-to-come through elaborate rituals including embalming and mummification, were indeed the very core of the work of the priests. Some of the most important religious texts of ancient Egypt have been called *The Book of the Dead*. The Torah, on the other hand, never speaks about these things except to warn us against any cultic practices regarding the dead. Isaiah also indicates that there were people among the Israelites who inquired of ghosts and looked to "the dead on behalf of the living" (Isaiah 8:19). The rejection of such practices was so complete, the cult of the dead so abhorrent to Israelite belief, that concepts of life after death, beyond that of some shadowy realm called "Sheol" only came into Judaism at a much later period. These later concepts, however, did not negate the Torah's prohibition of worship of the dead, and we should be very cautious about creating cults in which we elevate the dead to positions of semi-divinity.

The revolution of belief that Mosaic monotheism wrought was far-reaching. It freed the concept of God from physical limitations and it separated the cult from sexual rituals and from worship of the dead. Instead it stressed sexual purity and the value of life. Kohanim were not there to serve the dead, but to tend to the living. They were not surrogates for the Divine, nor could they work magic. Rather they represented Israel before God and taught Israel God's commands. In order to do this they were required to adhere to strict regulations of purity.

Kohanim have long since lost their status as the religious leaders of Israel and retain at the most certain ritual privileges. Their place as religious teachers has been taken by rabbis, and while rabbis do not have to adhere to the ritual requirements the Torah spells out for the priests, they do have to adhere to the spirit of these laws — namely that anyone who speaks in the name of religion must be above reproach and above suspicion. The same, however, is true for all Jews. Commanded as we are to "be holy," representing God and God's Torah, we must be careful in our actions and demonstrate the ethical purity of Judaism in all we do. Otherwise we too are guilty of profaning the name of God.

2. The Cycle of the Year

One of the most relevant sections of this reading is the listing of the special days of the year and the way in which they are to be observed, the cycle of the Jewish year (Leviticus 23). In nature, days are undifferentiated. No one day is more important than another. The Torah, however, imposes a system whereby each seventh day has greater significance — in no way corresponding with any natural phenomenon such as the cycle of the moon. Similarly, specific days of specific months are singled out as holy and set aside from other days. Obviously the seasons of the year play a part in this, for the two most significant months are the first, spring, and the seventh, another "turn of the year."

Although we generally think of these holidays in terms of our history, it is

obvious that there is a strong agricultural, natural, basis for them. In the listing in this reading, incidentally, only Sukkot is given any historical background: "in order that future generations may know that I made the Israelite
people dwell in booths when I brought them out of the land of Egypt" (Leviticus 23:43). All the rest are simply listed in reference to the seasons of the year.
In the early days of Zionist settlement of the land of Israel, the settlers, especially those in kibbutzim, attempted to reemphasize the agricultural side of
the holidays and invented new rituals connected to the seasons and the earth.
In some cases they substituted these for historical reasons and even omitted
any religious significance or reference to God.

Although they may have gone too far, their innovations were not without
reason. Living in exile, uprooted from the land and far from agrarian life Jews
tended to overlook the agricultural aspect of the holidays. Reconnecting to
the land gives us the opportunity to redress the balance and make of these
days an appropriate combination of the two. Pesah is the holiday of freedom,
but it is also the holiday of spring. Shavuot — which in the Torah has absolutely no historical basis whatsoever — became the holiday of Revelation but
is essentially the holiday of the harvest of new grain. And Sukkot reflects our
wandering, or rather the protection God granted us when we were wandering, but is also the holiday of thanksgiving for the harvest and anticipation of
the rain.

There is symmetry in the Jewish year. At the beginning of the year and at
the beginning of its second half, on the day of the full moon, a *hag* (festival) is
held for seven days. This is followed by a concluding event: Sh'mini Atzeret
after Sukkot in the autumn and Shavuot after Pesah in the spring. The first
and seventh months themselves are special times. On the first of the seventh
month the shofar is blown, proclaiming the importance of the time. Later this
became the holiday of Rosh Hashanah. The tenth day of the same month,
Yom Kippur, was the time to purify the Sanctuary so that the rites of Sukkot
could be held properly. Later it was connected to Rosh Hashanah to create the
period of time known as "the days of awe." The tenth of the first month,
Nissan, was the time of taking the lamb to be used on Pesah. The symmetry is
extraordinary.

The meaning of *hag* is often overlooked. It is not simply a festival but a
pilgrimage holiday. In Arabic the cognate word *hajatun* retains that meaning.
As Baruch Levine commented, "This means that any festival called *hag* could

not be fully celebrated at one's home, but required one's presence at a cult site. In earlier times, the pilgrimage might have brought a family to a nearby altar, but subsequently Deuteronomy ordained that all sacrificial offerings were to be brought to one central Temple, which necessitated a much longer pilgrimage for most Israelites" (*The JPS Torah Commentary: Leviticus*, p. 156).

Such a pilgrimage has an electrifying effect upon the individual and the community. As the Sages often pointed out, "The glory of the King is felt where there is a multitude of people" (Proverbs 14:28). Coming together in large numbers from different places has the effect of making one feel part of a larger whole and closer to the Divine. It is true that God is present everywhere, but a sanctuary can create the feeling of intense closeness to God. This is especially so if there are historical events related to that sacred place. We know from descriptions of the pilgrimages during the days of the Second Temple how impressive the event was and how it helped to unify the Jewish people who, even before the destruction and the exile, were spread throughout the world far and wide.

Today we have returned to almost the same circumstances which existed before the destruction. Jews live freely in their own land, but many live in other places throughout the world, not because they are dispersed by force, but because they wish to live there. Nevertheless, they should have special ties to the land if they are to feel a part of one people. What better way than through pilgrimage to the sacred sites, to Jerusalem? And what better time than the sacred seasons, Pesah and Sukkot?

One more aspect of the calendar remains to be explored, and that is the special place given to Shabbat. Shabbat has neither of the attributes of the festivals. It has no historical connection, except in Deuteronomy 5:15 where it is a remembrance of freedom from slavery, and it has no agricultural connection. Yet its importance is unparalleled. It comes at the beginning of the list (Leviticus 23:3) and it is mentioned time after time in the Torah — in Genesis 2:3, in Exodus 16:23, before the giving of the Torah and throughout the rest of the books. The uniqueness of Shabbat is in the fact that it is essentially a-historical. It directs our attention not to ourselves and our history but to God alone and to the wonder of the world that God has created. In the original Ten Commandments, the rationale for Shabbat is remembrance of Creation (Exodus 20:11). It is interesting, however, that here in Leviticus no reason is mentioned. Rather we are simply told that it is "a Shabbat of the

Lord" (Leviticus 23:3). The emphasis is upon dedicating a day to the worship and contemplation of God. According to this the command to cease from work and rest is not only for the sake of rest itself, important though that may be, but in order to permit us to be free to devote ourselves to God.

In a larger sense this indicates to us that concern with everyday affairs, with work, with business, with making and doing, does not permit us the leisure to contemplate things of higher importance and attune ourselves to the spiritual aspects of life. What a pity it is that so many in our society today have lost this precious opportunity and have chosen instead to make Shabbat the primary shopping day of the week. There is something very sad about the abandonment of this opportunity to rise above the mundane and enter a realm in which time, contemplation and values are of greater concern than material things.

All the sacred times listed in this portion are intended to hallow our days, bring meaning to our lives, call attention to God, impart devotion to values and instill in us an appreciation of the world that God has given us. These matters are no less vital today than they were when first mentioned thousands of years ago. On the contrary, they are more important than ever. With our return to our own land, these times can be revitalized and renewed and can help cement the unity of Jews wherever they may live.

B'har

בהר

Leviticus 25:1–26:2 | ויקרא כה:א-כו:ב

1. The Wandering Jew

The origins of a people often determine its future and its character. Two historical facts connected with our origins have left their enduring mark upon the people Israel and its Torah: landlessness and slavery. At the beginning of our history we experienced both of these; this is reflected in the laws of the Torah and the concepts that underlie them.

Our ancestors were wanderers who detached themselves from the land of their birth — Mesopotamia — in order to set forth to an unknown destination. When they arrived there, it was not in their possession but merely a place where they were temporary residents. Thus it is that Abraham had to plead with the Hittites to purchase a gravesite explaining, "I am a resident alien [*ger v'toshav*] among you" (Genesis 23:4) and request the right that was not his to buy land.

We are reminded of this every year at our Pesah seder when we read both the passage from Joshua 24:2-4, which tells us that our ancestors were idol worshippers who lived beyond the Euphrates and were led from there to Canaan, and the verse from Deuteronomy 26:5: "My father was a fugitive Aramean. He went down to Egypt with meager numbers and sojourned [*vayagar*] there." This last verse was recited by each Israelite when bringing his first fruit to Jerusalem, so that he would realize the full impact of the fact that the wandering and sojourning had been brought to an end by the fulfillment of the promise to bring them to Canaan.

But in a sense the people were still strangers even within the land. In this portion we learn about the consequences of this type of landlessness. Before

185

they even embark on their journey from Sinai to Canaan (which they assume will be a matter of a few months at the most) the Israelites are commanded to regard the land as a sacred trust which must be shared equally and which belongs ultimately to God, not to them: "But the land must not be sold beyond reclaim, for the land is Mine; you are but strangers resident [*geirim v'toshavim*] with Me" (Leviticus 25:23). This is exactly the expression that was used concerning Abraham — but with a difference. He was a resident alien with the Hittites. The people of Israel are resident aliens with God. The land does not belong to us. Thus we remain landless in our own land because we are here as tenants and God is the true and sole owner. As a result of this landlessness, this condition of being a "stranger" (*ger*), the Torah teaches us time and time again to love the stranger and to treat the stranger well.

There are two legal ramifications of this, according to the Torah. One is that God can command us not to work the land every seventh year (Leviticus 25:4-5) — that becomes "a sabbath *of the Lord*" because it is, after all, God's land, not ours. The other is that we cannot permanently sell the land because we do not own it. It was distributed to us equally by God through Moses upon entering the land and can never be simply sold (see Numbers 33:54). Of course the underlying social reason for that is clear: land was the prime source of wealth; if one had to sell land because of poverty or debt, this would result in inequity in society, in a society in which some would have great property and be rich and others would live in perpetual poverty. If the land is returned to the original owners every fifty years, as prescribed by Leviticus 25:13-17, this will not happen.

Although this utopian plan cannot be carried out today — we have long ago lost any knowledge of the original owners of the land — it does have a message for us: that a situation in which there is both great poverty and great wealth contradicts our contract with God. It is not a simple thing to realize the goal that the Torah sets forth, but Jews loyal to the Torah cannot ignore it when making their choices concerning the social and economic policies that will determine the nature of Israeli society.

2. From Enslavement to Servitude

The other historical fact of our origins, slavery, has also influenced the regulations found in this portion. One verse in this portion encapsulates the idea: "For it is to Me that the Israelites are servants: they are My servants, whom I freed from the land of Egypt" (Leviticus 25:55). Here too paradox reigns. Just as we were given a land but remained landless, so, too, although freed from servitude we remained servants — slaves — but with a difference. Then we were slaves to Pharaoh. Now we are slaves, servants, to God — the same God to whom the land belongs! As slaves to God, we cannot also be slaves to human beings. Therefore the Torah commands that an Israelite who has become poverty-stricken (and has probably lost his land) and must sell himself into slavery is not to be treated as a slave. He must be a "hired or bound laborer" who must be freed completely in the Jubilee (fiftieth) year (Leviticus 25:39-43). Deuteronomy goes even further and requires that any Hebrew "slave" serve no longer than six years and be freed on the seventh (Deuteronomy 15:12). Thus the Torah abolished all slavery for Israelites, leaving instead an institution of indentured servitude that was little more than a long-term contract with severe limitations concerning the treatment of that servant.

The character of our people was thus formed by the experiences of the past, experiences of landlessness and slavery. As a people that has known suffering and oppression — not only early on but also unfortunately throughout our history — we have developed norms that sensitize us and cause us to want to create a society of equality, of freedom and security, a society in which all are treated humanely and in which the stranger is afforded equal rights. This portion envisions a society without master or slave, without rich or poor, without landed and landless. Little remains of this vision today except for certain symbolic observances. Even within the Torah itself this had to be modified to take into consideration conditions of urban living that are so different from those of a totally agricultural and pastoral society (see Leviticus 25:29-30). Perhaps it is beyond human reach. But the ideal and its underlying concepts should still speak to us and make us examine our society carefully.

B'ḥukotai בחקתי

Leviticus 26:3–27:34 | ויקרא כו:ג-כז:לד

1. Dire Warnings

Anyone expecting Leviticus to end with some particularly uplifting moment will be disappointed. The concluding portion of the book is overwhelmingly concerned with a frightening exhortation warning Israel of the terrible consequences of disobeying God. Of the first forty-three verses, eleven describe the blessings God will bring if Israel follows God's laws and commandments. All the rest speak of the "misery" that will follow disobedience.

This section is known as the *tokhaḥah* (the reproach) and is customarily read quietly as if to say, "We don't really want to hear this!" or, "Heaven forefend that this should ever come to pass!" A similar, even longer, section is found in Deuteronomy 28:15–68, when Moses warns the Israelites prior to entering their new land of the consequences of breaking the covenant made with God. Thus the priestly book of Leviticus and the Deuteronomic code are in complete agreement that terrible consequences will follow Israel's breaking of the covenant with God.

These verses make difficult reading. They are also problematic. Are we to take them to mean that every time there is a national tragedy this is a punishment from God? We have seen that happen when "literalists" explain terrorist attacks or other tragedies as punishment for some lack of ritual observance — faulty *mezuzot* or Shabbat desecration. We have also heard these charges made in regard to the Shoah — that it was God's punishment for some sin or another — secularism, Zionism, etc.

These simplistic accusations not only defame innocent people; they also ignore the fact that while Judaism has taught that God punishes evil (as in the stories of the flood and Sodom and Gomorrah), it has also acknowledged that there are times when the righteous suffer. Judaism has taught that one may not infer from a person's suffering that it was a deserved punishment because of some sin. The entire book of Job is devoted to that doctrine and we must never forget it. In the words of *Pirkei Avot*, "We have no way of understanding why the wicked prosper and why the righteous suffer" (*Pirkei Avot* 4:19). We dare not blame the victims and thus in any way justify the crime perpetrated against them.

Nevertheless the importance of this doctrine cannot be so easily dismissed. In the first place it was a needed exhortation for those about to enter the land for the first time. During the latter days of the First Temple, it served to remind the people of Israel, who had strayed far from the pure faith Moses had taught, that their well-being depended upon their adherence to the laws of Godly morality. The teachings of the great prophets such as Amos and, later, Jeremiah were based on this doctrine; we should not forget that what they constantly emphasized was not one ritual or another but basic morality. As Jeremiah put it:

> No, if you really mend your ways and your actions; if you execute justice between one man and another; if you do not oppress the stranger, the orphan, and the widow; if you do not shed the blood of the innocent in this place; if you do not follow other gods, to your own hurt — then only will I let you dwell in this place, in the land that I gave to your fathers for all time. (Jeremiah 7:5-7)

The meaning of these exhortations for us must be that evil has consequences and that a society is only as strong as its morality. The late Rabbi Louis Jacobs, the outstanding British theologian, put it this way in his book *Principles of the Jewish Faith* (New York: Jason Aronson, 1988):

> Wickedness [carries] the seeds of its own destruction. We prefer to leave the details to God, who in His wisdom "searches all hearts," but so to conduct ourselves that all the ancient teachings on reward and punishment are still of the utmost relevance to our lives…in every possible way it is *ultimately* better for us to lead a good life and reject

an evil life. When we pursue evil we are at variance with God's purpose and this can never succeed in any ultimate sense. (p. 365)

There is one other teaching in this section that was and is of great importance in our history. This is the idea that after punishment will come repentance and forgiveness. Three times the text repeats this idea: "Then will I remember My covenant" (Leviticus 26:42 and 45), "I will not reject them or spurn them so as to destroy them, annulling My covenant with them" (Leviticus 26:44). These words were important in providing the prophets with a message of comfort to the people, a message that helped sustain Israel through seventy years of Babylonian exile and nineteen hundred years of the second exile. It was because of this message that Jews never lost hope for their redemption.

2. Blessings and Hope

The last portion of Leviticus, *B'ḥukotai*, is a fitting conclusion to the previous laws. As we have seen, it details the consequences of following or disregarding them. The covenant with God is a contract and contracts have consequences. If the contract is violated, there is a penalty. If it is upheld, there are rewards. But the message is an important one, even if it is couched in terms that reflect ancient views. The underlying meaning is very simple: a society is only as strong as its morality. A nation that is corrupt and uncaring will crumble from within and lack the strength to resist challenges from without.

The opposite is also true. If we follow the ways of decency, we will be strong and able to endure hardship and eventually to triumph. If we are loath to heed the curses, we are thrilled to hear the blessings for they truly encompass our most precious dreams and hopes.

> I will grant peace in the land, and you shall lie down untroubled by anyone; I will give the land respite from vicious beasts, and no sword shall cross your land. You shall give chase to your enemies, and they shall fall before you by the sword. (Leviticus 26:6–7)

Does not such a prospect encompass our dearest hopes? The loss of the land is the worst punishment that can be envisioned, but the portion ends with comfort because it assures us that after exile, when Israel repents, "I will remember My covenant…and I will remember the land" (Leviticus 26:42).

We are living at a time when this comfort has become a reality, but we are also living at a time when the challenges of the covenant face us daily. A sovereign people in its own land has the greatest responsibility of all — the responsibility to mold and sustain a society that is just and caring. The Torah may not be the law of the land, but its ethical teachings can and must guide our actions both as a nation and as individuals. In this way we prove ourselves worthy of being tenants — "strangers resident"- in the land that belongs to God.

Rather than dwelling on the punishment, then, let us conclude by looking at the blessing with which the section begins — a blessing that will come upon us if we are true to God's ways. It is not long, but it is powerful. It begins by describing the blessings of nature — rain that will bring with it great yields of fruit and grain (Leviticus 26:4-5). It continues with an even greater blessing — peace resulting from victory over our enemies (Leviticus 26:6-8) — and a promise of fertility (Leviticus 26:9) and finally with the assurance of the Presence of God in our midst and a renewal of the covenantal relationship, "I will be your God and you shall be My people" (Leviticus 26:12).

And so we conclude our reading of Leviticus with the hope that we will be worthy of having these blessings come upon us speedily and in our days.

NUMBERS

B'midbar

B'midbar

במדבר

Numbers 1:1–4:20 | במדבר א:א-ד:כ

1. Counting the Ranks

The fourth book of the Torah has two names — *B'midbar* (In the Wilderness), which is the fifth word of the book and an apt description of the contents of the book, and *Ḥumash Hapekudim* (The Book of the Countings), thus the English name "Numbers." The first portion in the book describes the "counting" — the census that was taken in order to determine the number of Israelite men aged twenty and above. These were the men who could be counted upon to be part of the fighting force needed for the conquest of Canaan as well as to fight against any enemies who might be encountered in the wilderness on the way to Canaan. In order to be successful, the Israelites could not simply be a wandering column of nomads but rather an organized, disciplined, armed camp ready to meet any eventuality.

The historical situation in which we find ourselves at the beginning of the book is the very moment when all other preparations have been completed at Sinai in order to proceed toward the goal — the settlement in the land of Canaan. The covenant had been made between God and Israel, further laws had been expounded, the Tabernacle had been erected with all its vessels to serve as a portable Sinai, the "dwelling place of God," in which the Ark would rest. The spiritual, moral and legal basis of a society had been formed. The needed physical structure had been erected.

The Israelites had been encamped at Sinai since "the third new moon after the Israelites had gone forth from the land of Egypt" (Exodus 19:1). The Tabernacle had been set up in "the first month of the second year, on the first of the month" (Exodus 40:17). It was now, on the "first day of the second month, in the second year following the Exodus" (Numbers 1:1) — one month later — that the time had come to make the very last preparations that would permit them to move on. (The entire book of Leviticus takes place in that one month!) As Moses later recounted it, "The Lord our God spoke to us at Horeb, saying: 'You have stayed long enough at this mountain. Start out and make your way to…the land of the Canaanites'" (Deuteronomy 1:6–7). So on the "second year, on the twentieth day of the second month" (Numbers 10:11) they set out on the journey that they thought would be brief, but that actually lasted forty years!

What were these last-needed preparations? Only after all else was in place was it possible to set up the military order that was needed. The census and the exact arrangement of the camp were now prepared, giving each tribe its proper place to be stationed in relation to the Tabernacle, which stood at the center of the camp. It was guarded by the tribe of Levi, which was entrusted with the special task of caring for the Tabernacle, taking it down, carrying it, setting it up and guarding it against any intrusion (Numbers 3:8).

The Torah gives the Levites the task of serving as armed guards, something that, as Jacob Milgrom points out, was not done by Levites in either the First or Second Temples, thus attesting to the antiquity of this book: "The Levite guard of the Tabernacle were armed, ready to strike down any encroacher, a fact that explains the action of Phinehas at Baal-Peor who slew the encroaching couple in his capacity as chief of the Levitical guards. Armed Levitical guards are not, however, attested for the two Jerusalem Temples" (*The JPS Torah Commentary: Numbers* [Philadelphia: Jewish Publication Society of America, 1990], p. xxxiii).

In his commentary, Milgrom points this out as one of many other indications of institutions of great antiquity, reflecting ancient practices found in Numbers that are not to be found in later Israel. Without actually defending the historicity of every specific detail found in the Torah, his commentary indicates that there is sufficient reason to believe in the historical basis of the Biblical account.

In contrast, when a certain professor of Bible at one of our Israeli universities was asked if he believed that the Exodus from Egypt had ever taken place, he answered categorically in the negative. Among the reasons that he offered for this judgment was the fact that the census figure we have in our portion — 603,550 men aged twenty and above (Numbers 2:32), not counting the Levites — would imply that there had been millions of Israelites. Such a number could not possibly have been sustained in the wilderness.

It is one thing to contend that the numbers themselves are not to be taken literally. Even classical commentators have been known to speak of exaggeration in the Bible. It is quite another, however, to state on those grounds that the entire story of the Exodus is a later myth with no basis in fact. That would mean that virtually nothing in the Torah from the time of Jacob and onward ever happened. Not only would there have been no Exodus — there would also have been no Sinai, no Ten Commandments, no Tabernacle of any sort.

One would have to ask, in that case, why anyone would make up this story and all the elaborations that accompany it. Why would a people that had never been in Egypt want to say that it had been? Why would a people never enslaved want to describe itself as enslaved? Why all the stories of their unfaithfulness in the wilderness? Why the story of the death of that rebellious generation on the journey? Why give details of institutions that do not match what later existed but that are similar, as Milgrom points out, to early institutions of other civilizations? One can understand elaborations, various versions of the ancient story, even exaggerations — but an entire fabrication with no historical basis? Fortunately the majority of Biblical scholars today do not agree with these radical assessments, even while pursuing historical truth with all the instruments of critical study available to them.

Reading this portion we have every reason to feel that we are in the midst of the saga of our people's history, on the verge of their journey into the wilderness that the book of Numbers will describe in detail, the good and the bad together. Unlike some myths of the origins of nations, we have never tried to gloss over our faults nor depicted our ancestors as glorious heroes without shortcomings. The kernel of historical truth is sufficient for us.

2. The Burden of Responsibility

It is striking that the steps taken to prepare for possible warfare, practical steps, are described here in such specific detail. One might have expected that the protection offered by God would have been sufficient. Instead we see that although they have God's promise of protection and assurance that He will bring them to the land, the Israelites are not to expect miracles along the way.

They are commanded to take responsibility for their own safety. What happened in Egypt was not going to be repeated. There the Israelites did nothing. They did not fight their way out; they were released because of the plagues that had come upon the Egyptians. This is emphasized in the Torah: "That very day *the Lord* freed the Israelites from the land of Egypt, troop by troop" (Exodus 12:51). Even at the sea, they did not have to fight. "*The Lord* will battle for you; you hold your peace" (Exodus 14:14), Moses said to them before they entered the sea. And afterwards we are informed, "Thus *the Lord* delivered Israel that day from the Egyptians" (Exodus 14:30). But now these miraculous events that allowed them to be passive are over. Now they have to take responsibility for themselves and for their own future and their own safety.

This portion is critical, then, for it indicates that now the Israelites are taking their destiny into their own hands. Their success or failure will depend upon their ability to organize themselves properly and to defend themselves. The Hebrew proverb puts it well: *ein somkhin al haness* (one does not depend upon miracles). Or in the words of the English saying, "God helps those who help themselves."

The preparations begin with the taking of a census, as discussed above. The Levites, who are singled out as replacements for the firstborn who had previously been designated as dedicated to God's service (Numbers 3:12), are also counted and assigned their specific duties of caring for the Sanctuary when it is being transported and guarding it from encroachment.

As ancient as these words are, they have a modern ring to them, for they speak to the situation of the State of Israel since its creation and until today. As miraculous as the rebirth of a Jewish nation was, it did not come about because of the suspension of natural law, but because Jews took responsibility for their own destiny and for the defense of their own lives. The miracles that brought Israel into existence and that have permitted it to continue to exist against overwhelming odds are the "miracles that are daily with us," in the words of our prayers. They are those same miracles that permitted the Maccabees to triumph: proper planning, courage and determination. In this we see the hand of the Almighty, but it is in His guidance, not in supernatural interference.

I believe it was Agnon who was reputed to have said that in the Six-Day War Israel could have won in one of two ways: the natural way, which would have been the direct intervention of God, or the miraculous way — that the Israeli Army would do it by itself.

The Torah portion gives all the Israelites (at least the males) equal responsibility. Each has a task, each has a place. Each one is responsible for the physical safety of the Israelites' camp and community. In modern times this is true as well. No one physically and mentally capable of participating in Israel's defense has the right to shun that task. Hundreds of years later the Sages emphasized and expanded this to include women when they stated that although the Torah temporarily exempted certain people from military service (Deuteronomy 20:5–8), this was only in wars that were for expansion — wars of choice — not for wars of defense. At such a time all must participate, "even the groom from his chamber and the bride from her *ḥuppah*" (*Sotah* 8:7). Thus each Israeli, man and woman alike, is religiously obligated to defend our land and our people.

In this portion, the tribes are encamped around the central Sanctuary, the symbol of the religious values of Judaism, ready to defend the nation and the Sanctuary. So too must we place the values of our tradition at the center of our nation, even if we differ in the ways in which we interpret that tradition. We must dedicate ourselves to the continuation of the tradition and to the physical as well as the spiritual defense of the people Israel.

Naso

נשא

Numbers 4:21–7:89 | במדבר ד:כא-ז:פט

1. Promoting Domestic Peace

The law concerning the suspected woman — *sotah* — (Numbers 5:11–31) is an anomaly in the Torah. It is the only trial by ordeal to be found in our tradition. Although such trials were common in the ancient world and remained so at least through the Middle Ages, they have no place in Jewish law where "it is not in heaven," but rather guilt must be proven in a human court through witnesses.

This law is the exception. The priest presides over a ceremony in which the suspected woman drinks bitter water, water in which the ink with which curses were written has been dissolved. If she has defiled herself, she will show certain specific physical signs and be deemed guilty. But since this is a trial "by God" and not by a human court, even then she is not put to death.

At the end of the first century CE this law was declared null and void. The Mishnah teaches:

> When adulterers increased, the "bitter waters" ceased. Rabban Yohanan ben Zakkai stopped them. (*Sotah* 9:9)

When adultery was common, or when men were guilty as well, there was no point to the ceremony, which had two main reasons: to persuade the woman to admit her guilt if she were guilty and to convince the husband of her innocence if she were innocent.

The motivation of the law is clear. If a husband is jealous and suspects his wife of unfaithfulness, he will either divorce her or, even worse, he will take matters into his own hands and harm her physically. Othello is a classic case in point, but there are all too many instances today in which this happens in real life. This law wishes to alleviate suspicion and thus permit husband and wife to resume a normal life. It was to be used only where there was doubt and no way of proving either guilt or innocence. Rabbinic law was very clear in trying to limit its use and make certain that it was invoked only where there was good reason for suspicion.

One comment by Rabbi Meir, the second-century Tanna, is very telling. He noted that the name of God is so sacred that we do not erase it or destroy it. Any document with God's name is hidden away in a genizah or buried, yet here the document that contains God's name is immersed in water and the name is destroyed! Said Rabbi Meir:

> God permitted His name to be obliterated by water in order to bring peace between man and wife. (*Numbers Rabbah* 9:21)

Rabbi Meir made this comment after the following incident: There was a woman who regularly attended Rabbi Meir's sermons against her husband's will. The husband quarreled with her and stated that he would not forgive her unless she spat in Rabbi Meir's eye. When he heard of this, Rabbi Meir told her that he had an eye infection that could only be cured if she spit in his eye seven times. When his disciples were upset at this, he explained to them that if God could permit His name to be eradicated to bring peace between husband and wife, surely Rabbi Meir could endure this indignity for that purpose!

The concept of peace — of harmony among people, between two neighbors and between husband and wife — is of the highest significance. The magnificent blessing of the priests — which is also found in this portion — concludes with the word "peace": "The Lord lift His countenance to you and grant you peace!" (Numbers 6:26). Indeed the Sages advised that every prayer should end with a request for peace (*Sifre Numbers* 42).

The participation of the priest in the *sotah* ritual may be seen as part of his function as a peacemaker. Hillel went so far as to advise that the priesthood in general should devote itself to bringing peace. He taught:

> Be of the disciples of Aaron — loving peace and pursuing peace, loving human beings and bringing them to the Torah. (*Pirkei Avot* 1:12)

The rabbis interpreted this to mean that Aaron would look for every opportunity to bring people together. He even went so far as to bend the truth in order to do so. For example, when two men had quarreled, he would tell one of them that the other was sorry and terribly upset — so that he would forgive him. Then he would tell the same thing to the other, thus bringing them together. He did the same with a husband and wife who had quarreled (*Avot d'Rabbi Natan A* 12). Undoubtedly Rabbi Meir had this in mind when he suffered the humiliation described above to bring about domestic peace.

Hillel lived at a time when the priesthood was notoriously corrupt, divorced from the common people and generally unconcerned with the welfare of society. Therefore he taught that it was not important who your physical ancestor was. What mattered was following Aaron's example. A descendant of Aaron who was not a man of peace was not following Aaron's ways. Priests and all others, he said, should learn from Aaron and should love one another, love peace and, in that way, bring people to love and observe the Torah.

This ideal of the religious leader as a person of peace, who cares for all human beings and their welfare, who wants to create harmony and not cause quarrels, who persuades people of the beauty of Torah but does not use force and coercion to enforce it, was a revolutionary ideal that had great influence in Judaism. It is this kind of religious leadership that is needed today as well when there are such deep divisions within Judaism and many are looking for meaning and values but are not willing to have observance forced upon them.

Toward the conclusion of the morning service we read an interesting passage from the Talmud that teaches:

> The disciples of the Sages — *talmidei ḥakhamim* — increase peace in
> the world. (*Berakhot* 64a)

Perhaps this passage should be read backwards as well: Those who increase peace in the world can be called the disciples of the Sages — and those alone. Those who increase contention, no matter what their learning, are not true disciples of the Sages.

When all of us — religious leaders included — follow the ways of Aaron, Hillel and Rabbi Meir, we will be on the way toward creating the kind of society that the Torah envisions, a society in which we will be blessed with peace.

2. The Sanctuary of Peace

The newly consecrated Sanctuary housing the Ark of the Covenant continues to play a central role in our text and is the framework of this entire Torah portion. The census that was begun in the previous portion continues here; however, it is concerned not with the general population, but with those specific clans within the tribe of Levi that were responsible for carrying and caring for the Tent. The portion concludes with a description of the gifts the various tribes gave "on the day that Moses finished setting up the Tabernacle" (Numbers 7:1), including wagons that would be used to carry the dismantled parts of the Sanctuary.

In between these two sections there are various laws that concern the priests who function within that Tabernacle. The first of these discusses the exclusion of the unclean from the camp (Numbers 5:1-4). Their purification and return to the camp depended upon rituals conducted by the priests. Following that, we learn about the way in which payment for defrauding a person goes to the priest if that person is no longer alive or if there is no kinsman who can receive it (Numbers 5:5-8). Of special interest here is the fact that the law of repayment is different for one who not only admits the crime but also regrets it and confesses it. As Milgrom points out, this is a precursor to the concept of *teshuvah* — the revolutionary idea that repentance can affect and even cancel out punishment (*The JPS Torah Commentary: Numbers*, pp. 397-8).

Two major laws in which the priest plays a central role, both of great importance in ancient times, are then presented. The first is the law of the *sotah* — the woman suspected of adultery (Numbers 5:11-31), discussed above. The second is the law of the Nazirite — the man or woman who makes a special vow for a limited period of time to take upon him or herself specific prohibitions and thus consecrate him or herself to God (Numbers 6:1-21).

The institution of the Nazirite was a method for permitting ordinary Israelites to devote themselves to God, even if they were not priests or Levites. It should be noted, however, that unlike the practice in some other religions, the Nazirite was not separated from the community and did not become celibate. Here too it was the priest who played an important role in terminating the Nazirite's vows. It is interesting that the Torah specifies that this vow could be taken be "anyone, man or woman" (Numbers 6:2). Women did not function within the Tabernacle as priests or Levites, probably because of the desire to remove all sexual rites from Israelite worship in contrast to the practices of the Canaanites and others, but there were women prophets and women could also be Nazirites. Thus the desire of women to attain greater levels of holiness and closeness to God was recognized and given an outlet. They were not to be excluded from religious experience.

The last of this list of commandments is the priestly blessing (Numbers 6:22–27). The order is probably not accidental since this forms the climax of the functions of the priests. In all of the others the priest has a function whenever a specific case arises, but he is not the central person concerned. This command, however, is directed to the priests themselves: "Speak to Aaron and his sons saying, 'Thus shall you bless the people of Israel; say to them'" (Numbers 6:23). As the Sages later taught, blessing the people was the duty of the priests — a positive commandment given to them. It was not something done only once is a while; rather, it was done in the Tabernacle and later in the Temple whenever people came to worship and it is done today in synagogues daily in Israel. (Customs differ elsewhere as to when the priests recite this blessing.)

The blessing itself is constructed of three verses, each one longer than the previous one, so that they are like steps — three words, five words and then seven words, the sacred number. They speak of God "blessing" and "protecting," "shining His face," "being gracious," "favoring" and "granting peace." What more could one want? And the Torah also makes it very clear that the blessings themselves come not from the priest but from God alone — "and I will bless them" (Numbers 6:27). The priest is the conduit to express the blessing, not the source of it. For all of their importance, priests, as we saw earlier, were severely limited in their functions and were never thought to be endowed with magical or supernatural powers.

Finally, at the end of the reading, the gifts are given, an expression of the portion that each tribe had in the Sanctuary. It is only then that the Sanctuary is ready to begin its central role as the place where God will speak to Moses. He enters the tent and hears "the Voice addressing him from above the cover that was on top of the Ark of the Pact between the two cherubim" (Numbers 7:89). How beautiful it is that the climax of the building of the Tabernacle is not simply that God's Presence is there, but that God communicates from there to Moses. God had first spoken to him at Sinai. There is no more need for Sinai. The Tabernacle takes its place as the site connecting God with human beings.

B'ha'alotekha   בהעלתך

Numbers 8:1-12:16 | במדבר ח:א-יב:טז

1. The Human Side of Moses

The Torah is a combination of active and passive sections. Active sections are those narrative portions in which there is movement — something is happening. Passive sections are commandments or descriptions of what is to be done either immediately or in general — laws and regulations.

After a string of passive portions, we finally come to several active sections. One of great significance is the announcement that the Israelites are finally moving away from Sinai and beginning their journey to their new-old home, Canaan: "In the second year, on the twentieth day of the second month, the cloud lifted from the Tabernacle of the Pact and the Israelites set out on their journeys" (Numbers 10:11-12). Perhaps we should mark that day each year on our calendar — the twentieth of Iyar, two weeks before Shavuot — as the anniversary of that epic event.

Unfortunately, this positive forward motion was soon to be accompanied by a negative event, the forerunner of many negative events that were to become the trademark of the journey: "The people took to complaining bitterly before the Lord" (Numbers 11:1). These first events of the journey from Sinai, which should have been so triumphant, are not very encouraging. Following a pattern that we have already witnessed in the book of Exodus, the people are rebellious, complaining, nostalgic for the food they had in Egypt! In little over a year the memory of Egypt has already become euphoric — "The fish that we used to eat free" (Numbers 11:5) — as if they had not been slaves who worked without recompense. Exodus 16 described how immediately after the great triumph at the sea the Israelites complained about the lack of meat. They were then given quail to eat as well as the manna that would accompany them throughout the journey. Now they are complaining again. Manna is not good enough. Like spoiled children, they want meat — "real food"! Not only is God angry, but Moses is fed up as well and wants to know why God "laid the burden of all this people upon me" (Numbers 11:11).

The way in which Moses responds to this crisis and the incident which follows it in chapter 12, in which Miriam and Aaron criticize Moses because of his marriage to a Cushite woman, shed light on the character of Moses. He appears to be all too human when he responds to the whining complaints of the Israelites by wishing that he were either relieved of the responsibility of caring for them or dead (Numbers 11:10-15)! Moses has suffered at the hands of the Israelites before. Soon after the Exodus, for example, they complained about water and Moses said to God "Soon they will stone me!"(Exodus 17:4). Nevertheless he managed to continue his work. Now — a year later — he would rather resign. One can hardly blame him.

God's reply, as Martin Buber so astutely pointed out, is a play on the Hebrew word *ruah*, which means both wind and spirit: "and I will draw upon the spirit [*ruah*] that is on you and put it upon them" (Numbers 11:17), "A wind [*ruah*] from the Lord started up, swept quail from the sea" (Numbers 11:31). The *wind* will bring them quails — the meat they are lusting for while the *spirit* of God will rest upon seventy elders who will be able to take some of the burden of leadership from Moses. (This may well be another version of the story of the appointment of judges that is told in Exodus 18:17-26.) See also Genesis 1:2 where it is difficult to know which meaning is intended. Some translations say "the spirit of God" and some say "a wind from God."

In what way do God's actions respond to Moses' complaint? In the first place Moses says, "Where will I get meat for them?" (Numbers 11:13) and God's response is to send a *wind* that will bring the flesh (Numbers 11:31). Then Moses complains, "I cannot deal with this people by myself" (Numbers 11:14) — so God responds that He will place His *spirit* on these seventy elders who will then share the burden with Moses (Numbers 11:17).

What is most striking is that when two additional people are affected by God's spirit and begin to prophesy, which Joshua sees as a threat to Moses, Moses' reply is, "Would that all God's people were prophets and that God would place His spirit upon them!" (Numbers 11:29). Indeed, if they were all under the influence of the spirit of God there would be no need to worry for there would be no more complaints.

The incident that follows is perhaps even more painful for Moses for it involves his own brother and sister. They speak against him "because of the Cushite woman he had married" (Numbers 12:1). It is not clear if he has taken a second wife or if Zipporah is the "Cushite woman" they are referring to. The first possibility seems more likely, but in any case their real complaint is the fact that Moses is the leader while they occupy only secondary positions.

When Aaron and Miriam say, "Has God spoken only to him?" (Numbers 12:2) it becomes obvious that the complaint about the wife is nothing more than an excuse to challenge Moses' leadership. We can understand Miriam's feeling since she seems to play no role at all in the leadership. Aaron, however, certainly has an important role as high priest, even though he is not equal to Moses. All of this presages other events that are to come, in which the leadership of Moses will be challenged. It is almost as if the Torah is giving us a preview of coming events. This is what you have to expect — complaints, challenges to leadership. We can see that it is going to be a bumpy ride indeed.

When Miriam is severely punished with leprosy for the sin of speaking evil, Moses does not rejoice in this vindication of his position. Rather he pleads with God to heal her in the shortest Biblical prayer on record: "Please God heal her please!" (Numbers 12:13). No wonder the Torah says of Moses, "The man Moses was the most humble of men" (Numbers 12:3).

Once again we are presented with a multifaceted picture of this greatest of all leaders. He is human. He can feel inadequate. He can want to give up his task — indeed he never wanted it in the first place! He can be angry — but he can also be humble and forgiving, looking to the good of his sister and to the welfare of his people. Even the greatest prophet is human, with the same weaknesses that beset us all. The religious leaders of our people never have been and are not today divine, perfect or infallible. The worship of human beings is foreign to Judaism. God alone is above human failings.

2. Not in Heaven

In a totally different vein, there is an episode in this portion that is very telling in regard to the way in which Jewish law (*halakhah*) was to develop. When the Pesah holiday is to be celebrated for the first time a year after the Exodus, there are some people who are unclean and therefore prohibited from offering the Pesah sacrifice (Numbers 9:6–7). What are they to do? Nothing in the instructions they were given dealt with this dilemma. They ask Moses, but he too does not know the answer. Therefore he decides to turn directly to the source (Numbers 9:8) and is then given instruction by God. They are to offer their Pesah on the fourteenth of the second month, thus establishing "Pesah Sheni" (Second Passover).

We learn from this that questions that were not covered in the instructions the people had received were referred to the prophet, Moses, who turned directly to God. God's answer was then incorporated into the Torah and into the corpus of what later was referred to as *halakhah*. It would seem that this continued as long as there were prophets who received and conveyed messages from God, prophets who could say, "Thus says the Lord." The source of *halakhah* in those early days was direct revelation from God.

There came a time, however, when this was no longer the case, when it was decided that Jewish law could only be based on the Torah (not even on the writings of the Prophets) and that it could only be determined by authorized teachers using specific methods of Torah interpretation. And it was the Sages, rabbis, who interpreted those rules and regulations according to very specific methods. Human interpretation replaced divine revelation. As the Torah states, "It is not in heaven" (Deuteronomy 30:12).

The use of this phrase is illustrated by the justifiably famous story of the "oven of 'Aknai'" (*Baba Metzia* 59b). A case came before the Sages concerning the ritual purity of an oven. Rabbi Eliezer pronounced it clean while the other Sages, a clear majority, declared it unclean. When the other Sages refused to accept Rabbi Eliezer's arguments, he proceeded to invoke miracles to prove his point. "Let the carob tree prove it," he said, and the carob tree was torn out of its place. "Let the stream of water prove that the *halakhah* agrees with me!" he exclaimed, and the stream flowed backwards. Eventually he called upon God to uphold his ruling and a heavenly voice called out, "Why do you argue with Rabbi Eliezer? The *halakhah* always agrees with him!" It was at this point that Rabbi Joshua exclaimed, "It is not in heaven!" *Halakhah* is decided by the majority vote of the Sages, not by miracles and voices from heaven. The postscript to this story states that later Elijah appeared and told Rabbi

Nathan that at that time God laughed with joy and said, "My sons have defeated Me!"

This remarkable story encapsulates the final victory of the process of human logic over reliance upon divine intervention in the determination of the meaning and application of the Torah's commandments. Reliance upon miracles or even upon prophets could result in dangerous teachings. How does one prove that a miracle is not a fraud? How does one make certain that a "prophet" speaks God's will? Judaism established a very wise principle: the Torah represents divine revelation. Once it has been given to us, "it is not in heaven," and its understanding and application are determined exclusively by the Sages, the scholars of Torah.

Even at the time of Moses it was necessary to find answers to questions concerning the fulfillment of the commandments. Even then they had to be applied to new conditions. How this was done changed over the centuries from direct turning to God to investigation and interpretation of the sacred text. Without the ability to expand and be interpreted, halakhah would be frozen and would lose its relevance to new times and new situations. Fortunately it does have that ability, for it is not in heaven, but available here on earth. How happy we should be that we do not depend upon soothsayers and magicians, nor upon any one individual who can determine what Jewish law is with absolute authority, but upon those learned individuals who are loyal to the tradition yet also committed to making it meaningful and usable in the modern world.

Sh'laḥ

שלח

Numbers 13:1–15:41 | במדבר יג:א-טו:מא

1. The Fear of Freedom

Surely no people has ever recorded as negative a picture of its own history as has Israel. What begins as a seemingly intelligent act — sending scouts to see the lay of the land before the imminent invasion — ends in tragedy. The results are the delay of the invasion for forty years and the death of the entire generation that left Egypt after years of meaningless wandering in the wilderness. With two exceptions, all adults who participated in the Exodus will perish without setting foot into the Promised Land.

Of course it could have been even worse. After the spies return, God threatens to destroy the entire people immediately and replace them with the family of Moses (Numbers 14:11–12). This is the second time that God has uttered such a dire decree. The first was after the sin of the golden calf (Exodus 32:10). In both instances Moses argues with God — taking a leaf from Abraham's book — and succeeds in annulling the severe decree. The same Moses who in the previous portion begged God to kill him if He would not relieve him of the burden of leading this rebellious people now argues for their continued existence (Numbers 14:13–19)!

Who is at fault? Some would say that Moses erred in sending the scouts in the first place. What need was there for their report when God Himself had assured them that they would enter the land and conquer it? Although our portion begins by saying that "The Lord spoke to Moses. Saying, 'Send men to scout the land of Canaan'" (Numbers 13:1–2), Deuteronomy 1:22 records that the request came from the people who said to Moses, "Let us send men ahead to reconnoiter the land," and Moses approved of the plan

(Deuteronomy 1:23). Some commentators see a hint of this here in the wording *shlaḥ lekha* (send *for yourself*), i.e., since you have asked, send them on *your* responsibility (*Numbers Rabbah* 16:4).

Certainly the ten spies were at fault. Moses sent them with six questions, all concerning the nature of the land and the people in it (see Numbers 13:18-20). When they return, they answer these questions, but they do so in a way that makes it clear that they are also recommending that the invasion not take place. After describing how good the land and its fruit are, they say, "*However* the people who inhabit the country are powerful, and the cities are fortified" (Numbers 13:28). That word "however" and the tone of the description that follows very clearly indicate their opinion. It's a nice place — but...! And then, after Caleb has said that they should go up, the others say, "We cannot attack that people, for it is stronger than we" (Numbers 13:31). Who asked them? They were asked six questions and answered seven.

We could compare this to a case in which the government asks the intelligence branch to supply certain information, and the branch not only gives the information but also tells the government what action it should take or not take — and does it publicly over the television and radio, causing a panic.

Even worse, the information they give is not accurate. It is, at best, a half-truth. The Torah makes this clear by saying, "Thus they spread a false report among the Israelites about the land they had scouted, saying, 'The country that we traversed and scouted is one that devours it settlers'" (Numbers 13:32). On what basis did they determine that they would be subject to perpetual warfare?

What motivated the scouts to do this? Perhaps they shared the same fears and feelings as those expressed by the community when they hear this calumny. The people are incensed against Moses. They wish they had remained in Egypt or died in the wilderness (an unknowing prophecy of what was to come!) and they determine to go back to Egypt (Numbers 14:2-4). They prefer the safety of slavery to the challenge of freedom.

Of course this is nothing new. In the previous portion we had their complaint about food in which they remembered "the fish that we used to eat free in Egypt" (Numbers 11:5), as if their enslavement had been one big feast! All of that is forgotten. Remember that immediately after the Exodus, before the splitting of the sea, they had said, "Let us be, and we will serve the Egyptians, for it is better for us to serve the Egyptians than to die in the wilderness"

(Exodus 14:12). After their salvation at the sea they complained again, "If only we had died by the hand of the Lord in the land of Egypt, when we sat by the fleshpots, when we ate our fill of bread" (Exodus 16:3). So there is a history of this longing for Egypt, a record of their false nostalgia and their fear of facing the hardships of the journey. Their actions now are only the climax of a long series of such incidents.

Was God not aware of this all along? There is more than a hint that He was in the fact that at the time of the Exodus itself we are informed that God "did not lead them by way of the land of the Philistines, although it was nearer, for God said, 'The people may have a change of heart when they see war, and return to Egypt'" (Exodus 13:17). Why take them out, or why expect that they will be able to invade the land? Of course we are on dangerous and difficult ground when we begin to speculate upon what God knows and does not know, for we face the contradiction between human free will and God's absolute knowledge. This was expressed well in *Pirkei Avot* in Rabbi Akiba's saying, "Everything is foreseen, yet freedom of choice is given" (3:19). This is a paradox that we have no way of understanding. The important part of it, however, is the absolute conviction that choice *is* given. The Israelites — regardless of their fears and their slave mentality — *could* have changed. They *could* have learned from all that happened to them that they had the ability — with the help of God — to make their way to Canaan and to inherit that land. They chose otherwise and the result was a tragedy for them.

But God's purpose was not sidetracked, for if they would not enter the land, their children would — a generation born or at least brought up in the wilderness, far from the fleshpots of Egypt, ready to undertake the task that their parents had feared, ready to live as free human beings.

2. The Greatness of Moses

We owe a great debt of thanks to Moses. Had he simply bowed his head in obedience when God threatened to destroy Israel because of the sin of the spies and substitute the descendants of Moses for them, most of us would not be here today. There would be a nation of "Mosaists" or perhaps "Mosites" rather than the descendants of Israel. How Moses must have been tempted! It was not long before that that he himself had complained about the Israelites and the burden they placed on him. He had even asked to be relieved of his position: "I cannot carry all this people by myself, for it is too much for me. If You would deal this with me, kill me rather, I beg You, and let me see no more of my wretchedness!" (Numbers 11:15). Who would want to lead such a stiff-necked group, always complaining about their conditions, showing so little gratitude for the gift of freedom that Moses had helped them attain?

Now, in a dramatic and ironic turnabout, it is not Moses who may perish, but that "stiff-necked group." For all of his complaints, however, Moses will not stand by and let that happen. The greatness of Moses is revealed in the fact that when these two offers are made, he immediately refuses them and uses every argument at his command to — as it were — change God's mind. Like Abraham before him who argued with God regarding the destruction of the cities of Sodom and Gomorrah, Moses argues against destroying Israel. But his arguments — which are the same in both instances — are not based on God's justice, as were Abraham's, but on God's fidelity to His promise to the Patriarchs, on the negative effect this would have on God's own reputation among the nations and on God's merciful nature.

Perhaps the Israelites were deserving of this punishment, but if God was truly merciful, as He had indicated in the Ten Commandments (Exodus 20:6), then He should forgive even this transgression. After the golden calf, God reiterated His merciful nature and even expanded upon it in the famous statement that is known in tradition as the "thirteen attributes of God" — "The Lord! The Lord! — a God compassionate and gracious, slow to anger, abounding in kindness and faithfulness, extending kindness to the thousandth generation, forgiving iniquity and transgression and sin" (Exodus 34:6–7). It is on that basis that Moses turns again now to God: "Therefore, I pray, let my Lord's forbearance be great, as You have declared, saying, 'The Lord! Slow to anger and abounding in kindness; forgiving iniquity and transgression....'" (Numbers 14:18). God's immediate response is, "I pardon, as you have asked" (Numbers 14:20), words we repeat on Yom Kippur.

In this case, however, the forgiveness is limited to letting them live. They will not be permitted to enter the land of Canaan. They will perish in the wilderness. What was to have been a brief sojourn from Egypt to Canaan, a matter of mere days, turns now into forty years of wandering, forty years that have no purpose but to permit that generation to die so that a new generation that has not rebelled will be able to enter the land (Numbers 14:21–35). Against this decree Moses does not lift his voice.

Two questions trouble me about this story. One is: how serious is God's offer to make of Moses a great nation? The other is: why does Moses not try to intercede against the decree of forty years of wandering and death in the wilderness?

Regarding the first, the Sages remarked that concerning the golden calf God said, "Let Me be"(Exodus 32:10), as a hint to Moses that he should argue with Him. As they put it, was Moses indeed holding on to Him that He asked "Let Me be?" (*Exodus Rabbah* 42:9). Furthermore, to make of Moses a great nation would have taken generations — as indeed it did with Abraham. It hardly seems to have been a practical notion. What would happen? Everyone would die and only Moses and his immediate family would remain there alone in the wilderness? Is this then simply an opportunity for God to encourage Moses to defend his people? An opportunity to understand more deeply the forgiving, merciful nature of the Almighty?

Regarding the second question, is this a flaw in Moses' nature? Although he does not want to see them perish as a nation, is he somehow pleased or at least willing to accept their punishment? After all, they have never been appreciative of his work. They have complained about him and have murmured time and time again. Why should he not think that punishment is due to them? The Sages characterized them as people who, if they saw Moses rising early, would say, "He got up early because he is not happy at home." And if he got up late, they would say, "He sits at home in order to plot more decrees against us!" (*Sifre Deuteronomy* 12). But perhaps the real reason is simply that Moses had come to the realization that God was right.

Whereas God had eventually forgiven the sin of the golden calf — a terrible incidence of infidelity to God — the sin of the spies, the refusal to go to the land God had promised, resulted in a severe punishment. Perhaps the reason was that this sin revealed a character flaw in this generation that simply could not be remedied.

This generation was not ready for the task of coming into the land. They were too steeped in the mentality of slaves. One could not expect them to be the real generation of freedom. They would have to die in the wilderness. There was no point in disputing that. In his magnificent poem "The Dead of the Wilderness," Bialik sympathizes with them and has them proclaim themselves "the last generation of slavery. The first generation of redemption!" But perhaps they were not yet truly redeemed and "the first generation of redemption" was yet to arise. That was their true tragedy.

Korah קרח

Numbers 16:1–18:32 | במדבר טז:א-יח:לב

1. A Tale of Two Rebellions

This is certainly one of the most painful sections of the Torah. What a bleak narrative the book of Numbers turns out to be! The alternating laws and narratives tend to mitigate the severity of what is going on, but from the point of view of the actual events, we have no sooner experienced the incident of the spies, with its consequent decree that the generation of the Exodus must die in the wilderness, than we come to these multiple rebellions that also result in death and destruction.

As Jacob Milgrom points out in his commentary to the book, there is indeed a connection between these unhappy events:

> Israel's fortunes have reached a low ebb. Demoralized by the majority report of the scouts and condemned by their God to die in the wilderness, the people are psychologically receptive to demagogic appeals to overthrow their leadership and return to Egypt. (*The JPS Torah Commentary: Numbers*, p. 129)

All the bright hopes have turned to ashes. The people that marched triumphantly out of Egypt and through the sea proclaiming "I shall sing unto the Lord" (Exodus 15:1) has no hope and no future. True, the next generation will attain the goal, but that is not enough to satisfy the current generation, and so they become easy prey to false leaders and false claims.

The chief rebel is the one whose name becomes the name of the portion — Korah. His motivation is transparent. He wishes to replace Aaron as the high priest. As a Levite, Korah already has a special status, but this seems not to be enough for him. As Moses says to him, "Now that He has advanced you and all your fellow Levites with you, do you seek the priesthood too?" (Numbers 16:10). The *Targum* goes a step further and translates the word "*kehunah*" as "high priesthood." Like some corrupt modern-day politician, Korah attempts to appeal to the lowest level of the populace in order to attain his goal and has no scruples about bending the truth to his own purposes.

Korah gathers malcontents about him — Dathan, Abiram and On, all from the tribe of Reuven, the firstborn, who wonder why their tribe was not chosen to lead, and others in leadership positions who are not satisfied with what they have but want to rise higher and higher (Numbers 16:1-2).

Two accusations are made against the leadership of Moses and Aaron: one pertaining to religious matters, the other to secular ones. Korah accuses Moses and Aaron of "raising themselves above the congregation" and states that "all the community are holy!" (Numbers 16:3). Dathan and Abiram phrase the accusation in more secular terms, "Would you also lord it over us?" (Numbers 16:13), and remind everyone of the painful fact that Moses and Aaron promised to lead them to a land of milk and honey and are not doing so. They conveniently forget to mention that the only reason for their failure to reach Canaan was the rebellion of the people, who refused to go to the land when commanded to do so!

"All the community are holy" is clever demagoguery. The people were commanded to be holy time and time again (see especially Leviticus 19). They were told that God had brought them to Sinai to be "a holy nation" (Exodus 19:6). So now, if they are a holy people, why should they need anyone to assume a position that implies greater holiness? Should we not all be equal? (See the next section for a further discussion on this point.)

Moses answers both charges. To the charge of "holiness" he responds that this is an argument against God, not against him or Aaron, for it was God who had chosen Aaron (Numbers 16:11). He says that God will demonstrate who is chosen and who is not.

Regarding the charge against the quality of his leadership, he responds that he has been scrupulously honest: "I have not taken the ass of any one of them, nor have I wronged any one of them" (Numbers 16:15).

Although Moses is anxious to have God demonstrate that he and Aaron are the true leaders, he nevertheless is equally anxious to defend the innocent. Twice he intercedes with God. Once he and Aaron cry out, "Oh God, source of the breath of all flesh! When one man sins, will You be wrathful with the whole community?" (Numbers 16:22) — an echo of Abraham's defense of Sodom and Gomorrah. And then again he instructs Aaron what to do in order to prevent a plague from killing them all (Numbers 17:11). Even under these most trying circumstances Moses remains true to his nature as a caring leader, a true shepherd of his flock — even when they are rebellious.

The story of Israel in the wilderness is not a happy tale, nor one that redounds to the glory of our people. Accusations have been made that most of these narratives are "spin," meant to serve the purposes of the monarchy of the seventh century BCE. It seems to me that if that is so, these ancient spin doctors did a miserable job, at least on the story of the wilderness period. What self-respecting propagandist would want to depict his people as so rebellious and unreliable as the group we read about in Numbers? Unfortunately, whether all of the details are accurate or not, this story seems all too true and has been repeated too often in the history of humankind.

2. We Are Lost!

The narrative of this portion depicts a total demoralization of the people and a total breakdown of society. Israel stands on the brink of anarchy. It seems clear that the punishment they received as a result of their reaction to the report of the spies — their doom — has so affected them that they are disintegrating as an organized group. They fall easy prey to demagoguery and turn from being a "holy people" into a rabble of rebels.

We must not be fooled into thinking that their rebellion was justified as some attempt at primitive democracy. At Sinai, Israel had accepted upon itself the rulership of God. God is the King of Israel. Moses is merely the one to whom the divine king reveals His will. All of the institutions and laws needed for a good, just, orderly society have been established. Now all of that is undermined by individuals who are seeking their own power and elevation and who persuade the masses to follow them. They have very little to lose, since they are not going to reach the land in any case, so they permit themselves to be misled.

And clever demagoguery it is. The section begins with "And Korah... took" (Numbers 16:1) — which the rabbis interpreted as "Korah took words."

With words he manipulated his listeners. Rhetoric can be effective — especially in the mouths of tyrants and rebels. In *Julius Caesar*, Mark Antony is
able to foment a rebellion against Caesar's assassins using nothing but the
words in his speech over Caesar's corpse. The result is that he "lets loose the
dogs of war." So too Korah, who leads some two hundred fifty prominent
people against Moses and Aaron with the words, "You have gone too far! For
all the community are holy, all of them, and the Lord is in their midst. Why
do you raise yourselves above the Lord's congregation?" (Numbers 16:3).

Indeed the very last command that had been given to the entire people of
Israel at the conclusion of the section concerning *tzitzit* was "you shall be holy
to your God" (Numbers 15:40). The problem is not only that Korah states
that they *are* holy while the command is in the future — you *shall be*, you
must constantly strive to attain holiness — but that the word *kadosh* is being
used in two different ways and the people cannot discern that distinction.
Korah uses it in the sense of being singled out for the ritual service of God. In
that way the priests are holy. Remember that the high priest wore a frontlet
that said "*Kodesh* [holy] to the Lord" (Exodus 28:36). Whereas "you shall be
holy" simply means you shall follow God's commands and in that way be
distinguished from other peoples.

One is reminded of the way in which Communist ideologues spoke of the
rulership of the proletariat and promised a society in which all would be
equal. Yet the result was simply to put different people into positions of
wealth and power. One elite replaced another. Korah would be very happy to
replace Aaron. Moses sees through him and knows that, not content to be a
Levite, what he really wants is to be a kohen (Numbers 16:10). And as for
Moses' leadership, every step of the way he has proved himself to be a man
dedicated to the good of his people. How many times did he step in to argue
with God in defense of Israel?

The greatest demonstration of Moses' love of Israel comes in one of the
most perplexing incidents — the plague that God lets loose on the community when the entire community "railed against Moses and Aaron" because of
the two hundred and fifty who had perished in the previous rebellion
(Numbers 17:6). God indicates clearly that He intends to annihilate all of
them. If we are to understand this literally, it means that God was going to
destroy not only those doomed to perish in the wilderness but everyone. He
lets loose a natural disaster — a plague — that will destroy anyone who comes

near it. Therefore He tells Moses and Aaron to "remove yourselves from the community" so that they will not perish as well (Numbers 17:10).

Moses quickly commands Aaron to take the incense and stand in the midst of the congregation "to make expiation for the people" (Numbers 17:12). There are times when ritual actions achieve atonement. Perhaps we should understand them as prayers without words, actions that beg for divine mercy and are answered by the cessation of the plague. With no thought to his own safety, Aaron does so. Yes, thousands die, but the people is saved.

It is now a sad and depleted congregation that remains and will continue the journey. As they themselves say, "Lo, we perish! We are lost, all of us lost!" (Numbers 17:27). Triumph has turned to tragedy, but the new generation will survive and will reach the land. Because of Moses and Aaron, the people will fulfill its destiny.

Ḥukkat

חקת

Numbers 19:1–22:1 | במדבר יט:א–כב:א

1. Time Goes By

The chronology of events in the Torah is frequently unclear. Time is not always easily measured and frequently does not coincide with narrative length. The entire book of Leviticus, for example, occupies but one month, while Numbers spans some forty years. As a matter of fact, nearly forty years may very well go by in this one portion. The death of Miriam is reported in Numbers 20:1 as having taken place on the "first new moon" — but of what year? Aaron's death, on the other hand, is also recorded in this portion (Numbers 20:27–29) and later on is specified as having occurred "in the fortieth year after the Israelites had left the land of Egypt, on the first day of the fifth month" (Numbers 33:38).

Some scholars believe that all of the events in this portion took place in the fortieth year. Others think that Miriam's death and the subsequent story of the water and the rock took place near the beginning of the journey. The narrative of the story of the water that led to their punishment does seem to imply that it took place near the beginning of that period because of the nature of the people and the words they use to describe themselves. They speak about how their "brothers perished at the instance of the Lord" (Numbers 20:3), a clear reference to those who died in the rebellion of Korah (Numbers 17:14) described in the previous portion. Furthermore they speak of themselves as having actually left Egypt (Numbers 20:5), which means that these are the same rebellious Israelites we have encountered all along — the so-called generation of the wilderness that must die out before Israel can enter Canaan. This is not the new generation that has overcome the slave mentality.

In that case, nearly forty years stand between the death of Miriam and that of Aaron, with very little being said of what happened in between. That silence in itself says something about those years of wandering — years with no purpose except to wait for death to eliminate an entire generation. Perhaps silence is the best way to describe such an interval. But if that is so, it also means that both Moses and Aaron knew their fates as well during that entire period and had to live out all of those years with the knowledge that they would never enter the land!

There is only one more incident in which the Israelites are depicted as complainers, Numbers 21:4–5, and the chronology of that is also uncertain. As the Sages often remarked, "The Torah does not follow chronological order."

2. The Sin of Moses and Aaron

All of us have goals and aspirations in life. Sometimes we are able to fulfill them; sometimes we are not. The history of the world is filled with the stories of great leaders who did not fulfill their dreams. Lincoln was cut down before he could effect the reconciliation so badly needed and the integration of the newly freed slaves into society. Martin Luther King stood on the mountain but did not enter the integrated land he worked to achieve. Franklin Delano Roosevelt did not see the achievement of the defeat of the Axis that he had worked so diligently to attain. Yitzhak Rabin was assassinated before he could achieve the peace he longed for. And of course the three leaders of the children of Israel did not reach the Promised Land, as we learn in this portion.

In this one section we read of the death of two of them while the death sentence of the third is pronounced. How unfair it seems. Miriam is the first to depart this world: "The people stayed at Kadesh. Miriam died there and was buried there" (Numbers 20:1). As we have seen, this seems to have occurred in the third year after the Exodus, so that Miriam actually did not accompany them in the forty years of wandering in the wilderness. Had she lived, would she have been allowed to enter the land? She had been punished for speaking against Moses (Numbers 12:1–15), but there is no indication that her death was the result of this folly.

The record of Miriam's death seems laconic. The death of Moses is treated with much greater detail (Deuteronomy 34), as is that of Aaron (Numbers 20:27). Rashi says of Miriam, "She too died by a [divine] kiss. Why then does not the text say 'by the mouth of the Lord' as it does with Aaron [Numbers 33:38] and Moses? Because this would not show proper respect for God" (Rashi Numbers 20:1).

When Moses died, he was mourned for thirty days (Deuteronomy 34:8). When Aaron died "all the house of Israel bewailed Aaron thirty days" (Numbers 20:29). Did no one mourn for Miriam? We do not even know if she had descendants. There is no record of her marrying. She was, as the midrash points out, a brave woman who was instrumental in saving the life of Moses (*Mekhilta B'shalaḥ* 1). The Rabbis also taught (*Sifre Deuteronomy* 305) that because of Miriam's merit there was a miraculous well that accompanied Israel on the journey and that when she died it ceased to give water, which is why immediately after her death we read that "The community was without water" (Numbers 20:2). She was a prophetess who led Israel in song and thanksgiving, but seems to have led a lonely, childless life. So while we shed a tear for Aaron and for Moses who were doomed to die without entering the land of Canaan, we should also bewail Miriam.

Unlike Miriam, Moses and Aaron *were* punished for a transgression and therefore were not allowed to live beyond the fortieth year when Israel entered the land. The story of the rock is a tragic one. The generation that left Egypt was already condemned to die in the desert. Now the leadership — Moses and Aaron — are to suffer the same fate. It hardly seems fair that these two leaders should not be able to enter the land and thus witness the fulfillment of all their work. We know that the sin of the Israelites was grave. Their rejection of the very purpose of the Exodus, their inability to trust God, brought upon them this severe punishment. God terms it "harlotry" (Numbers 14:33) — i.e., unfaithfulness. He says of them that "they have no faith [*ya'aminu*] in Me" (Numbers 14:11). But what have Moses and Aaron done to deserve this fate?

The nature of their sin has long been a source of discussion among ancient commentators and modern scholars alike. The facts are clear. When the people complain because of thirst, these two leaders are told to "order the rock to yield its water" (Numbers 20:8). They then assemble the people and say to them, "Listen, you rebels. Shall we get water for you out of this rock?" and Moses strikes the rock twice (Numbers 20:10–11). They are then told of their punishment "because you did not trust [he'emantem] Me enough to affirm My sanctity in the sight of the Israelite people" (Numbers 20:12). It is important to note that in Hebrew the same root a-m-n is used both regarding the people and regarding Moses and Aaron, although the translations are different ("faith" and "trust").

Among the many suggestions concerning the nature of their sin are these:

1. Moses struck the rock when he should have spoken to it.

2. Moses struck the rock twice in anger.

3. Moses called Israel "rebels."

4. Moses said "shall *we* get water for you" rather than attributing it to God.

God's words make it clear that their sin had to do with sanctifying God publicly, what we would call *kiddush hashem* (the sanctification of God's name). It is also clear that it is a sin of omission, "you did *not* trust Me." The first three suggestions do not fit the text, but the fourth does. It is both in what Moses said and in what was not said that their transgression can be found. Saying "shall *we*" implies "*we* shall." There is not a word about God either before or after the rock yields water. They should have said, "The Lord will provide water for you from this rock." That would have been *kiddush hashem*. But Moses and Aaron were too annoyed and too self-centered at that moment to sanctify God's name. In neglecting to ascribe this to God and God alone, they showed a lack of trust and ascribed magical power to themselves. Although Moses performed all of the actions alone, Aaron was equally guilty for not insisting that they speak about God's power. He silently acquiesced in Moses' terrible error.

And terrible it was, for it contradicted everything they had been teaching since their first encounter with the Divine. All along, Moses and Aaron had performed miracles: the ten plagues, the previous incidents concerning water, the quails, the manna. But never had they ascribed any of these things to their own power. It was always done in the name of God. They could not do this alone or force God to do any of it. They were not, as were Pharaoh's people, magicians. They were God's messengers and nothing more. Now, suddenly, they depict themselves as the ones who can miraculously extract water from a rock.

God's words of condemnation are rather clear and purposely echo His description of the Israelites: "Because you did not trust Me enough [did not have faith in Me] to sanctify Me in the sight of the Israelite people" (Numbers 20:12).

All of their lives Moses and Aaron had taught the people to believe in God, to trust in God. And yet at this critical moment they waver. Instead of once more stating as they had before that God would provide for them (as they did for example in Exodus 16:8, "Since it is the Lord who will give you flesh to eat in the evening and bread in the morning to the full"), here they do not even mention God's name.

Moses had taught the repudiation of magical powers. There is no power except that of God. The prophet is not a magician who uses incantations to bring about supernatural events. Yet here Moses acts in a way which could easily be interpreted as contradicting all of that. It is as if he and Aaron had such powers.

Thus Moses' words are a repudiation of all that he has taught these many years. Did he mean them that way? Of course not. They were the outcome of thoughtlessness, anger or frustration. But even so one might say that God, depicted always as forgiving, should have been forgiving in this case as well. Indeed in the book of Deuteronomy (3:23-26) we see Moses pleading for such forgiveness but it is not forthcoming. This is because those with greater responsibility are held to greater accountability. As Moses himself says to Aaron when explaining the death of Aaron's sons who offered strange fire before the Lord, "Through those near Me I show Myself holy and gain glory before all the people" (Leviticus 10:3). Here too God says that they "did not sanctify Me [show My holiness]." That which is forgivable in an ordinary person is unforgivable in a leader — priest or prophet. Such a person is held to a higher standard.

If one wishes to lead, one must have only the highest standards and be extremely careful of what one says and what one does. This applies to religious leaders and to public figures as well. As Avtalyon taught, "Sages, be careful of what you say!" (*Pirkei Avot* 1:11).

That lesson is as applicable today as it was then. Anyone who purports to lead — be it secular or religious leadership — must be above suspicion and must be constantly held to the highest standards. Those who aspire to religious leadership certainly have no right to do so unless all their actions contribute to *kiddush hashem*, the sanctification of God in the sight of all the people.

The death of these great leaders of Israel is an occasion for sadness, especially when we realize that they were cut off before realizing their dreams and aspirations. Nevertheless, their accomplishments were astonishing and it is to be hoped that before they passed away they realized that they had indeed helped God to create a people dedicated to holiness, leading them out of slavery to freedom and directing them to their own land.

Balak

בלק

Numbers 22:2-25:9 | ט:במדבר כב:ב-כה

1. The Blind Seer

There could hardly be a greater contrast than between the two sections of this portion — the first, the story of Balaam, the seer who is asked to curse Israel and blesses them instead (Numbers 22:2-24:25), and the second, which relates the sin of the Israelites with the Moabite women (Numbers 25:1-9). The first is a lengthy, semi-comic, satirical legend, the second a brief serious description of the sin of the new generation of Israelites. The common thread that ties them together is that both of them were generated by the same man — Balaam. This is made clear later in Numbers 31:16: "Yet they are the very ones who, at the bidding of Balaam, induced the Israelites to trespass against the Lord in the matter of Peor."

Balaam is a complex character, so much so that some scholars have seen in his story two separate narratives later joined together. In one Balaam is a loyal servant of God who refuses to curse the Israelites against God's will. In the other he is a schemer who tries in every way to thwart God's will. Later Jewish tradition also had a difficult time making up its mind about the true nature of Balaam. Sometimes he is called "Balaam the wicked." At other times it is said that although no other prophet arose in Israel like Moses, one did arise like Moses among the nations — Balaam! (*Sifre Deuteronomy* 427).

His fame is attested to by the fact that stories are told about him in a non-Israelite eighth-century BCE inscription found in the Jordan valley that presents him in a way that jives with our story. The story that is told here in Numbers contains one of the few examples of humor or satire in the Bible. The idea of a "seer" who cannot see as well as his animal can and of a king who wastes his resources on countless sacrifices and runs from place to place trying to curse Israel is really quite humorous. Yet the story also has its serious side and actually ends in tragedy for Israel. Like a Chaplin film, comedy and gravity, laughter and tears, are mixed in one composition.

The impression left is that the first story is meant to be a satire on paganism and pagan beliefs. One is reminded of the way in which idolatry is characterized in the psalms:

> They have mouths, but cannot speak; eyes, but cannot see. They have ears but cannot hear; noses but cannot smell. They have hands but cannot touch, feet, but cannot walk; they can make no sound in their throats. (Psalms 115:5–7)

Here too, they have a seer, but he cannot see, a curser who cannot curse.

Nor is his advice very wise. He tells his master Balak to keep building altars and sacrificing animals in great quantities — a matter of no little expense — yet all of this is to no avail (Numbers 23:1). God cannot be moved. The curse cannot be uttered. And so Balak squanders his wealth on a futile enterprise that only ends up in blessing Israel. The pagan king thought that the threat of Israel could be thwarted by magical spells — the normal pagan way. He learns that there is "no augury in Jacob, no divining in Israel" (Numbers 23:23). The God of Israel is not some idol that can be toyed with and coerced.

But when Balaam utters his blessings, we are not reading something of no value but rather magnificent poems that stay in our memory and that characterize Israel in words that have never been forgotten. So wonderful are they that they have found their way into our liturgy. With the words of this pagan we worship daily: "How fair are your tents, O Jacob, Your dwellings, O Israel!" (Numbers 24:5).

What a shock it is therefore to descend to the second part of the portion, chapter 25, and to read there of an immoral, idolatrous Israel. What happened to the people with the beautiful tents described before? To the people whose "kingdom shall be exalted" (Numbers 24:7), the people that "is triumphant" (Numbers 24:19), the people of whom Balaam said, "May I die the death of the upright, may my fate be like theirs" (Numbers 23:10)? Instead we read of twenty-four thousand of them dying in a plague as a punishment for their immorality (Numbers 25:9).

What led them to this terrible fate? Balaam had enough understanding of human nature to realize that they could indeed be defeated — not by magic, but by playing upon their human weakness. Their destruction would not be caused by God, but by themselves. They could be induced to sin; they could be seduced into immorality and idolatrous worship by human weakness. At the end of *Parashat Sh'laḥ Lekha* we read, concerning the wearing of *tzitzit*, "so that you do not follow your heart and eyes in your lustful urge [*asher atem zonim aḥareihem*]" (Numbers 15:39), and here we read "The people profaned themselves by whoring [*vayaḥel ha'am liznot*) with the Moabite women who invited the people to the sacrifices for their gods" (Numbers 25:1–2). Evidently in this case the *tzitzit* were not effective in preventing them from following their urges.

The lesson of this is clear. Magic has no effect. Curses are meaningless. God is all-powerful and cannot be coerced into damning and harming Israel through the magical means, spells and incantations, that were so common in the pagan world. But Israel can be corrupted because sin and temptation are under human control, not divine control. Since we have free will, there is no way in which we can be prevented from corrupting ourselves unless we ourselves decide not to succumb. Furthermore, God can prevent Balaam from cursing, but not from giving evil counsel. Even Balaam has free will to do good or evil.

There is some comfort in knowing that Balaam met his comeuppance. According to Numbers 31:8, in the fight against the Midianites "they also put Balaam son of Beor to the sword." He may have said nice things about them, but his counsel was an evil counsel that betrayed his true nature. He was no friend of Israel, but an enemy who seized upon human weakness to destroy the Israelites. In the long run it is not words that count, but deeds. That is how one can tell an enemy from a friend.

In a real sense the Israelites were brought low not by an enemy force and not by God, but by their own weaknesses. There are times when we are our own worst foe and when the enemy we must resist is not external, but internal. It is also sad to realize that those who succumbed here were probably not the generation of the wilderness, most of whom should have died off by that time, but their children, the new generation that was worthy of entering the land. They may have been a more worthy group than their fathers, less afraid, less slave-like, but they obviously were not stronger in the way that counts the most — in being true to the ideals of their religion and in being capable of winning the struggle against their baser selves. As we read in *Pirkei Avot*, "Who is a hero? One who can overcome his evil impulse" (4:1).

2. The Blessings

Let us explore the "blessings" that Balaam utters. There are four of them and each of them testifies to the nature of Israel. The first (Numbers 23:7–10) is very brief. In addition to stating the fact that Balaam has no power to bless and curse, but can only relate whatever God has decided, it characterizes Israel as "a people that dwells apart, not reckoned among the nations" and as a great and populous people. At that time Israel was indeed set apart. It was the only nation that embraced monotheism, and as such it could not easily assimilate among the nations since it could not adopt their gods and their beliefs. In the Havdalah prayer we stress this by saying, "You distinguished between Israel and the nations." Of course throughout our history we have not dwelt alone, but among the nations, always influenced by others. The question then, as now, was: how do we retain that which distinguishes us while still sharing the culture that is around us?

The second oracle (Numbers 23:18–24) again begins by affirming that human beings, even seers, cannot manipulate God: "There is no augury in Jacob, no divining in Israel." Israel is powerful and will defeat its enemies because God is with the people. The idea of God as Israel's king is stressed. Another aspect of the uniqueness of Israel at that time was that it was not ruled by a human king, but by God whom the people proclaimed king at the sea, "The Lord will be king for ever and ever" (Exodus 15:18). Even when human kings were appointed, they too were subservient to God and had to obey the rules of God.

The third oracle (Numbers 24:3–9) repeats the idea that Israel will be victorious and adds that not only is Israel not subject to curses, but those who curse it will be cursed, and those who bless it will be blessed. This echoes God's promise to Abram, "I will bless those who bless you and curse him that curses you" (Genesis 12:3). Most importantly, Balaam looks upon the tents of Israel spread before him in their camp and utters the famous line "How fair are your tents, O Jacob, your dwellings, O Israel" (Numbers 24:5). The rabbis interpreted this to mean that he saw how they each respected the privacy and modesty of the other (Baba Batra 60a). Some applied these words to our institutions of learning and worship. The beauty of Israel is not in its magnificent buildings, but in its ways of life, in its morality, in its learning, in its devotion. It was this which Balaam attacked in his plan to entice Israel into immorality.

The fourth oracle (Numbers 24:15–24) is a prediction of the fate of the nations that are enemies of Israel who, in the future, will be defeated by Israel. Again he stresses the supreme power of God's will.

In short, in his oracles, Balaam proclaims that Israel is a unique, strong people, destined to overcome its enemies, ruled by God, the liberator and divine king, not subject to magic. It is an ordered society, anchored in morality and replete with institutions of learning and worship. This is an accurate assessment of the status of Israel at that time and paints a picture of our people that we should take as a blueprint for our society. The subsequent history of Israel's apostasy and descent into immorality casts a dark shadow on these beautiful words and reminds us repeatedly how fragile society and civilization are and how easy it is even for a well-organized and grounded society to lose it way.

Pinḥas

פינחס

Numbers 25:10–30:1 | במדבר כה:י–ל:א

1. The Beginning of the End

Although two more portions of Numbers and the entire book of Deuteronomy remain, this portion really marks the beginning of the end. Forty years have passed. The generation of the wilderness has perished. Of those who left Egypt all who remain are Moses, Joshua and Caleb (Numbers 26:65). This portion deals with this new situation and attempts to attend to the final preparations needed to bring the story of the journey to Canaan to an end. It does that by requiring another census — the very "numbers" that give the book its name (Numbers 26:2); by apportioning the land according to the results of the census (Numbers 26:52–56); by appointing a successor to Moses who can lead the people into the land (Numbers 27:18) and, finally, by establishing the calendar of the year for the rituals to be carried out in the land (Numbers 28:1–30:1). It is, then, a very practical section that deals with the concrete steps that have to be taken to ring down the curtain on this chapter and to raise the curtain on the new chapter — the conquest.

All of this comes at the conclusion of a very traumatic event — the apostasy of the Israelites in the matter of Baal-peor that was described in the previous portion (Numbers 25:1–5). That tragic event concluded with a plague that killed twenty-four thousand Israelites, a plague that was stopped only when Pinḥas slew Zimri, one of the leaders of the tribe of Simeon, together with the Midainite woman, Cozbi (Numbers 25:14–15). And it is that event that serves as the background for this section.

The sin of Baal-peor was the third major incident in which the Israelites betrayed their covenant with God. The first was the golden calf, which almost resulted in the destruction of Israel (Exodus 32); the second was the spies, which caused that entire generation to die in the wilderness (Numbers 14:20-24). Sadly, the new generation fell prey to a similar sin. Those who remained must have wondered how serious the consequences would be. Now they see that, although thousands died, there is no threat to prevent them from going on. On the contrary, now is the time to make these final preparations. Now is the time to count their numbers in preparation for the conquest. Now is the time to insure continuity of leadership. Now is the time to give each tribe the feeling that they have a portion in the land. No matter what has happened, Israel will enter Canaan — now.

One of the important actions taken by Moses in concluding the business of dividing the land equitably among the tribes is bringing God's answer to the request of the daughters of Zalophehad: their father will not be disinherited even though he had no sons (Numbers 27:6-11). This may not exactly have been women's lib, but it was the beginning of the serious consideration of the role of women in Jewish law, a discussion that continues in our own day.

Another matter that is dealt with is cultic in nature — the holy days of the year and the sacrifices that are to be brought upon them (Numbers 28:1-39). This tabulation tells at a glance what the structure of the year is to be, month by month, emphasizing the sacrifices that are to be brought each day. The sacrifices, brought in the name of the entire people, symbolize the close relationship between God and Israel. Even on ordinary weekdays there are two sacrifices, the *Tamid* offerings of the morning and of the late afternoon, so that the tie between the people and God is never forgotten. There is no question but that the Torah always places morality above ritual and that the prophets emphasized time and time again that bringing sacrifices without obeying God's moral code was worse that nothing, it was an annoyance to God (see, for example, Amos 5:21-25). Nevertheless, assuming that ethical behavior and concern for their fellow human being accompanies it, regular ritual practice serves an important purpose in reminding the people of its obligations to God and in establishing an orderly way of life that unifies the entire people around one central act of collective worship.

2. Appointing the Successor

It is at this very critical moment that God reminds Moses that although he is preparing Israel for its entry into Canaan, he — Moses — will not participate in that event. He is told to ascend the mountain from which he will view the land, but "when you have seen it, you too shall be gathered to your kin, just as your brother Aaron was" (Numbers 27:13). Both he and Aaron suffer the same fate for the same reason — because "you disobeyed My command to uphold My sanctity" (Numbers 27:14).

Two of their three leaders are already dead and now Moses is about to meet his death as well. What will happen to the people without him? He has been a pillar of strength, an intermediary who brought God's word to Israel and who pleaded for Israel before God. He has led them in battle, legislated for them, governed and judged them. There was never anyone like him before and will never be anyone like him again (Deuteronomy 34:10), but the people cannot be left leaderless.

What is very interesting here is Moses' reaction to this news. One might have expected that this would be the moment when Moses would ask forgiveness and request that the decree against him be annulled. Later on, in Deuteronomy 3:23, Moses records having done just that. But now, at this immediate moment when he realizes that he will not be the leader, his first thought is not for himself but for the people. He asks God to "appoint someone over the community" so that they will "not be like sheep that have no shepherd" (Numbers 27:16-17).

Indeed the true measure of a leader is his concern for his people. The reference to the shepherd here is particularly poignant since Moses himself was a shepherd before his appointment by God (Exodus 3:1). The midrash stressed this by teaching that it was because Moses was so concerned with caring lovingly for his sheep that God decided he would be a good leader of the people: "Since you are so merciful to the sheep belonging to human beings, you shall shepherd My sheep — Israel!" (*Exodus Rabbah* 2:2). Indeed he proves himself so here by showing this concern. His attitude is not "After me — the deluge!" but "After me — a leader who can care for them as I did."

Although Moses may have an idea of whom that leader should be, he does not dare to make a suggestion, leaving it to God to pick his successor. He asks God to "appoint someone over the community" who will lead them and bring them into the land (Numbers 27:16-17). Moses does not himself make the appointment. He was chosen by God to lead the people, and he assumes that God will now choose someone to replace him. The mantle falls upon Joshua. We may assume that God finds him worthy because of his faithfulness in standing up to the spies (Numbers 14:6-10) and also because of his abilities as a warrior — abilities that Moses himself did not possess. Each generation needs its own leader, one who possesses the qualities that are required at that moment, and Joshua is definitely the man for this hour.

The midrash takes the opportunity to expand upon this event and in so doing emphasizes Moses' concern for Israel and the proper way in which the transition was effected. The Sages pictured Moses as though he were one of them (after all they did call him *Moshe Rabbenu*, Moses our teacher). Therefore they have Moses appointing a spokesman for Joshua, someone with a loud voice who could convey Joshua's words to the entire assembly since there were no loudspeakers, letting Joshua give instruction while Moses was yet alive so that he would have authority after Moses' death and even placing him physically in such a way that Moshe himself, as well as all Israel, would have to look up to him. Joshua, for his part, pays respect to his predecessor, proclaiming, "Blessed be the Lord who has given Torah to Israel at the hands of our master Moses" (*Sifre Deuteronomy* 305).

What a contrast this is to much that we see in our days, when leaders, religious and secular, are often concerned only with their own power and their ability to maintain positions of honor rather than thinking of what must be done to assure proper leadership for the community. We see battles for succession rather than preparation for turning over the reins to the right successor.

Again the midrash paints a poignant picture of Moses at this sad moment in his life:

> Moses said to Joshua, "These people that I am giving into your care are still like young lambs, still mere infants. Do not be too strict with them about all that they do, for even their Divine Master has not been strict with them about all their deeds, as it is said 'When Israel was a child then I loved him' (Hosea 11:1). I do not have permission, but if I had permission, I would bring them in to dwell beside the tents of the

shepherds [i.e., in the land of Canaan where the patriarchs dwelt]."
(*Sifre Deuteronomy* 305)

It is important to note who was not chosen to succeed Moses. There is no thought given to a family succession, nor to giving it to the high priest, either of which would have resulted in a very different future for the people of Israel. The chain of leadership which was later described by the Sages as leading to them (see *Pirkei Avot* 1), begins here when Moses "laid his hands upon him and commissioned him" (Numbers 27:23), the beginning of the tradition of *hasmakhah* (rabbinic ordination). The priest has his role to play in ritual. Later on the king has a role in governance, but the spiritual leader is made, not born.

Moses may not have been a perfect leader. Had he been, perhaps he would have entered the land. No human being is perfect; we leave perfection to God. But he was a leader who placed the needs of his people and the good of his people above his own personal concerns. He thought of them before he thought of himself and even at the moment of his greatest personal tragedy, he looked for the way in which Israel could be led to the Promised Land, though he himself would never get there. Moses set an example and a standard for leadership that should inspire all of us and direct all our leaders to follow in his ways.

Mattot-Massei   מטות-מסעי

Numbers 30:2-36:13 | במדבר ל:ב-לו:יג

1. The Borders of the Land

Although these are two Torah portions, they are almost always read together and are best considered as a unit.

There are many troublesome parts in this double portion. There is the description of vows taken by women that places women in an inferior position, under the rule of fathers or husbands (Numbers 30:4-16). There is a story of warfare that does not conform to our standards of morality (Numbers 31:14). There is a description of the boundaries of the Promised Land that excludes much of the current State of Israel and areas that were at various times part of the kingdoms of Judah and Israel, while including sections of Lebanon and Syria that never were in Jewish hands (Numbers 34:1-12). It also contradicts the borders that are described in other Biblical tales such as Genesis 15:18-21 — which only goes to show how difficult it is to use the Torah as a guide to the borders of the state. In each instance we are confronted with a problem that can only be solved when we are willing to study and understand the Torah against the historical background of its own time.

Concerning the borders, it is difficult to decide what is and what is not within the Holy Land because there are different descriptions of the borders. On the one hand, we have a very broad definition of "from the river of Egypt to the great river, the river Euphrates" (Genesis 15:18) which is echoed in Deuteronomy 1:7 and in Exodus 23:31. On the other hand we have the definition in Numbers which is much more limited, "from the wilderness of Zin, alongside Edom. Your southern boundary shall start on the east from the tip of the Dead Sea. Your boundary shall then turn to pass south of the ascent of Akrabbim and continue to Zin, and its limits shall be south of Kadesh-barnea, reaching Hazar-addar and continuing to Azmon. From Azmon the boundary shall turn toward the Wadi of Egypt and terminate at the Sea. For the western boundary you shall have the coast of the Great Sea…. For your eastern boundary…the boundary shall then descend along the Jordan and terminate at the Dead Sea" (Numbers 34:3–12).

Neither of these definitions fits current-day Israel or even "Greater Israel." The expansive definition is far beyond anything we have or could imagine having. The narrow definition excludes the area south of the Dead Sea but includes much of Lebanon and Syria. Scholars have discovered that the narrow definition fits the boundaries of the Egyptian province of Canaan, which would be most appropriate for the time of Moses. As they stand ready to enter Canaan, the Canaan that they recognize is that which was defined by the geo-political realities of the time. The actual borders when they conquered the land were somewhat different and they changed over the centuries as reality changed.

2. The First Diaspora

One thing is clear: according to the book of Numbers, the other side of the Jordan was not part of the Promised Land. Therefore the desire of certain tribes to settle there is considered to be a refusal to enter the land that God had promised.

Although their request seems innocuous enough, Moses' reaction to it is extreme. He accuses the tribes of committing a sin as great as that of the spies, which resulted in the decree that an entire generation would perish in the wilderness — and one that could result in a similar fate for the new generation! "If you turn away from Him and He abandons them once more in the wilderness, you will bring calamity upon all this people" (Numbers 32:15).

What exactly had they done that warranted such an accusation? Various possibilities have been suggested:

1. They turned away from God by deciding to live in a land other than the one He had promised them.

2. They put materialism above all else. Their reason for wanting to dwell there was that these lands "were a region suitable for cattle" (Numbers 32:1). In their plans, they even put animals above their own children: "We will build here sheepfolds for our flocks and towns for our children" (Numbers 32:16). When Moses does grant them permission to stay there he changes the order: "Build towns for your children and sheepfolds for your flocks" (Numbers 32:24).

3. They were separating themselves from the community of Israel by choosing to live outside the land that was sanctified.

4. They were indifferent to the fate of the people of Israel, choosing not to participate in the battles that would have to be fought in order to conquer the land.

There is a certain amount of truth in each of these explanations. But from the words of Moses himself and from the answer that is given by those tribes it would seem that what troubled Moses the most was the thought that they would not fight alongside the others. The first thing that he says to them is: "Are your brothers to go to war while you stay here?" (Numbers 32:6). And their immediate reply is: "And we will hasten as shock-troops in the van of the Israelites until we have established them in their home" (Numbers 32:17). Moses, in turn, replies to them that they can have this territory "if you go to battle as shock-troops" (Numbers 32:20).

One wonders what caused these tribes to do what they did. It could not have been fear of the Canaanites, for they were willing to fight. Perhaps it was the lure of the lushness of the land they saw, as opposed to the uncertainty of the land they had not seen. Even though they had been assured that it was a good land, they knew what they had and could only speculate about what they had not seen. A bird in the hand… Whatever the reason, in a sense these tribes created the first Diaspora community.

There is something ironic in the fact that the first "Diaspora" was established even before the entry into the land of Canaan. The problem of Jewish unity and Jewish responsibility arose at the very beginning and has never departed from us. It can be dealt with only by intensive measures and a strong desire to solve it on the part of all Jews, wherever they may be.

In the end Moses does not forbid the tribes to live there. He grants them the land they want, but with the proviso that they must participate in the conquest of Canaan.

In the book of Joshua we have the account of these men being sent back to their homes when the mission of conquering the land is completed. Joshua also speaks to them and warns them to "be very careful to fulfill the Instruction and the Teaching that Moses the servant of the Lord enjoined upon you, to love the Lord your God and to walk in all His ways" (Joshua 22:5). Is Joshua afraid that in being separated from the rest of Israel, they will be easy prey to temptations and forget the purpose of their existence?

What follows is very interesting, for these tribes build "a great conspicuous altar," or perhaps "an altar for show" would be a better translation, on the other side of the Jordan (Joshua 22:10). When the Israelites within the land hear of it they are so incensed that they are ready to go to war. It is absolutely forbidden to have an altar and sacrifices anywhere but within the land itself! The tribes finally explain that they did not build it for sacrifices, but only out of concern that the time would come when the children of the tribes in the land would say to those outside the land, "you have no share in the Lord" (Joshua 22:25). By showing the altar, an altar that is never used, they will be able to indicate that they are part of the Lord's people. It will be "a witness between you and us" (Joshua 22:28).

The problem that they were concerned with is one that is with us today as well. How does a Jew in the Diaspora maintain his identity as a Jew and feel one with Jews in the land of Israel? And equally important, how can we be certain that those in Israel will feel that Jews outside of the land have an affinity with them? The Diaspora has been with us from the beginning. It existed before the settlement in the land. To find the ways to strengthen these relationships, to preserve Jewish identity in the land and outside of it and to preserve Jewish unity is the challenge that faces us today. It requires great sensitivity and mutual respect, but also the building of a common understanding of what it means to be a Jew and how to fulfill our responsibilities to one another.

We may extrapolate from this story that Jews are not forbidden to live in the Diaspora — i.e., outside of Israel — but there is a proviso: they should always remember that they have an obligation to see to it that the homeland of the Jews, the center of world Jewry and of Jewish life, is safe and strong. Furthermore they should remember that every effort must be made to make certain that they retain a strong connection to the land and those who live there, as well as to Judaism. They must be part of one people with a feeling of unity, even if they live in different places. They too must erect symbolic altars — institutions and symbols that will bind them to the Jewish center.

DEUTERONOMY

D'varim

D'varim   דברים

Deuteronomy 1:1–3:22 | דברים א:א-ג:כב

1. Revisiting the Past

This portion begins the fifth and final book of the Torah — *D'varim*, known as "Deuteronomy," a word that stems from the ancient Hebrew appellation of the book, *Mishneh Torah* (The Repetition of the Torah). Indeed the book is an exercise in *déjà vu*. It retells many of the incidents of the years since the Exodus, not in chronological order and not always exactly as they were told the first time.

Deuteronomy is unique in that it does not have an anonymous narrator, as do the other books. Rather it is entirely (with few exceptions, such as the few verses at the end of the book) a series of speeches given by Moses at the end of his life just before Israel is to enter the land of promise. Even the various laws and commandments that are found in this book, some of which are found nowhere else, are spoken by Moses, not directly by God. Whereas in other books we will find the words "The Lord spoke to Moses saying, 'Speak to the children of Israel and say unto them,'" here we have the much more circumlocutious phrase "And this is the Instruction — the laws and the rules — that the Lord your God has commanded [me] to impart to you" (Deuteronomy 6:1). Because of this it is frequently said of Deuteronomy that it is the most humanistic — in the sense of human-based and human-centered — of all the books of the Torah.

The Sages considered this book to be a work of rebuke to Israel (*Sifre Deuteronomy* 1). They see it as Moses' "deathbed blessing." Just as Jacob called together his children when he was dying, spoke to them of all their past misdeeds and charged them how to act, so Moses rebukes the people for their misdeeds (or the misdeeds of their fathers) and tells them what is expected of them in the future. This is, as it were, Moses' last chance to speak to them and to influence them

This portion, the first of Moses' discourses, begins with a retelling of the most horrendous incident in the history of the Israelites — the story of the spies that resulted in their wandering for thirty-eight additional years rather than entering the land almost immediately after the Exodus. We may well wonder at this and ask ourselves why Moses does not begin with the Exodus itself, or even with Mount Sinai. Why choose the most painful part of their history? Obviously that is just the point. He is not simply retelling old stories around the campfire. He has a lesson to teach. The point is: you are still here today because of the mistake your ancestors made thirty-eight years ago when they rebelled against God. Were it not for that, you would have been long settled in the land. Remember that and do not repeat it.

As Jeffrey Tigay points out in his commentary to Deuteronomy (*The JPS Torah Commentary: Deuteronomy* [Philadelphia: Jewish Publication Society of America, 1996]), this story and many others are related differently from the first tellings. Traditional commentators always try to reconcile the different versions. Biblical critics see them as two different versions of the same events from two schools of thought. Whatever the truth may be, it is also possible to look at them as a kind of "Rashoman" phenomenon, in which the same event is told quite differently depending on who recalls it. What we are hearing in Deuteronomy is Moses' recollection or reconstruction of events long past. How often do we seek to recall our own life stories and find that when we come to tell something that happened forty years ago it may differ from someone else's recollection of the same event? This happens not because we are trying to lie, but because our minds have a way of reinventing the past in light of our own experiences or our own desires and beliefs.

Taking the story of the spies as an example, in the book of Numbers the idea of sending the spies comes from God: "The Lord spoke to Moses, saying, 'Send men to scout the land of Canaan'" (Numbers 13:1–2). In Deuteronomy it is the suggestion of the people: "Then all of you came to me and said, 'Let us send men ahead to reconnoiter the land for us'" (Deuteronomy 1:22). God has no part in it. Moses approves the plan and carries it out alone (Deuteronomy 1:23). In Deuteronomy the task of the spies as articulated by the people is to "bring back word on the route we are to follow and the cities we are to come to" (Deuteronomy 1:22). There is no word about the route in Numbers. Moses remembers it as his telling the people, "Go up, take possession" (Deuteronomy 1:21). But instead of readying themselves to do that, they replied that they would like to send spies and have some more information. That was not the way to react to God's command. Certainly remembering it this way or telling it this way places much more of the burden on the people. It is no longer that God had them do something that then turned out to have a bad result, but that from the very beginning they lacked faith. They wanted to send spies to see how they should proceed, when God would have guided them without that.

And Moses, looking back, further blames himself because he agreed to this plan (Deuteronomy 1:23). He should have dismissed it as a slap in the face to God, but he did not. Now he sees that mistake as the reason for God's anger against him and the decree that Moses too could not enter the land, something not mentioned in Numbers where the incident at the rock is the cause of Moses' punishment (Numbers 20:12).

And so this book of admonition begins with the most serious admonition possible, telling it in such a way as to emphasize the exclusive role of the people in their own fate. But we should not forget that it then immediately recounts a positive story, the way in which the new generation has carried out God's commands, fighting their way through enemy territory and acquiring some land on the eastern side of the border (Deuteronomy 2:1–3:20). Unlike their ancestors, who rebelled and refused to go up to the land, this generation has listened and is poised for its great adventure. If they continue that way and avoid the pitfalls of those who went before, then they, under Joshua, will do that which Israel under Moses could never do — enter the Promised Land and live therein.

2. Now Is the Time

"I am not a man of words [d'varim]," said Moses to God when he was commanded to appear before Pharaoh and deliver God's message (Exodus 4:10). Yet now, some forty years later, Moses begins one of the longest orations in history — the entire book of D'varim (words).

Deuteronomy, as we have seen, is Moses' recapitulation of the events from the time the Israelites left Egypt until this moment, when they are poised to cross the Jordan — but it is also more than that. Moses' purpose is to prepare Israel both for its immediate task of entering the land and for the long-term task of living as God's covenanted people. For this purpose, words (*d'varim*) — and many of them — are necessary. They are the tools by which Moses hopes to forge the nation. Therefore the man of no words transforms himself into a man of many words.

Most of this first section of his discourse is devoted to the subject of taking possession of the land. As discussed above, Moses describes the rebellion of the previous generation and their punishment for listening to the negative report of the spies (Deuteronomy 1:26-40) and then skips to the recent battles undertaken by the new generation on their way to the land (Deuteronomy 2:1-3:20). These battle accounts have an almost ritualistic effect. Each one repeats the same formulas: either a command not to harass people of a certain land because they are somehow related or have been given their land by God, or a command to conquer them, with God's promise that He will deliver the enemy into Israel's hand (Deuteronomy 3:2). This is followed by a brief account of the successful battle, including the way in which all the inhabitants were destroyed and the cattle and booty that were taken (Deuteronomy 3:6). This victory, achieved by human beings, is nevertheless ascribed to God, "and the Lord our God delivered him to us and we defeated him" (Deuteronomy 2:33).

So much else happened during those years, but references to those events must wait until later in the speech. At this point Moses wants no other distractions. He is focused on a single theme and he wants to make a deep impression upon his listeners. That theme is this: The major battle is before you. Do not fear. God has given you assurances that He will be with you and you will succeed. Remember the past and learn from experience. When your ancestors did not listen, they were defeated. They paid a terrible price and perished in the wilderness. When you listened and obeyed in the battles against Og and other kings you succeeded.

The point of reviewing these events, which were already described in great detail in the book of Numbers, is not simply to retell the events, but to use them didactically in order to teach this new generation and to inspire them. The message is summed up succinctly in the last line of this portion when Moses says to Joshua, "Do not fear them, for it is the Lord your God who will battle for you" (Deuteronomy 3:22).

As we have seen, at times there are differences between the accounts that we have here in Deuteronomy and those in Numbers. Another example is the story of the two and a half tribes who settled on the eastern side of the Jordan. As related here, Moses omits the fact that he was angry when they first asked to settle there (Numbers 32:6) and only permitted them to do so when they themselves suggested that they would be willing to lead the forces in battle and only then return to these lands (Numbers 32:17). Here it is described as if Moses simply assigned those lands to them as a matter of course (Deuteronomy 3:16) and commanded them to be at the head of the troops (Deuteronomy 3:18). Has Moses decided that settling that side of the Jordan was a good idea and therefore does not wish to remind anyone of the negative things that were said? Perhaps at this moment, on the very eve of battle, he wishes only to strengthen the resolve of these men who are going to bear the brunt of the battle by giving unconditional legitimacy to what they have done. He accomplishes this by telling a shortened version of what happened.

Another major difference that occurs for the first time in this section but is repeated twice elsewhere (Deuteronomy 3:26 and 4:21) is that Moses was denied entry into the land of Canaan not because of some sin of his own, but "because of you" (Deuteronomy 1:37), because of the sin of the people in listening to the spies and not being willing to undertake the conquest. Exactly why Moses is guilty is not clear. Certainly in Numbers the decree is connected to the incident with the rock (Number 20:12) and not to the spies. Perhaps there were multiple explanations for Moses' punishment. By connecting it here to the refusal to go up to the land, Deuteronomy strengthens the severity of that action and, by inference, the importance of not repeating that catastrophic error.

Moses' speech to Israel is a long and complicated one that has many facets to it. It begins, however, with one essential message: It is time to accomplish the goal which was the very purpose of the Exodus, the goal that has been postponed for all these wasted years because of the actions of the generation of the Exodus which became the generation of those who died in the wilderness. The time is ripe. Do not let the opportunity slip through your hands.

Va'ethanan ואתחנן

Deuteronomy 3:23–7:11 | דברים ג:כג–ז:יא

1. Purity of Belief

There is probably no portion that is more important as a source of Jewish belief than this section. It contains both the Ten Commandments (more accurately "the Ten Utterances," Deuteronomy 5:6–18) and the first section of the Sh'ma (Deuteronomy 6:4–9).

Moses continues his discourse to Israel, in which he constantly refers back to the events of the past forty years. He takes them back to the revelation at Sinai — not only to reiterate for them the terms of the covenant made with God but also to exhort them to avoid idolatry and to remain true to the Lord and be careful in observing all of God's commands. In the section we call the *Sh'ma* he goes beyond that and urges them to love God and to serve God with their entire beings.

Several times Moses reiterates the fact that at the theophany at Sinai they saw no form: "The Lord spoke to you out of the fire; you heard the sound of words but perceived no shape — nothing but a voice" (Deuteronomy 4:12); "Be most careful — since you saw no shape when the Lord your God spoke to you at Horeb out of the fire" (Deuteronomy 4:15). Time and time again he stresses that they heard a voice — meaning that the entire experience of God at Sinai was verbal and not visual. They saw no form (see Deuteronomy 4:33, 36; 5:19). The description of the Sinai revelation in Exodus does not emphasize this at all. As a matter of fact it states, "For on the third day the Lord will come down, in the sight of all the people, on Mount Sinai" (Exodus 19:11), which could be interpreted as describing a visual Presence. In Exodus

24:10-11 it is even stated that Moses, Aaron and the leaders of Israel "saw the God of Israel."

There is very little doubt that the Torah and other books of the Bible take it for granted that God has a form, a physical manifestation. It was only under Maimonides that the doctrine of God having no physical form was finally promulgated and generally accepted in Judaism. In our portion too Moses does not specifically deny that. He is only emphasizing that even at Sinai — the moment of greatest revelation — they did not *see* any form. They only heard a voice. He stresses this in order to strengthen the prohibition against making idols — including, and perhaps especially, idols that would represent the Lord Himself. *All* physical representations are forbidden.

This idea is found, of course, in the Ten Commandments themselves: "You shall not make for yourself a sculptured image, any likeness of what is in the heavens above, or on the earth below, or in the waters below the earth" (Deuteronomy 5:8). In his farewell sermon Moses emphasizes this and greatly expands it. Lest there be any misunderstanding, he tells them not to "make for yourselves a sculptured image in any likeness whatever: the form of a man or a woman, the form of any beast on earth, the form of any winged bird that flies in the sky, the form of anything that creeps on the ground, the form of any fish that is in the waters below the earth" (Deuteronomy 4:16-18). Nothing could be clearer. He repeats this prohibition in Deuteronomy 4:23 and 4:25.

Why is he so adamant on this subject? Because they are about to enter Canaan where they will encounter a civilization that is based upon idolatry; the temptation to copy it will be very great. The Israelites already have a history of succumbing to the worship of physical representations of God in the incident of the golden calf and in the story of Baal-peor. The temptation to make a physical representation of the God of Israel will be great, but it is forbidden, and if they do create such as image, says Moses, it will result in exile or worse: "You shall soon perish from the land that you are crossing the Jordan to possess; you shall not long endure in it, but shall be utterly wiped out" (Deuteronomy 4:26). Unfortunately this seems to be exactly what did happen toward the end of the period of the First Temple, the time when, according to the interpretation of most Biblical scholars, the book of Deuteronomy was discovered and authenticated (see 2 Kings 22:8-20).

The terrible thing about idolatry is that it brings with it the belief that if you have the physical representation of God you can somehow use this to magically force God to do your will. As Jeffrey Tigay has written:

> In idolatry, the purpose of an idol was to draw the presence of a deity to the place where the statue stood. It assumed that by a kind of sympathetic magic, like that connected with voodoo dolls, a being was somehow present in its representation. Here Moses forbids Israel to use idols to attract God: since no form was seen in the original contact with Him, none is to be made for future contacts. (*The JPS Torah Commentary: Deuteronomy*, pp. 48–49)

The great revolution in belief that Moses taught was that the Lord is not limited and not subject to magic and incantations. Not only is there only one divine power, but that divine power is supreme above all else. Any physical representation of God will naturally lead to limitations upon God and upon God's will and power. Deuteronomy — through the words of Moses — stresses this above all other books and spells it out in detail.

But if this section stresses this negative teaching — not to make or worship idols — it also adds the positive command that we recite twice daily in the Sh'ma, "You shall love the Lord your God with all your heart and with all your soul and with all your might" (Deuteronomy 6:5). Alone of all the books of the Torah, Deuteronomy teaches and stresses the love of God, a love that is total and requires willingness to serve God with one's entire being, a love that leads to action and fulfillment of God's will.

Outlawing idolatry lays the foundation for a true and pure belief in God, one that eschews all magic and superstition, one that liberates us from the belief in myths and in ideas that would limit God, setting us on the path toward a worthy concept of God. But that in itself is insufficient. To it must be added a positive motivation toward the active service of God — love. These two ingredients, combined in this one Torah portion, created Judaism and set a standard against which all religious teachings must be measured.

2. The Love of God

Of all the commandments in the Torah, "You shall love the Lord your God" (Deuteronomy 6:5) may be the most unusual. Can love be commanded? Love

is a feeling, an emotion, not an action. Emotions are not so easily controllable. As we read in Song of Songs, "For love is fierce as death...if a man offered
all his wealth for love, he would be laughed to scorn" (8:7). Regarding love of
other human beings, the Torah's exact command in Hebrew is not "Love your
fellow as yourself" but "Be loving *toward* your fellow as yourself" (Leviticus
19:18) i.e., act in a loving manner to others. We cannot be forced to love
others, but we can be commanded to act toward them in the same loving
manner in which we would want others to act toward us. We are not even
commanded to love parents, only to honor them (Deuteronomy 5:16).

The command to love God is found only in Deuteronomy, not in any
other book of the Torah. The closest we come to it elsewhere is in the first
appearance of the Ten Commandments in Exodus 20:6 where there is
mention of "those who love Me," but even there it is not a command. It is
more common to think of God in terms of awe, reverence or even fear. Even
in this portion when Moses recalls the revelation at Sinai, he says, "I stood
between the Lord and you at that time to convey the Lord's words to you for
you were afraid of the fire" (Deuteronomy 5:5).

The midrash was aware of this and therefore taught that "only in regard to
God do we find love combined with fear [reverence] and fear combined with
love" (*Sifre Deuteronomy* 32). Moses himself constantly combines the two.
For example, "And now, O Israel, what does the Lord your God demand of
you? Only this: to *revere* the Lord your God, to walk in His paths, to *love* Him,
and to serve the Lord your God with all your heart and all your soul" (Deuteronomy 10:12). Nevertheless the midrash also teaches that while the performance of commandments out of fear is acceptable, performance because of
love is preferable by far.

The fact that the emphasis on loving God is found only in Deuteronomy
is not accidental. Deuteronomy is different from the other books in that it is
largely composed of the words of Moses rather than the direct speech of God.
Indeed this "command" — "You shall love the Lord your God" — does not
come from God but from Moses. It is not prefaced by the words, "The Lord
spoke to Moses saying, command the children of Israel" but is part of Moses'
grand oration to Israel on the eve of his death. It is Moses who urges Israel to
serve God out of love and to do so completely, "with all your heart, with all
your soul and with all your might." And it is obviously something in which he
believes deeply, for he repeats it time and time again: "Love, therefore, the

Lord your God" (Deuteronomy 11:1); "loving the Lord your God" (Deuteronomy 11:13; 11:22), and so on.

It is no accident that the Song of Songs, a book expressing the love
between men and women, was interpreted by the Sages, especially Rabbi
Akiba, as depicting the relationship between God and Israel. "All the books of
the Scripture are holy and Song of Songs is the holy of holies," taught Rabbi
Abika (*Yadayim* 3:5). As the late Gershon Cohen wrote, they did not interpret
Song of Songs in that way because they were embarrassed by the frankness of
the poetry of that book but because they were in search of a book that would
truly express the love, the mutual love, between Israel and God. The love of
man and woman is the most intense expression of that feeling and therefore
the depiction of that human love in Song of Songs can best indicate the love of
Israel for God and God for Israel:

> The conclusion is inescapable that the work filled a gap, a void no
> other work in the Bible could fill. Its very daring vocabulary best
> expressed, and was, perhaps, the only way of expressing what the Jew
> felt to be the holiest and loftiest dimension of religion — the bond of
> love between God and His people. In the final analysis, it is not the
> canonization of the Song of Songs that needs to be explained but the
> Jewish conception of the bond of love between God and Israel that
> made the canonization possible. ("The Song of Songs and the Jewish
> Religious Mentality" in *Studies in the Variety of Rabbinic Cultures*
> [Philadelphia: Jewish Publication Society of America, 1991], p. 5)

On the one hand, the Torah is very insistent that God is not to be thought of
as a human being. God has no sexuality, just as God has no physical needs,
nor is God subject to birth or death (all of this in contrast to the way in which
pagan gods were depicted). The use of the masculine to refer to God is only a
convention, not a description. On the other hand, God is not to be considered an abstract force, but an object of love, a love that is a response to God's
love of Israel.

Our liturgy demonstrates the importance of love by incorporating the
words of Moses in the Sh'ma that is recited twice daily. Our prayers also
emphasize the mutuality of this love and the fact that the command to love
God comes as a response to God's love of Israel, a love demonstrated by His
granting us the Torah and the commandments. Thus before we recite the

Sh'ma we say, "With everlasting love have You loved Your people Israel, teaching us Torah and *mitzvot*, statutes and laws."

We must be careful, however, not to mistake love of God for sentimentality. The love of God that Moses describes is not merely an emotion or some abstract feeling, rather it is love that leads to action, to the fulfillment of God's will and to a life dedicated to the pursuit of the good: "Love, therefore, the Lord your God, and always keep His charge, His laws, His rules, and His commandments" (Deuteronomy 11:1).

Judaism has often been described as a stern religion, a religion of fear. It is not. Judaism displays a realistic awareness of God's greatness and therefore of the need to approach God with a feeling of awe and reverence, but it also teaches that love of God is the highest of all relationships and the best motivation for the service of God. Love translated into concrete ways of life, following the pattern of the Divine, is the love that Moses urged upon all Israel. It is his bequest to all of us as well.

Ekev   עקב

Deuteronomy 7:12–11:25 | דברים ז:יב–יא:כה

1. To Be Worthy of the Gift

One of the best-known oratorical devices is repetition, saying the same idea over and over until your point is made. *Ekev* is a good example of that. In his oration to the people of Israel at the brink of their entry into the land of Canaan, Moses has a message he wants to deliver and he says it over and over again: "If you obey these rules and observe them carefully" (Deuteronomy 7:12); "You shall faithfully observe all the Instruction that I enjoin upon you" (Deuteronomy 8:1); "Take care lest you forget the Lord your God and fail to keep His commandments" (Deuteronomy 8:11); "And now, O Israel, what does the Lord your God demand of you? Only this: to revere the Lord your God, to walk only in His paths, to love Him, and to serve the Lord your God with all your heart and soul, keeping the Lord's commandments and laws" (Deuteronomy 10:12–13); "Keep, therefore, all the Instruction that I enjoin upon you today" (Deuteronomy 11:8).

All of this and more is climaxed by the second section of the Sh'ma (Deuteronomy 11:13–21), which is recited twice daily, beginning with "If, then, you obey the commandments that I enjoin upon you this day, loving the Lord your God and serving Him with all your heart and all your soul." This section was characterized by the Rabbis as *kabbalat ol mitzvot*, the acceptance of the yoke of the commandments. In it we are assured that Israel will be blessed with much needed rain as a reward for observing the *mitzvot*.

We may have some difficulty in accepting literally the connection between observance of the commandments and the blessing of rain. The Sages themselves taught that "the world pursues its natural course"- i.e., there is such a thing as natural law which is not dependent upon human conduct. "An illustration: if a man stole a measure of wheat and sowed it in the ground, it would be only right that it would not grow — but the world pursues its natural course" (*Avodah Zarah* 54b). Nevertheless we should have no difficulty in accepting the concept that the strength of a nation or of a people depends upon its values and morality and that nations crumble when they lack that foundation. That is the underlying meaning of the passage.

Moses goes out of his way to remind the people that they have done little up to now to merit the gift of the land. On the contrary, he reiterates the two incidents in which their unfaithfulness would have resulted in their total destruction had Moses not intervened — the golden calf and the spies (Deuteronomy 9:6-29). It was the merit of the ancestors that caused God to grant them the land, not their own merit (Deuteronomy 9:5). But now they must become worthy of this gift by remaining faithful to God and to God's teachings. Only in that way will they earn God's blessings and remain in the land.

Too often our instinctive reaction to these admonitions is to connect them with ritual observances alone. We forget that Torah and *mitzvot* are composed of moral and ethical demands as well. As Abraham Joshua Heschel once remarked, why are we concerned with having a *mashgiah* for kashrut but not for gossip and malicious speech? Within this portion itself there is a hint that God's concern is with our conduct toward others. God is characterized here as the One who "upholds the cause of the fatherless and the widow, and befriends the stranger, providing him with food and clothing — you too must befriend the stranger" (Deuteronomy 10:18-19). To imitate God is the highest virtue. "As He is merciful, so must you be merciful," taught the Sages (Sotah 14a).

The prophet Jeremiah, whose thinking was greatly influenced by the book of Deuteronomy, made the point very clear when he castigated the worshippers at the Temple who believed that they could violate all the ethical principles of God's law and still expect God to save them if only they brought the right sacrifices and worshipped at the holy shrine. In what must surely have been an act of colossal chutzpah, Jeremiah stood before them at the Temple gate and spoke in the name of the Lord and told them that only "if you execute justice between one another; if you do not oppress the stranger, the orphan, and the widow; if you do not shed the blood of the innocent in this place; if you do not follow other gods, to your own hurt — then only will I let you dwell in this place" (Jeremiah 7:5-7).

Moses is depicted in this portion as a man who is afraid — afraid that the people will not learn the lessons of the past, afraid that they will continue to be stiff-necked, afraid that they will not remain faithful to God, afraid that the moral and ethical ways he has taught them will not be obeyed. He foresees two dangers — the outer danger that they might come to follow the ways of the Canaanites and the inner danger that their own prosperity would make them forget their dependence upon God. As the Sages put it, "Prosperity causes rebellion" (*Sifre Deuteronomy* 43).

It is all too easy to dismiss these teachings as applying to an ancient situation but having nothing to say to us today. Yet as we look around us at the society in which we live we would do well to ask the question, how faithful are we to the Instruction of God? This does not mean only how many *mezuzot* we affix and how strictly we observe Shabbat. It means loving the stranger, caring for the widow, doing justice and imitating God's ways of mercy and love.

2. A Modest Request

When anyone says to you "I just want to ask you a little favor" — watch out! I remember that as a parent those were always the hardest requests to fulfill. I was reminded of those "little favors" my children used to ask for when I read the words Moses speaks to Israel as they stand poised to enter Canaan after forty years of wanderings: "And now, Israel, what does the Lord your God ask of you? *Only this*: to revere the Lord your God, to walk in all His paths, and to love Him, and to serve the Lord your God with all your heart and all your soul, keeping the Lord's commandments and laws, which I enjoin upon you today, for your good" (Deuteronomy 10:12-13). "*Only this*"!? That's all? Love, reverence, service, observance of 613 *mitzvot*...just a small favor.

And it is phrased as a favor. There is something rather poignant in the wording. It does not say "demands" or even "requires," simply "asks." This implies that Moses — or perhaps even God — realizes that some things cannot be forced. You cannot force love and reverence even though the

Sh'ma, "You shall love the Lord your God," seems to command it. You can only ask for it.

Love and reverence are critical. Regardless of all the threats and curses of dire consequences listed in the Torah if we do not comply with the commandments, fear is not enough to guarantee observance. If fear is all there is, the moment that fear evaporates, the entire system evaporates and anarchy reigns. The observance of the commandments themselves must be based on love and reverence or their observance will not continue. Furthermore, if they are observed only because of fear of punishment, they are not really being observed properly. The implication of "only this" in Moses' request is that everything else that is found in the Torah, all of the lists of ritual and ethical practices, of do's and don'ts, are really expressions of revering and loving God and serving Him with all your being. This is a wonderful antidote to the school of thought that teaches: Just follow the laws, even without understanding. Don't bother to look for reasons, for ethical principles. Just do it. Moses' statement here proves to the reader that praxis — blind action — without devotional understanding is insufficient.

Following Moses, many others searched for the essence and meaning of the commandments by asking, "What does God ask of you?" The prophet Micah, after telling the people that offering animals or even children as sacrifices was no way to gain favor with God, then asked: "What *does* the Lord require of you? Only to do justice and to love goodness and to walk humbly with your God" (Micah 6:8).

Again "only." Notice the resemblance to Moses' words. Both talk about walking in the ways of God or with God. True, Micah's words are fewer and less detailed, but what he asks is not easy either. He asks for justice and goodness, the very essence of the good life.

The third-century Amora Rabbi Simlai, a renowned Galilean preacher, once addressed this question by trying to reduce the *mitzvot* to one essential element. He began by saying that God gave Moses 613 commandments, 365 negative ones corresponding to the days of the year (i.e., every day there are things you should not do!) and 248 positive ones corresponding to the parts of the body (i.e., there is always some action your body should be performing!). He then began the reduction: David reduces them to eleven in Psalm 15, Isaiah to six (Isaiah 33:15–16), Micah to three (as above), Isaiah to two — "Keep justice and do righteousness" (56:1) — and finally Amos to one: seek

Me and live (5:4). Another rabbi, Naḥman ben Yitzhak, suggested that the one should be "The righteous shall live by his faith" (Habakkuk 2:4; *Makkot* 23b-24a).

Obviously Rabbi Simlai was not attempting to eliminate 612 commandments and retain only one. Rather he was seeking the essence of Judaism, the rationale that is behind all our actions as believing Jews. He found it in Amos's words. Everything we do, every action we take, must be an expression of seeking a perfect harmony with God and God's will. And if the answers to dilemmas of living are not always clearly apparent, we must use our understanding to try to seek God's way. And we know from the other verses what these ways are — justice, righteousness, mercy, etc.

This reductionist exercise did not originate with Simlai. It had been tried earlier by Akiba, who taught that the great principle of the Torah was "Love your fellow as yourself"(Leviticus 19:18). His companion, Ben Azzai, preferred "This is the book of the line of Adam" (Genesis 5:1) since "fellow" might refer to your fellow Jew while *Adam*,"man," includes all humanity created by God (*Genesis Rabbah* 24:7). Before them, in the incident of the convert who wanted the entire Torah taught while standing on one foot, Hillel had no problem answering (in Aramaic): what is hateful to you do not do to your fellow — which is a negative formulation of "love your fellow" (*Shabbat* 31a). Wisely and slyly Hillel added, "The rest is commentary. Go study."

All of the commandments, then, according to Hillel, are expressions of "love your fellow." They are the commentary that must be studied. Without the commentary, the words have no meaning. How does one love one's fellow? The commandments are the guide to doing that. But the implication is profound: unless one loves one's fellow, all other observances are worthless. Or, as my revered teacher, Rabbi Louis Finkelstein put it, the observance of all the commandments, ritual as well as moral, is intended to produce a human being who loves his fellow, all human beings, as himself, and acts accordingly. That is the little favor that the Lord asks of us.

Re'eh ראה

Deuteronomy 11:26–16:17 | דברים יא:כו-טז:יז

1. The Basis of a Jewish Society

What are the elements that constitute an authentic Jewish society? This is the question that Moses tries to answer in this portion, although of course the word "Jewish" is unknown to him. He is speaking of the life the tribes of Israel should live when they enter the land of Canaan. When they cross the Jordan and occupy the land without him, what should they do and what should they not do?

At first glance the section sees to be an untidy potpourri of various laws and regulations with no particular order or logic. There is the command to destroy pagan places of worship (Deuteronomy 12:1-3) and the command to worship and sacrifice only in "the place the Lord your God will choose" — i.e., the exclusive nature of the Temple in Jerusalem and the consequences of that (Deuteronomy 12:4-27). We then have warnings against following other gods and those who try to lead Israel astray into idolatry (Deuteronomy 13:1-19)

This is followed by the prohibition of following pagan practices of mourning (Deuteronomy 14:1-2) and of eating prohibited animals (Deuteronomy 14:3-21). Then come laws of tithes (Deuteronomy 14:22-29), laws concerning the seventh year (Deuteronomy 15:1-11) and laws limiting slavery (Deuteronomy 15:12-18). Finally we have laws concerning firstborn animals (Deuteronomy 15:19-23) and a list of the festivals to be observed in the "place that He will choose" (Deuteronomy 16:1-17).

Some of these are innovations. In no other book of the Torah, for example, are worship and sacrifice confined to one place alone. Others are variations on regulations spoken of elsewhere, such as kashrut, the seventh year and slavery. Why has Moses chosen to put them together in this way at this time? Or is this merely a stream of consciousness, Moses talking about whatever comes to his mind?

A close examination shows that there is indeed method in this seemingly casual order. These regulations are prefaced by a general exhortation which immediately sets the theme, "See this day I set before you blessing and curse: blessing if you obey the commandments of the Lord your God...and curse if you do not obey the commandments of the Lord your God" (Deuteronomy 11:26–28). This is the setting. You — Israel — have the choice. You can create a blessed land and a blessed society or a cursed one. The commands that follow will tell you what you should choose and which you should eschew. You decide.

What follows then is a four-fold blueprint for a blessed society. The first part (Deuteronomy 12:1–13:19) is completely concerned with the proper worship of *God*. Moses has spent his entire career as a prophet teaching Israel the true concept of God, the one God, the sole Creator, not to be worshipped in images, not to be worshipped in immoral ways, not subject to magic and manipulation. This is the very basis of the life of the people Israel. If, when they enter their land, they abandon that, all will have been for naught. Therefore: destroy the pagan altars which will lead you astray; do not listen to any who tempt you to idolatry, no matter how convincing they may sound, and have only one central altar, because that can be controlled and kept pure. A multiplicity of temples may lead to a corruption of the pure worship of the Lord.

The second part (Deuteronomy 14:1–21) deals with the ritual ways in which Israel can retain its identity as a holy people, being always aware of the need to separate itself from impurity and remembering always its task of being "a kingdom of priests and a holy nation," as it was commanded many times before. To do this the Israelites must avoid such degrading practices as those the pagans perform when in mourning, desecrating their bodies, and they must follow the laws of kashrut, which are designed to emphasize Israel's holy status.

Thirdly, "Open your hand to the poor and needy kinsman in your land" (Deuteronomy 15:11). Israel must establish a *society of equity and justice*, a society that cares for the poor, forgiving debts, loaning money to those in need, limiting the time of service of indentured servants (Deuteronomy 14:22–15:18).

The fourth section of the reading (Deuteronomy 15:19-16:17) closes the circle by returning to the first theme — the proper worship of God — but this time on a positive rather than a negative note. In the first part we were warned against idolatry. Now we are told to come to that one place God will choose three times a year and to "rejoice in your festival," along with all of your family and those who depend upon you, including "the Levite, the stranger, the fatherless and the widow" (Deuteronomy 16:14). And this last section echoes the first, which told us that we had a choice of blessing or curse by stating, "for the Lord your God will bless all your crops and all your undertakings, and you shall have nothing but joy" (Deuteronomy 16:15).

The message of Moses, then, boils down to this — choose the blessing: (1) worship the Lord properly and exclusively, (2) preserve your identity as a holy people, (3) establish a society of equity and justice, then (4) rejoice before God together with the needy for all the blessings He will bestow upon you.

The world of Moses seems very different from our own. Wherever they are, Jews today live in a secular society. For many this formula of Moses is unacceptable and even incomprehensible. It begins with God in whom many do not believe, and it includes holiness which many term irrelevant. That is indeed the gulf that separates us from traditional Judaism. Yet we must wonder if belief in God is really so far from us or if we simply have an erroneous concept of what such belief entails. Belief does not require one to abandon reason, logic and scientific thought. It certainly does not require one to accept some of the superstitious thinking that passes for religion today. There need be no contradiction between belief in God and modern knowledge, as a glance at the writings of such theologians as Heschel, Buber, Fackenheim, Rozensweig, Berkowitz, Soloveichik, Kook and Jacobs will reveal. Nor is holiness an outmoded concept when understood as reverence for life and a desire to live in accord with God's ways. And these two concepts, basing life on a pure belief in God and on the holiness of the Jewish people, serve as the platform upon which we can build a just and good society for all — a society which can bring joy to all who live within it. That is the message of Moses and that is the message we need today as well.

2. The Exclusive Sanctuary

In contrast to the previous sections of Deuteronomy, this portion is not a review of the past with a rebuke for Israel's actions nor is it an exhortation to obey *mitzvot* and love the Lord. Rather it begins a series of chapters in which Moses gives the people laws that are either completely new or that supplement previously given laws. These laws continue through the end of chapter 26. All of these regulations, discussed in detail above, are important for the Israelites since they pertain to their lives in the land they are about to enter. All of these laws are given in a style that is unique because it contains exhortations as well as legal prescriptions. It is not enough simply to tell people what they are to do or not to do. They must be urged to follow God's ways and they must be brought to understand why this is so important.

The most revolutionary law found here is the one that distinguishes Deuteronomy from all other books of the Torah: the demand that there be only one sanctuary where the Lord may be worshipped through sacrifices (Deuteronomy 12:4–16). This is framed as a repudiation of Canaanite practices. They — the Canaanites — worshipped "on mountains and on hills or under any luxuriant tree" (Deuteronomy 12:2). Israel must worship God "only in the place that the Lord will choose in one of your tribal territories" (Deuteronomy 12:14). The place is not specified, but it was understood later to be the Temple Mount in Jerusalem, variously known as Mount Zion and Mount Moriah.

Most Biblical scholars today believe that this law was either not known or not enforced during the early years of the settlement in Canaan, even after the establishment of the Jerusalem Temple. Archeological evidence shows that sacrificial sanctuaries existed in different places and only at a later period was there an attempt to eliminate them as improper. (See chapter 17 of Judges.) Josiah ordered the demolition of all such shrines once he had established the authenticity of the book that was found in the Temple, the book thought to be Deuteronomy (2 Kings 23:8).

The question that begs to be asked is why Deuteronomy insists that there should be only one sacrificial sanctuary. What would be so terrible if there were many sanctuaries so long as they are devoted exclusively to worship of the Lord and do not include pagan practices? Perhaps there was a fear that if there were many sanctuaries, it would be all too easy for some of them, far from any central authority, to incorporate pagan elements. Yet we know that idol worship was introduced even into the Jerusalem Temple under some kings. Perhaps the feeling was that given the concept voiced in Exodus that somehow God's Presence dwelt in the Sanctuary (Exodus 25:8), if there were many sanctuaries, each would claim the Presence of God, which could lead to polytheism.

Yehezkel Kaufmann, had a different idea. He felt that the concept of one exclusive sanctuary was

> one of the intuitive symbols through which Israelite religion sought expression…. The Deuteronomic idea founds the entire cult on the idea of divine election…. Pagan sanctity is rooted in nature and may therefore be found everywhere. Israelite sanctity is a creation of the will of God; it originates always in a historical election, a revelation of God's word. The earlier embodiments of this concept are the idea of the sanctifying election of the people and land of Israel, of Jerusalem, the temple, and the house of David. The idea of the election of Jerusalem and the temple did not at first imply the prohibition of the rural altars. But in the course of time the Judean priesthood drew this ultimate inference. (*The Religion of Israel*, p. 289)

In other words, sanctity is found only where God decrees it to be found. It is not inherent in any place. God chose Jerusalem and only Jerusalem, so all sacrifices should be brought only to that place.

Ironically, it was the very fact of the exclusivity of the Jerusalem Temple that brought about one of the greatest innovations of Judaism, which has influenced other religions as well — the idea of a place of worship *without* sacrifices: the synagogue. The Torah forbids bringing sacrifices elsewhere. It does not forbid praying elsewhere. Certainly when Jews were dispersed to other lands it was not sufficient for them to send gifts to Jerusalem or to participate from time to time in a pilgrimage to Jerusalem. Or consider the situation following the destruction of the Temple in 586 BCE. What were the Jews in Babylonia to do? Even before that, when there was a Temple, people in Israel who lived far away from Jerusalem were virtually cut off from the possibility of worshipping God. The solution was to worship without sacrifice, to pray and read the sacred word — the Torah — wherever they lived.

Nowhere was it prohibited to offer prayers and psalms in public squares or in special buildings. Thus the synagogue was born.

Jewish life today — as for the past two thousand years or more — is inconceivable without the synagogue. And so Deuteronomy provides us with the ultimate sanctity of a Temple in Jerusalem and inadvertently encourages the sanctity of multiple "small sanctuaries" wherever we live: synagogues. Without them, there would be no Judaism.

Shoftim   שפטים

Deuteronomy 16:18–21:9 | דברים טז:יח-כא:ט

1. Justice, Justice

Living as we do in the age of democracy, we tend to look down upon any system of government that is not based on the election of officials by popular vote. Certainly none of us would want to return to any other system and we rejoice whenever any country abandons totalitarianism and joins the democratic world. This is as it should be. But when we study the rules and regulations laid down in the Torah — as in this portion, which is a compilation of one law after the other on a variety of subjects — we should also appreciate the fact that although they do not set out the framework for a democratic government, they are extremely concerned that the government be a just one.

The key to these laws and to the society being set up by the Torah can be found in one verse: "Justice, justice shall you pursue, so that you may thrive and occupy the land that the Lord your God is giving you" (Deuteronomy 16:20). These are words that should give us pause as we look around at our society. Wherever we live we must ask ourselves if justice is always done or if some are favored over others. We must question if our governmental system is concerned enough that justice be done for all citizens, regardless of their religion or ethnic grouping. The word "justice" is repeated twice for emphasis. The rabbinic interpretation was that this means that justice must be pursued in a just way. Not only the ends but also the means must be just. There are no shortcuts to justice.

Most important is the fact that these judges are to be scrupulously honest. The Sages later remarked, "Woe to the generation that judges its judges" (*Ruth Rabbah* 1:1). When judges and rulers are corrupt, society is indeed in deep trouble. The Torah goes out of its way to forbid the taking of bribes or the showing of partiality. The verse quoted earlier — "Justice, justice shall you pursue, that you may thrive and occupy the land that the Lord your God is giving you" (Deuteronomy 16:20) — is an extreme statement implying that unless there is the active pursuit of justice, exile will result. We are worthy of the land only if justice prevails.

In order to reach this goal the portion begins by requiring that there be both "judges and officials" appointed in each city and village. A society without a system of justice is no society. The words *mishpat* (judgement) and *tzedek* (justice) are repeated over and over again in these opening verses (16:18–20). Judges — notoriously corruptible in the ancient world and even today — are warned that their task is to judge justly. They are not even allowed to take a fee for hearing a case lest it blind them and make them favor one of the parties over the other (16:19).

A "supreme court" — much later known as the Sanhedrin — was set up for especially difficult cases (Deuteronomy 17:8–12). It consisted of a larger number of judges, some from the priests of the Levitical tribe and some lay judges, to insure justice for all.

Indeed rabbinic law carries out these concerns. The rich may not be favored over the poor, but neither may the poor be favored over the rich. Each case must be heard for what it is and justice must be done. Throughout the ages Jewish communities have been known for this quality. Today, when we hear so many complaints regarding the way in which women are treated in some of our *batei din* (religious courts) and the problems that arise over divorces, we must ask ourselves if we are still carrying out the Torah's demand for true justice in the proper way and, if not, what should be done about it.

Another law in this section deals with witnesses. It stipulates that no one can be put to death on the testimony of only one witness. This is another strong fence to protect justice, for it is all too easy for one person's testimony to be obtained and for this to result in a miscarriage of justice. Certainly there are many cases in which a misdeed has been done but was not witnessed by two witnesses, but the Torah would prefer that that person go unpunished by human courts than that innocent people be punished because of a false witness. Furthermore this code specifically warns against false witnesses and orders that they be punished with the penalty they wanted to bring upon the accused (Deuteronomy 19:16–21). Human life is sacred and the Torah is careful to avoid any miscarriage of justice, especially in capital cases. This tendency was carried much further by the rabbis, who for all practical purposes made capital punishment impossible and warned witnesses that if they lied, the blood of the innocent person would be on their heads and the heads of their descendants until the end of time (*Sanhedrin* 4:5)!

The importance of justice is stressed in several other laws found in this portion. The first deals with a way to save the life of one who inadvertently kills another person. Taking cognizance of the ancient practice of the blood-avenger, in which blood relatives of a slain person killed the slayer, regardless of the circumstances, the Torah set up a system of cities of refuge. These cities were open to the inadvertent killer, and in them that person's life was inviolate (Deuteronomy 19). It would have been difficult if not impossible at that time to simply forbid blood-revenge. This way, the life of the innocent person was protected.

Then there is the law concerning the dead body found in the open, when the slayer is unknown. Here justice cannot be done, but the rulers of the closest city must enact a ritual purging them of guilt, declaring that they "did not see the blood nor did [their] eyes see it done" (Deuteronomy 21:7). They must declare not only that they were not the active perpetrators of the crime but that they were not guilty of passively permitting such a thing to happen.

There can never be a perfect system of human justice. Losses have to be weighed against gains, but the Torah attempts to arrive at justice in the best way possible.

Thus the Torah forged a society in which justice was paramount, in which the judges were to be scrupulous about ruling and judging without prejudice, in which witnesses had to be honest and in which the supreme ruler was subservient to God, the greatest Judge of all. Our society may have a different form of governance, but its motto should remain the same: *Justice, justice shall you pursue.*

2. Subservient Kings

It is all very well to discuss general principles and even specific regulations, as Moses has done. But how will this new society work? Who will run it? Who will govern it? In a sense, up until now, Moses was almost a one-man show.

He was prophet, legislator, judge, ruler. Of course he appointed others to assist him, and he has even seen to it that a successor was appointed for him, Joshua. In the long run, however, a stable society needs more than that. And so Moses begins by saying, "Judges and officials shall you appoint for your tribes, in all the settlements…and they shall govern the people with due justice" (Deuteronomy 16:18). This is truly a remarkable statement for its time. It leaves the appointment of these individuals, who seem to be both rulers and judges, to human beings, either the people as a whole or the elders of the tribes. Jeffrey Tigay points out that this is addressed "to the people… implying that they, or the elders on their behalf, are to make the appointments" (*The JPS Torah Commentary: Deuteronomy*, p. 160). Thus there is at least some democratic element in this law as well. We might have thought that the kohanim or the Levites would assume this position, but that is not the case. They have authority over sacrifices and ritual matters, but not what we would term today "civil law." In that way Deuteronomy is truly humanistic. There is a court for especially difficult cases that is under "the Levitical priests or the judge" (Deuteronomy 17:9), evidently the institution later known as the Sanhedrin. It seems to have had both laymen and priests in it, perhaps because it dealt with both ritual and civil matters.

Who holds authority in this society? Moses speaks about two types of people: the prophet and the king. The prophet is someone "raised up" by God (Deuteronomy 18:15). It is not an inherited position, nor one that can be learned. Of course there is always a difficulty in determining if a prophet is true or false, and this problem accompanied the institution of prophecy as long as it lasted, which was until the beginning of the period of the return from the Babylonian exile in the fifth century BCE (*The JPS Torah Commentary: Deuteronomy*, p. 164).

The concern for justice and for a just government reaches its peak in the laws concerning the possible appointment of a king. The powers of kings at the time of the Torah were absolute. It is only in recent centuries that kingly powers have been diminished so that most sovereigns today — at least in Western countries — are little more than window dressing with few significant powers. How different the kingship laws set out by the Torah!

Rulership lies with the king, but Deuteronomy has a very ambivalent attitude toward the kingship. It indicates that the people of Israel will ask for a king in order to be like all the nations, and if they do, they may appoint one.

In other words, it is optional, not mandated by God. As a matter of fact we know that when they did appoint a king, God regarded it as a rejection of His kingship (1 Samuel 8:7). But the important thing is that Deuteronomy severely limits the powers of the king. He may not multiply horses, wealth or wives (Deuteronomy 17:16-17). Exactly what kind of a king is that? Certainly not the mighty rulers of Egypt and Babylonia of that time. Furthermore, he is required to have a copy of the Torah, which must be kept with him. He had to "have a copy of this Torah written for him on a scroll by the Levitical priests. Let it remain with him and let him read it all his life.... Thus he will not act haughtily toward his fellows or deviate from the Instruction to the right or to the left" (Deuteronomy 17:18-20). In a manner totally unlike that of any other ancient kings, Deuteronomy made the king subservient to the laws of the Torah.

Whereas in most societies the king was the author of the laws, as was certainly the case with the famous code of Hammurabi, in Israel the king was subservient to the laws that came from God. He was not permitted to change them at will.

It was because of this fact that prophets could denounce kings and not be executed for it. Thus Samuel castigates Saul (1 Samuel 15:17-23), Nathan rebukes David for his sins (2 Samuel 12:1-12), Elijah reprimands Ahab (1 Kings 21:20-24) and Jeremiah speaks against a whole series of kings (Jeremiah 22:24-30).

The concepts of society taught by Moses differed fundamentally from those of the surrounding nations not only in the basic understanding of the nature of God, but also in the nature of society. Israel was not to be ruled by despotic kings who considered themselves divine and above the law. Nor was it to be put into the hands of all-powerful priests. Rather, if it was to have a king at all, he would have to be a limited monarch who followed the instructions of the Torah. There could be prophets speaking in the name of God, but they too had to adhere to those basic teachings. Most importantly, society was to be founded on justice, with judges and officials above reproach, figures who took no bribes and did not side with interested parties but were concerned only with justice itself, and whose courts were run with integrity and with reliable witnesses.

Ki Tetze   כי תצא

Deuteronomy 21:10–25:19 | דברים כא:י-כה:יט

1. The Sensitivity Code

What purpose do laws serve? Are they simply for the regulation of society so
that there will be fairness and equity, or do they go beyond that into molding
the character of a people? Judaism is, without doubt, a religion of law —
although the very word "law" may be misleading. Our laws are *mitzvot*, not
cold regulations. The Torah is not "law" as the Greek translation, the Septuagint, has it, but "instruction," a guide to life. One of the main points of dispute
between Judaism and early Pauline Christianity was the value of the *mitzvot*.
Paul saw them as laws and believed that the laws of the Torah were a burden,
encumbrances that had to be abolished and replaced by faith alone. Judaism
has insisted that living by *mitzvot* is the way to fulfill God's will. Torah and
mitzvot are not a burden but a blessing and a privilege.

We can see this clearly in this portion, as Moses continues to outline the
regulations by which Israel must live when entering the land. The range of
legislation is extremely broad, dealing with captives in war, marital relations,
divorce, rape, lost animals, building regulations, proper and improper clothing, conduct in an army camp, harvesting, rebellious children and so much
more. The vast majority concern civil law; a few deal with rituals.

This section is reminiscent of Leviticus 19, the Holiness Code, a seemingly unrelated series of regulations ranging over both ethical and ritual
matters. The main difference is that in Leviticus the *mitzvot* are given by God
and have as their purpose "You shall be holy," whereas here they are conveyed
by Moses and the word "holy" never appears. Certainly Deuteronomy also
envisions Israel as a holy people (Deuteronomy 26:19), but the emphasis here

is not so much on that exalted state as on the conduct of everyday life that makes for a good society.

This collection of regulations goes far beyond that. No law can take into account every situation, but these ways of life can teach us how we should approach the art of living. There are provisions that are intended to mold character, not simply to regulate actions. Perhaps this section could be deemed not a Holiness Code but a Sensitivity Code, for time and time again it attempts to inculcate in us sensitivity to others — human and animal alike. To borrow a phrase from Martin Buber, we are asked to look at the other not as an "It" but as a "Thou."

For example, chapter 22 requires us to return any lost objects or animals we may find and cautions "You must not remain indifferent" (Deuteronomy 22:1-3). We see here, as in so many other instances in this book, the way in which Deuteronomy turns dry legislation into moral imperative. It was not sufficient to say to the Israelites "This is the law"; rather they had to be exhorted to mold their character in such a way that these things would be second nature. The chapter then continues by telling us that if another person's animal has fallen, we must help him raise it (Deuteronomy 22:4) — again with an exhortation, "Do not ignore it."

Judaism's attitude toward those who are weak and helpless finds expression in many of these *mitzvot*. Fugitive slaves are not to be returned to their masters (Deuteronomy 23:16-17), the complete opposite of the accepted laws in the ancient Middle East, where the return was an imperative. This very issue was still a bone of contention in the United States prior to the Civil War. The Torah also goes out of its way to teach that the needy and destitute laborer "whether a fellow countryman or a stranger" must be paid his wages before the sun sets "for he is needy and urgently depends on it" (Deuteronomy 24:15).

Even such regulations as not abhorring Edomites and Egyptians (Deuteronomy 23:8), not taking a part of a mill stone which would make the instrument useless in pawn, "for that would be taking someone's life in pawn" (Deuteronomy 24:6) by depriving him of his means of making a living, and not muzzling an ox when it is threshing (Deuteronomy 25:4) are all instances of sensitivity and consideration of other that go far beyond a mere legal code.

"You shall not subvert the rights of a stranger or the fatherless; you shall not take a widow's garment in pawn.... When you reap the harvest in your field and overlook a sheaf in the field, do not turn back to get it; it shall go to the stranger, the fatherless, and the widow — in order that the Lord your God may bless you in all your undertakings" (Deuteronomy 24:17-19). These are not simply laws, but an attempt to mold the character of the individual, to sharpen our sensitivities so that in any situation we will first think of the implications of what we are doing and how it will affect other people.

The regulation concerning not taking birds until the mother has been sent away (Deuteronomy 22:6) is also an attempt to inculcate sensitivity. It is an injunction that many Sages interpreted as teaching us sensitivity and mercy to animals (see the discussion in Bavli Berakhot 33b and Yerushalmi Berakhot 5:3).

Even the way in which one must treat a person to whom one has given a loan shows sensitivity. You have come to take the garment that is his pledge for the loan, but you may not go into his house to get it. He must be allowed to bring it out to you (Deuteronomy 24:11). In this way his dignity is preserved. And if he is poor and has only that garment to sleep in, you are required to give it back to him at night (Deuteronomy 24:13). A laborer has to be paid on the day that he works. You cannot withhold his wages even overnight because he needs it (Deuteronomy 24:15).

Moses was not merely a great lawgiver — he was a great teacher and the laws he taught were instructions in ethical living, intended to sensitize us to others. Now that the Jewish people once again has a sovereign state of its own, it is imperative that the Jewishness of Israel be manifested in having leaders no less sensitive to human needs than was Moses. Compassion is the essence of Torah and a Jewish state or community that lacks compassion is an oxymoron.

2. Difficult Regulations

It is also true, however, that this portion contains some regulations that are difficult if not impossible for us to accept, laws that offend our modern sensibilities. And yet if we examine them closely we can see that these too fit the general pattern of morality and ethical living that characterizes Judaism. Several examples of this can be found in the opening sections of our portion.

The very first law concerns the taking of a captive woman as a wife

(Deuteronomy 21:10–14). We may indeed be repelled at the very idea. It is certainly not something we would want to see done today. When we go to war, we do not take civilian prisoners and we certainly do not bring back captive women and marry them against their will. The importance of this law, however, is not in what it permits, but in what it forbids. At that time such treatment of women captives was commonly accepted. The Torah did not take the radical step of eliminating it, something that would undoubtedly have been impossible, but it did the next best thing and limited the actions of the captor. Soldiers commonly did whatever they wanted with captive women. The Torah limits the rights of the soldiers by legislating certain methods of treatment. It gives the captive woman rights. It limits the man's ability to do with her what he will. It requires him to marry her, not simply to cohabit with her, and it obligates him to either treat her as a wife or to liberate her. If thereafter the soldier sends the woman away, he must "release her outright. You must not sell her for money: since you had your will of her, you must not enslave her" (Deuteronomy 21:14). She is even given time to properly lament what is happening to her. Sensitivity is shown "even" to the captive woman. In its day, this was a far-reaching reformation of existing practice that other nations would have scorned.

Similarly we would not want to see parents have the right to have their child put to death for being "wayward and defiant" (Deuteronomy 21:18) — no matter how badly the child behaves or irritates. But what we forget is that the accepted law in so many societies then was that parents had absolute rights over their children. Here the law limits the parents' rights to punish a child. They must bring the child to a court and only the court can decide whether or not to punish the child (Deuteronomy 21:19). The execution was not performed by the parents but by the people of the town (Deuteronomy 21:21). For its day, this was progressive legislation designed to protect the child. Needless to say, rabbinic legislation went even further in limiting these laws, in some cases in effect making them inoperative. See for example *Sanhedrin* 71a: "There never has been a 'wayward and defiant son' and there never will be. Why then was it written? So that you may study it and receive a reward."

In these cases, and in so many others, limitations are placed upon the rights of people in power (the captor, the parents) to keep them from acting as they might wish. A legal process is invoked which will help to prevent miscarriages of justice.

When reading a section such as this it is always important to see it not in absolute terms but against the background of its time. In this way we can appreciate those laws that still remain valid as well as those that are no longer appropriate but still indicate the Torah's concern to rein in lawlessness and cruelty and demonstrate the Torah's attitude of mercy and concern for human beings and human rights.

When the Torah enjoins us not to "subvert the rights of the stranger and the fatherless" (24:17), or commands us to leave certain parts of the produce of our fields for the "stranger, the fatherless and the widow" (24:19), both because we ourselves were strangers in Egypt and so that "the Lord your God may bless you" (24:19), it is setting a standard for our conduct that is not only valid for today but that reflects everything we stand for as Jews.

Examples of laws that demonstrate acute sensitivity to others and attempt to mold an Israelite personality of care, concern and love toward others abound. The supreme sin is indifference to others, ignoring their needs, looking the other way and avoiding the necessity to help others. No wonder the Sages termed our people "merciful people, modest people, doers of acts of loving kindness" (*Yevamot* 79a). These are the basic values of the Torah that should inform our lives.

Ki Tavo

כי תבוא

Deuteronomy 26:1–29:8 | דברים כו:א-כט:ח

1. The Ultimate Reproof

This is a portion most of which we would prefer not to hear. And indeed the practice is to read the sections containing curses and descriptions of terrible things that may occur in a whisper. No sane person wants to listen to descriptions of disaster. Yet one might very well say that the entire book of Deuteronomy has been building up to these unpleasant verses. As has been noted, the Sages who wrote the official interpretation of Deuteronomy, the *Sifre*, over fifteen hundred years ago intuitively called it a book of reprimands and reproofs. In preparation for the entry into Canaan, Moses not only gives the people many laws that they must follow there; he also warns them time and time again that they must not repeat the sins of the past, but love God and follow God's commands if they are to be worthy of living in the land. The blessings and the curses, the last being much longer and more detailed than the former, are intended to impress this upon them in ways that they will never forget.

Moses understands well the use of symbolism and dramatic ceremony. Simply saying these things, no matter how effective the oratory, is not enough. Therefore he outlines here two impressive ceremonies that are to be held. In the first, they are to set up great stones together with an altar on Mount Ebal as soon as they cross the Jordan. Mount Ebal, located near Shechem, is the highest mountain in the area. These stones are to be plastered over and upon them are to be written, "all the words of this Teaching" (Deuteronomy 27:3), i.e., sections of Deuteronomy. What better way is there to impress upon them the fact that their entry into the land is intimately connected to their observance of these words? Surrounded by the words of Torah, for the very first time they will offer sacrifices to the Lord on the soil of the land promised to their ancestors.

But this is not sufficient. To the visual impression will be added the auditory one. The people are to be divided into two groups; six tribes shall stand on Mount Gerizim and six on Mount Ebal (Deuteronomy 27:12-13). The first group will proclaim the blessings that will come for faithfulness, the second the curses that will follow disobedience. Immediately thereafter the Levites will proclaim twelve curses and the people must answer "Amen" to each of them (Deuteronomy 27:14-26).

Surely the things prohibited in these twelve curses are not the only things to be avoided, yet they encompass matters of great concern and represent the entire group of commandments, which are referred to in the twelfth curse, "he who will not uphold the terms of this Teaching and observe them" (Deuteronomy 27:26). Of the other eleven, only the first is concerned with our relationship to God, forbidding the making of images (Deuteronomy 27:15). All the others concern human relationships and moral conduct, including a curse upon anyone who subverts the rights of "the stranger, the fatherless and the widow" (Deuteronomy 27:19). These are all words that should speak to us today as they did to our ancestors and that should be impressed upon us, informing the way we live and the way in which governments approach the needs of society.

Now, while still in Moab, Moses does not wait until they cross over to invoke blessings and curses. He describes to them the blessings and curses that will come upon them if they do or do not obey the covenant. Thus he concludes a second covenant with them — renewing and revitalizing the covenant made at Sinai (Deuteronomy 28:1-69).

Some of this is disturbing to us. We prefer to think that the best way to influence human conduct is through positive reinforcement. The Israelites should be ready to observe the commandments and the moral ways of the Torah because of their intrinsic value and out of the highest motives, not because of threats that if not they will suffer the consequences. Evidently Moses does not believe that that will work. Perhaps he knows them too well. He has been through so much with them, witnessing their stubbornness, their rebelliousness, their lack of gratitude. Therefore he feels that a good dose of fearful consequences will go a long way. One is reminded of the statement in *Pirkei*

Avot that were it not for the fear of the government, people would swallow one another alive (3:2). The reality of human nature calls for such measures as the threat that the policeman is watching and that jail is a possibility.

And yet Moses also has higher expectations of the Israelites. He commands that when they are settled in the land, they are to take their first fruits to the Temple and to make a declaration, one that is well known to us because it has found its way into the Passover Hagaddah:

> My father was a fugitive Aramean, He went down to Egypt with meager numbers and sojourned there; but there he became a great and very populous nation. The Egyptians dealt harshly with us and oppressed us; they imposed heavy labor on us. We cried to the Lord, the God of our fathers, and the Lord heard our plea.... He brought us to this place and gave us this land, a land flowing with milk and honey. (Deuteronomy 26:5–10)

The declaration makes absolutely no mention of the trials in the wilderness, the sins and difficulties. Perhaps this indicates that there is a difference between the time before entering the land when warnings and admonitions were required and the time after settling there. Once settled, our emphasis need not be on the negative side of our experiences, but upon the kindnesses of God. We are to view our productive life in the land of Israel as the fulfillment of our history and we are to be grateful.

Although most of us today are not farmers and have no actual first fruits to offer, the motivation behind this declaration can be equally meaningful for us. Whatever we accomplish, whatever work we bring to fruition, can be seen as our first fruits to be utilized for the good of our people. When doing so, we should review our history and be thankful that we have progressed from being a wandering people to a people living in the land that we have been given, "a land flowing with milk and honey."

2. To Serve God Joyfully

"Because you would not serve the Lord your God in joy and gladness over the abundance of everything, you shall have to serve — in hunger and thirst, naked and lacking everything — the enemies whom the Lord will let loose against you" (Deuteronomy 28:47-48). This perplexing verse is found in the midst of a long section of dire threats and frightening descriptions of the consequences of disobedience to God when Israel is settled in its own land.

One can well understand Moses' concern that once they come into the land, settle down and prosper, they will forget all about the teachings he has been promoting for forty years, all about the covenant with God, all about the fact that they are to live according to a different standard of morality than the people they are replacing. Therefore he concentrates on "blessings and curses" (Deuteronomy 27:11-15).

Yet the phrase "because you would not serve the Lord in God in joy and gladness over the abundance of everything" stands out and begs attention. Would it not have been sufficient to say "because you would not serve the Lord your God?" Why add "in joy and gladness"? With this brief phrase the Torah encapsulates an approach to observance and worship that is central to Judaism. True service of God is joyful and enthusiastic service. It is not cold and formal, merely following the details of laws and rituals, but service that comes from a joyful recognition of the wonders of life.

There are religious traditions that view all observance in dark terms, filled with fear and emphasizing a dour attitude toward life, built upon feelings of guilt and depression. Judaism is the very opposite.

Paradoxically, then, in the midst of warnings about punishment, the Torah delivers the message that if we serve only in order to avoid these punishments, that is not true service. True service is characterized by "joy and gladness." It is no accident that the Torah speaks of celebrating the festivals and says, "You shall rejoice in your festival...you shall have nothing but joy" (Deuteronomy 16:14-15). Of course no one can be commanded to be joyful, but you can be told that happiness should be the result of all the goodness and blessing of your lives; only an ingrate would not feel it.

Judaism did not have to wait for the modern Hassidic movement to know that true service must be accompanied by joy. It was inherent in the religion of Israel from the very beginning, although from time to time some may have forgotten it.

It is very interesting that in the list of holy days found in the Torah there is not one that is dour. The agricultural festivals are pure joy. Shabbat, Rosh Hodesh and Rosh Hashanah are tranquil times of celebration. Even Yom Kippur is solemn but not sad. Remember that the Talmud even says that "there was no happier days than Tu B'Av and Yom Kippur" (*Ta'anit* 26b). All the days of sadness are the result of events that happened to us later in history, days of mourning. They are not part of the divine scheme of worship but of the need for remembrance of history. The basis remains joy.

As a matter of fact, this portion itself begins not with curses but positively, with the need to acknowledge God's goodness. "When you enter the land" (Deuteronomy 26:1), we are told, after your harvest you are to take your first fruits, bring them to the Sanctuary in Jerusalem and make a declaration which expresses thanksgiving to God not only for the fruit but for being in the land altogether.

Happiness is stressed yet again in verse 26:11, "And you shall enjoy, together with the Levite and the stranger in your midst, all the bounty that the Lord your God has bestowed upon you and your household."

This declaration is followed by another concerning the giving of tithes, which stresses the fact that the Israelite has given to those who do not have land of their own — "the stranger, the fatherless and the widow" (Deuteronomy 26:13–14). Only then are we entitled to truly rejoice.

Elie Wiesel once wrote:

> The Gaon of Vilna said that "You shall rejoice in your festival" is the most difficult commandment in the Torah. I could never understand this puzzling remark. Only during the war did I understand. Those Jews who, in the course of their journey to the end of hope, managed to dance on Simhat Torah, those Jews who studied Talmud by heart while carrying stones on their back, those Jews who went on whispering *Zemirot shel Shabbat* while performing hard labor — they taught us how Jews should behave in the face of adversity. For my contemporaries one generation ago, "You shall rejoice in your festival" was one commandment that was impossible to observe — yet they observed it.

Our fortunate generation, which has had the privilege of witnessing the return to the land, should need no threats in order to rejoice. We must make certain that those in need can rejoice with us and then we must ourselves serve God with joy daily and turn our religious observance from routine and burden into "joy and gladness over the abundance of everything" with which we have been blessed.

Nitzavim-Vayelekh   נצבים-וילך

Deuteronomy 29:9–31:30 | דברים כט:ט-לא:ל

1. Exile and Redemption

These two portions usually read together bring to an end the series of lectures Moses delivers to Israel as they stand ready to enter the land. What remains is a "song" — *Ha'azinu* — and a blessing. The conclusion of Moses' major speech is found at the end of chapter 30. Moses sums up all that has been said in these words, "See, I set before you this day life and prosperity, death and adversity" (Deuteronomy 30:15). Love of God and obedience to Him will bring blessing (Deuteronomy 30:16). Worshipping and following other gods will bring exile (Deuteronomy 30:17-18). His last words in this oration are "by loving the Lord your God, heeding His commands, and holding fast to Him. For thereby you shall have life and shall long endure upon the soil that the Lord swore to your ancestors, Abraham, Isaac, and Jacob, to give to them" (Deuteronomy 30:20).

Moses had a task in life. It was given to him at the burning bush: to take the Israelites out of Egyptian bondage, to bring them to Sinai and to bring them to the land of Canaan (Exodus 3:16-17). Although his work remains unfinished, since he will die before they actually enter the land of Canaan, in a sense he has completed his task. They have left Egypt, they have experienced God at Sinai and they are prepared now for the entry into the land under the guidance of God with the help of Joshua.

Moses is concerned, however, that this will not be enough. They will come to the land, break the covenant that he is renewing with them now (Deuteronomy 29:11), and be punished with exile. He seems desperate to

293

avoid this and therefore he impresses upon them the choice that lies before them — life or death, blessing or curse, homeland or exile.

Did he succeed? Eventually the exile came, but it was not until hundreds of years had passed (586 BCE), so perhaps we can say that he did have a good measure of success.

It does seem, however, that Moses believed that at some point exile would come. He devotes ten verses (Deuteronomy 30:1–10) to a description of what will happen when they are sent into exile. It begins not with "*If* all these things befall you" but "*When* all these things befall you." It becomes Moses' sad task to call together the people and say plainly to them, "For I know that, when I am dead, you will act wickedly and turn away from the path that I enjoined upon you, and that in time to come misfortune will befall you" (Deuteronomy 31:29). If Moses was disappointed, this was the cause. The only reason that Moses did not succumb completely to despair was that he also knew that the misfortune would not bring an end to Israel, but that eventually they would return and be vindicated; thus paradoxically his message is not a discouraging one.

Moses describes the remedy before the illness has come. He tells the people that they will remember the message he is giving them now and, in the midst of their exile, they will finally take all of this to heart and "return to the Lord your God," loving God and obeying His commandments (Deuteronomy 30:2). The Hebrew for "return" here derives from the same root as the word *teshuvah* (repentance), a word that is in our minds particularly during the High Holy Day season which is when these portions are read. God's response to this is that He "will restore your fortunes and take you back in love" and bring you back to the land where you will prosper even more than before (Deuteronomy 30:3–5). Here too the word "restore" echoes the word *teshuvah*. When you return to God, He will return you to your land and your former status. The entire section emphasizes mutuality. You return to God, He returns you to your land. You love God, He loves you.

Indeed these verses are the source of the concept of "repentance" that plays such an important role in Jewish theology. The prophets take up the idea that is presented here and explicate it and emphasize it time and time again. In the Haftarah we read on Shabbat Shuva between Rosh Hashanah and Yom Kippur, for example, Hosea says, "Return [*shuvu*], O Israel, to the Lord your God, for you have fallen because of your sin. Take words with you and return to the Lord" (Hosea 14:2–3) and he tells them the words to say to gain God's forgiveness. Jeremiah, who lived before and during the first exile, similarly says to Israel, "Turn back [*shuvu*], rebellious children" (Jeremiah 3:14), "Turn back, O rebellious children, I will heal your afflictions" (Jeremiah 3:22). Turning back to God, returning to God, true repentance, will cause God to forgive and to heal.

This message from Moses is of extreme importance. He assures the people that even if they do that which he has been warning against and choose the way of the curse, the way of death, it will not mean the end of the people of Israel or the end of their inhabitation of the land of Israel. The exile, terrible as it may be, will not be the end of the story. Even though more than once the Lord has threatened to destroy them because of their sins in the wilderness, that will not happen. All they need do is to come to a clear realization of their faults and return to God and their exile will be terminated.

If we ask ourselves what gave the Israelites in Babylonian exile the strength to continue and the will not to give up their identity and simply assimilate into Babylonian society — which would have been easy enough — the answer may well be that it was Moses' promise of "return." And similarly, in the nearly nineteen hundred years of the second exile, what kept alive the spirit of the Jewish people and their will to live? Was it not the belief that the exile was not final but would end in a glorious return?

The return to Israel in the last century was indeed a vindication of Moses' message and should continue to give us strength and hope in times of adversity.

2. Instruction at Hand

Moses must have been a disappointed man. In this portion, his life is ending and he is unable to realize the one thing that he really longed for — reaching the land of Israel. And yet as we read these portions that describe his actions in his waning days, we do not sense that disappointment. He has stopped asking God to change the decree. Not only has he stoically accepted his fate, he is valiantly working to complete his discourse and to do all that has to be done before he departs from this world.

There is an urgency to whatever he does. He is deeply concerned about the future of his "teaching" — his instruction, *Torah*. It is of utmost importance to him that what he has taught through the years not be forgotten. He speaks to his people and urges them to take the teaching seriously and to realize how readily available it will always be to them.

> Surely, this Instruction which I enjoin upon you this day is not too baffling for you, nor is it beyond your reach. It is not in the heavens...neither is it beyond the sea.... No, the thing is very close to you, in your mouth and in your heart, to observe it. (Deuteronomy 30:11–14)

As was common in ancient times, important knowledge was transmitted and learned orally. Moses had already transmitted his instruction to the people. He emphasizes that all they have to do is remember it and follow it. They do not have to go in search of it. Israel has no need for esoteric knowledge in order to live according to God's ways. The commandments have been disclosed to them. The laws are known. There are no secrets. The way to serve God is not difficult. How different this is from many ancient religions that were based upon secret knowledge and mysterious rites that were the exclusive domain of religious functionaries. In those religions, the common people knew only what the priests wanted them to know.

Classical Judaism is the very opposite of these mystery religions. It does not advocate mystical rites, neither for the priests nor for the people. It does not depend on spells, amulets or secret knowledge that can be revealed only to initiates. It does not contain secret codes that reveal the future. It is open and revealed to all. And thus it remains to this day. Judaism is an open book to those who choose to read it.

Moses realizes, however, that oral knowledge alone has its limitations. It depends too much upon memory, which is often faulty. Therefore Moses also insists that his teaching be committed to writing. Some elements had already been written down; the Ten Commandments and some other teachings had been placed in the Ark (Exodus 25:16).

Now, at the end of the forty-year journey, Moses writes down the teachings he had been giving orally "and gave it to the priests, sons of Levi" (Deuteronomy 31:9). He charges the Levites: "Take this book of Teaching and place it beside the Ark of the Covenant of the Lord your God, and let it remain there as a witness against you" (Deuteronomy 31:26). This accords with the opinion stated in the Talmud (*Gittin* 60a) that "the Torah was given completed," which according to Rashi means "It was not written down until the end of the fortieth year when all of the sections had been uttered. Moses had put them in order orally year by year until he wrote them down."

Moses then instructs the people that these words are not only to be written down, they are to be read publicly to the entire people every seventh year. At Sukkot time, when all the people come to Jerusalem, everyone is to gather together — "men, women, children and the strangers in your communities" (Deuteronomy 31:12) — in order to hear the Teaching read. This public reading was the beginning of the regular reading of the Torah that became such a central part of Jewish worship. Again it emphasizes that the Torah is open and available to all. There is nothing secret that the laypeople cannot know. The emphasis on study and knowledge that has been so central a part of Judaism has its beginning in this practice. Perhaps then the mass of the people could not read, but they could listen to the words being read and therefore know — without the need for intermediaries — what it was that God wanted of them.

This ceremony, known as *Hakhel*, was not simply a ritual but an educational experience, an opportunity for the people to hear the Instruction and understand it. Many centuries later, after the return from the Babylonian exile, a similar ceremony was held in Jerusalem when Ezra had the text of the entire Torah read aloud to the people, men and women alike. "They read from the scroll of the Teaching of God, translating it and giving it sense, so they understood the reading" (Nehemiah 8:8). It was not the reading alone that was important, but the understanding.

Throughout Jewish history the strength of Judaism has been assured by seeing to it that these teachings would be known to all, not confined to a small elite. Women as well as men were included then and should be included today as well.

After doing all of this, Moses is informed that regardless of all his efforts, Israel will go astray, will break the covenant and will therefore be punished (Deuteronomy 31:16–21). He may have been disappointed, but life is filled with disappointments. God Himself was disappointed by human beings time and time again. But Moses also had reason to feel satisfied and — one hopes — as he climbed the mountain he thought not only of the failures, but also of the successes and of the fact that his Teaching, now committed to writing, would remain true and vital well into the future and would be passed on from generation to generation.

Ha'azinu   האזינו

Deuteronomy 32:1–52 | דברים לב:א–נב

1. A Song of Prophecy

The Torah contains two great poems. The first is the song of triumph sung at the sea (Exodus 15:1–18). The second is this poem recited by Moses to the people of Israel prior to his death, referred to by its first word, *Ha'azinu* (give ear). This latter poem is very different from the first. It is really prophecy. Most of the discourses of the prophets are written in the heightened language of poetry, as is this one. Although today we refer to Moses with the title that the rabbis conferred upon him — "Moses our teacher [rabbi]" — the Torah refers to him as a prophet: "Never again did there arise in Israel a prophet like Moses" (Deuteronomy 34:10). The prophet is God's spokesman and often tells what will happen in the future, usually as a warning. That is the theme of our portion.

The poem begins by asserting the righteousness of God, which can be seen in God's treatment of Israel. Not only did He favor them over all other nations (Deuteronomy 32:6–9), He also guarded, cared for and fed them generously when they were in a howling wilderness, Sinai (Deuteronomy 32:10–14). So far Moses is reiterating the saga of Israel's past. But the description that begins at this point is not of something that has happened but of something that *will* happen. These are matters that Moses has warned the people about throughout his speeches in this book, but here it sounds as if he foresees them as events in the future. He describes Israel as spurning God and taking up the worship of "no-gods" (Deuteronomy 32:15–18), beings worshipped as divine who have no true value. The result of this is that God becomes angry and, using a clever turn of phrase, permits a "no-folk" to come and conquer them (Deuteronomy 32:19-25). Nevertheless in the end God will punish the nations that come against Israel and will deliver and restore Israel (Deuteronomy 32:26-43).

When Moses recites these words to the people, he advises that they teach them to future generations "that they may observe faithfully all the terms of this Teaching" (Deuteronomy 32:46) so that they may long endure in the land of Canaan (Deuteronomy 32:47). The purpose of the poem, then, is to permit them to avoid what it foresees. If they take it to heart, they will not abandon God and worship idols, in which case no foreign nation will conquer them. But even if that does happen the poem gives them hope, for it assures Israel that God will not permit others to destroy them completely. Rather, at the end they will be restored.

Assuming that modern scholars are correct when they identify the book found during the days of King Josiah with Deuteronomy (2 Kings 22:8-20), we can understand Josiah's consternation at its words, for as Jeremiah, who lived at that time, testified, Israel had indeed forsaken God and gone after idols. Jeremiah wrote, "They have forsaken Me and sacrificed to other gods and worshipped the works of their hands" (Jeremiah 1:16). Indeed the prophecies of Jeremiah and the words of this poem are very much alike. Unfortunately, the people did not heed Jeremiah and did not heed Moses' poem. The result was disaster. But the hope that Moses held out sustained them and seventy years later the restoration began. *Shivat Tzion*, the return to Zion, did indeed take place.

2. Choices

There is something most appropriate about the fact that *Haʾazinu* is read on Shabbat Shuva, the Sabbath of repentance and return, although the poem never mentions repentance. That is a concept which, as we have seen, is hinted at in the previous Torah portions and made explicit by the prophets, such as Hosea whose words we read in the Haftarah, and the book of Jonah, which we read on Yom Kippur. The appropriateness of *Haʾazinu* is in its message: even though, from the very beginning of our history, we have abandoned God and been punished, the punishment has always come to an end and atonement has been made. The very last line of the poem uses the word "atonement" in its original sense of cleansing: "[God] will cleanse His people's land" (Deuteronomy 32:43).

The form of the poem is an oracle, as opposed to straight prophecy. In prophecy the prophet always ascribes his or her words to God: "Thus says the Lord." That is not the case here. Rather the speaker, Moses, depicts what he sees and envisions. It is very reminiscent of the way in which Balaam the seer spoke under divine influence. Balaam begins by speaking of himself: "Word of Balaam son of Beor, word of the man whose eye is true" (Numbers 24:3). Moses also begins with a personal reference: "Let my discourse come down as the rain, my speech distill as the dew...for the name of the Lord I proclaim" (Deuteronomy 32:2-3). Ironically, Balaam, the enemy of Israel, went on to describe the beauty of Israel. Moses, the lover of Israel, describes Israel's ungratefulness and apostasy! Perhaps there is a lesson in this: better the rebuke of a friend than the praise of an enemy.

Moses' oracle begins by speaking about God's nature and His relationship to the people of Israel. He reminds the people of all that God has done for them and describes the great gifts that they enjoy in the land that God has given them — honey, oil, milk, meat, wheat, wine (Deuteronomy 32:13-14). Of course none of this has happened as yet. Thus Moses is speaking as if he is witnessing the future. The same is true of what follows, a description of Israel enjoying all of these riches and instead of thanking God for them, growing fat and forsaking God for no-gods (Deuteronomy 32:15-18). This too has not yet happened. He is speaking to a wilderness generation that has not yet come to the land, much less enjoyed its fruits, a generation that has not gone after other gods. Again, he is depicting what he foresees in the future. He also foresees their defeat at the hands of enemies followed by their eventual vindication and victory — all through God's active intervention.

In many ways these words of Moses are similar to the prophecies uttered at later times, the words of Isaiah, Jeremiah and others, who may have used *Ha'azinu* as a model for their doctrines. Unlike those prophets, however, who stressed the moral deterioration of Israel, the lack of justice, the oppression of the poor, all of which are certainly explicit in other sections of the Torah and the teachings of Moses, in this poem the sins of Israel are basically confined to ingratitude to God and the worship of pagan deities. This does not mean that Moses was unconcerned with other matters as well, but the overwhelming challenge of Israel as it enters the land and in the early days of its settlement there was the enticement of paganism. Israel's monotheism, the revolution wrought by Moses, was a new and fragile creation. It stood alone against a world of idolatry, paganism and polytheism. Only Israel, a small, young people, believed in monotheism. The mighty empires surrounding it were filled with the pageantry of paganism. The land of Canaan was a center of fertility cults. Israel was now going to become a nation rooted in land and agriculture. Would it not be easy for them to be lured away into pagan rites rooted in the worship of nature?

If this is going to happen in any case, the value of telling it now is in teaching a lesson so that it will not be repeated. In other words, it will come to pass and the people will then realize that the reason for their suffering was their abandonment of the one true God and will not repeat the mistake. But if we take seriously the teaching of Judaism that we have free choice, something that Moses reiterated often enough — "Behold I set before you this day blessing and curse: blessing if you obey the commandments...and curse if you do not obey" (Deuteronomy 11:26–28) — then this entire vision must be understood as something that will happen if they make the wrong choice, but that can be avoided. In that case, Moses is talking to the right audience. He is addressing those who will enter the land, those who will benefit from all of its goodness and then be tempted to forget God and to follow the no-gods of other nations. Unfortunately we know that ultimately the warning was not heeded and the consequences were indeed similar to those Moses describes.

It is most interesting that the Sages who lived after the destruction of the Second Temple in the year 70 CE found in this poem more than just a description of what happened during the period of the First Temple. They also saw in it a prophecy of what would happen to the Second Temple and the destruction following Bar Kokhba's revolt in the following century as well as the eventual restoration that would take place. In the midrash composed at that time they wrote, "How great is this poem, for it contains references to the past and the future to come, as well as to this world and the world-to-come!" (*Sifre Deuteronomy* 333). Throughout their interpretation, they refer specific passages to events they had witnessed in their own time as the Romans crushed the revolt and slaughtered hordes of Jews.

The main emphasis of the Sages, however, was upon the hope, the restoration. For example, they taught, "Just as vessels of clay cannot be restored after they are broken, so after the punishment of Israel ceases, it [the punishment] will never be renewed" (*Sifre Deuteronomy* 324).

These words were of great importance at that time, for the Jewish people faced two challenges — the challenge of the Romans who contended that their gods were mightier than the God of Israel since Rome had been victorious, and the challenge of the new Christian sect that contended that the defeat of Israel and the destruction of the Temple was a punishment from God for Israel's rejection of "the messiah." Through their interpretation of the prophecy of Moses, the Sages countered these claims. It was not the might of Rome but the guilt of Israel that had brought this victory. Yes, it was God's punishment upon Israel, but not because of any lack of belief in "the messiah"; rather it was due to a lack of sufficient belief in the one God. And — most important of all — none of this implied that God had rejected His people. Israel remained and would always remain God's people. They would be restored and the enemy — Rome — would be destroyed.

I thought of these words once when I stood at the Arch of Titus in Rome, a triumphal arch depicting the defeat of the Jews. But ancient Rome is now in ruins and ancient Jerusalem is now being rebuilt. In the words of this Torah portion, "For the Lord will vindicate His people and take revenge for His servants...and cleanse His people's land!" (Deuteronomy 32:36, 43).

V'zot Habrakhah   וזאת הברכה

Deuteronomy 33:1–34:12 | דברים לג:א-לד:יב

1. The Final Blessing

This final portion of the Torah — which we read on Simhat Torah together with the first part of the first book, Genesis — is entitled *V'zot Habrakhah* (this is the blessing). How fitting it is that Moses concluded his life with a blessing. It is an ancient tradition that before leaving this world a father confers his blessing upon his children. That is what Isaac attempted to do (Genesis 27:4) and what Jacob did (Genesis 49). Now Moses leaves his children — the people of Israel — with a blessing before he ascends the mountain to view the land he will never enter and then to die. And so too does he bestow a blessing upon all of us as we come to the end of the Torah.

This is especially significant when we consider that the prophecy he uttered just before this was a harsh one in which he spoke of their sins and the punishment that would come upon them (Deuteronomy 32:1–47). Although it had a silver lining in the promise of eventual restoration (Deuteronomy 32:36–43), it was nevertheless a harsh message. Here we have exactly the opposite. The entire message is one of blessing. He speaks of each tribe and, unlike Jacob who used the opportunity to castigate some of his sons, Moses now has nothing negative to say about them. Each one receives a blessing. It is as if at the end all sins are forgotten and all is forgiven. A stormy relationship ends in peace and tranquility. The symphony of his life ends not with a blazing crescendo but with notes that fade into a harmonious coda.

The language Moses uses emphasizes this positive view. He refers to God as One who loves them and Israel as a people that accepted God's teachings (Deuteronomy 33:3) and proclaimed Him king (Deuteronomy 33:5). This is

305

a very different picture from the rebellious people we have heard about previously. To each of the tribes he also has something positive to say. He speaks of
Reuben's ability to survive, using the word "live" (Deuteronomy 33:6). The
word "blessing" features prominently. He asks God to bless Judah (Deuteronomy 33:11). Joseph is called "blessed of the Lord" (Deuteronomy 33:13). The
word is repeated concerning Gad (Deuteronomy 33:20). Naphtali is "full of
the Lord's blessing" (Deuteronomy 33:23) and Asher is "most blessed of sons"
(Deuteronomy 33:24).

The coda of the blessing speaks of the entire people of Israel as, "O happy
Israel! Who is like you" (Deuteronomy 33:29) and describes how God delivers them, destroys their enemies and permits them to dwell in safety (Deuteronomy 33:27–29). Thus the last words of the prophet are words not merely of
comfort, but of assurance of their future safety. The rest is silence.

2. Moses Departs

Many of the prophets exhibit the duality we see in the case of Moses. On the
one hand, they speak harsh words of condemnation and warning. On the
other, they speak words of assurance and comfort. Perhaps this tells us a
profound truth about them as human beings. No matter how much they
condemn, as indeed they sometimes must do, underneath it all they
profoundly love the people and wish them only good and blessing.

Thus Moses leaves his people with these words of blessing and assurance.
After that he has no more to say. In what is surely one of the most beautiful
and poignant passages in all of world literature, chapter 34 describes Moses'
lonely journey upward from the plains of Moab to the heights of Mount
Nebo. This old man has climbed mountains before. He ascended Sinai several
times in order to receive the two tablets of the covenant, a journey that was
not only physical but also spiritual, into the realm of the divinity. Indeed the
Sages thought of it as a journey not only to the heights of the mountain but
into heaven itself. But this is a different mountain and a different ascent. Yet it
too has about it the feeling of a spiritual journey. Alone, in silence, with no
word from God, he fulfills the command he had heard before, "Ascend these
heights of Abarim and view the land that I have given the Israelite people.

When you have seen it, you too shall be gathered to your kin" (Numbers 27:12, repeated in Deuteronomy 32:48–52).

This is both a punishment and a reward. Death without entering the land is the punishment, but viewing the land is a reward for all his labors. At the very least, he will view it from the mountain and that will be enough.

The last words God speaks to Moses seem rather brusque: "I have let you see it with your own eyes, but you shall not cross there" (Deuteronomy 34:4). Yet the subsequent description of Moses' death is anything but, for the burial of Moses is performed by none other than God Himself: "He buried him in the valley in the land of Moab, near Beth-peor; and no one knows his burial place to this day" (Deuteronomy 34:6). And of course the moving description — one might almost call it a eulogy — of Moses at the end of this chapter demonstrates God's appreciation of the greatness of this man. The Lord, we are told, singled him out "face-to-face" and there never was another like him (Deuteronomy 34:10).

A magnificent midrash heightens the words of the Torah:

> When Moses died, Joshua wept, wailed and mourned bitterly.... He continued mourning over him for many days, until the Holy One, blessed be He, said to him, "Joshua, how long will you continue mourning? Does his death affect you alone? Does not his death affect Me? For from the day that he died there has been great mourning before Me...but he is assured of the world-to-come." (*Sifre Deuteronomy* 305)

Thus do we conclude the Torah and take leave of the greatest of all our leaders, Moses our teacher.

Epilogue

Completing the entire cycle of the Torah portions has taken us on a journey from the creation of the world to the death of Moses. We have narrowed our focus, moving from the origins of the universe and humankind to the saga of one people — Israel — as it prepares for life as a covenanted people in its own land. The story of the subsequent history of that people will be told in later books of the Bible. Indeed the Torah is an incomplete tale that does not encompass all the richness of Judaism. For that one must continue with the rest of the *Tanakh* — the Hebrew Bible — with the impassioned visions of the prophets, the inner beauty of the psalms, the anguished theodicy of Job and so much else; and with the post-Biblical creations, the Mishna, the Talmud, the many works of Midrash and all the commentaries, ancient and modern, that have added so much depth to the Torah itself.

These prefaces were intended to give direction and guidance to reading and understanding the Torah portions and, most importantly, to serve as an impetus to further reading and study, for there is no end to the wonders that can be found within the Torah. It is at the same time too easy and too difficult to read the Torah. It is too easy because one can breeze through it quickly and superficially, especially in translation, and assume that one has understood it. It is too difficult because there is no end to the depth and variety of meanings and interpretations that exist. That, however, is the true beauty of the Torah, for as the Sages remarked, everything is in it (*Pirkei Avot* 5:26).

The "hero" of the Torah is really God. Unlike pagan books, the Torah tells us nothing of the "life" of God, but it is concerned with the interaction of God and humanity and with understanding the concerns God has for humankind and the role that the people Israel is to play in history. True, we learn little about the essence of God, but we learn a great deal about God's demands for human compassion and righteousness, as well as God's love, mercy and justice. Of course we must also be wary of too literal an interpretation of anything written about God, for our language is constrained by anthropo-morphisms which can only point at God's reality and not encompass it.

As for the legal portions of the Torah, the commandments that it contains, these must be viewed both against the background of the times when they originated and with an eye to the way in which they were inter-preted and developed over the subsequent centuries. The Torah shows great care for human beings as well as special concern for the poor, the weak and those in need. It teaches not only the oneness of God but the equality of all human beings created in the Divine image.

In a very real sense the Torah is only the beginning and not the end of the development of Jewish ethics and ways of life. And if there are passages that cause us concern, we should be aware that this concern has been felt before and has been dealt with by ancient Sages as well as by modern religious think-ers.

Our understanding of the Torah has been immeasurably enhanced by archeological knowledge and the study of comparative ancient religions. We now view the Torah as a work of Divine inspiration filtered through human consciousness. When the Torah scroll is lifted in synagogues after having been read we recite the words, "This is the Torah that Moses presented to the people of Israel by the mouth of God through the hand of Moses." Indeed the core of the Torah is the teaching of Moses, a partnership — God and Moses, human and Divine.

Reading the Torah is a life-long task, one that never ends. We no sooner finish the last book than on the very same day we begin the first one again, over and over. There is always something new to discover therein. Its contents are the basis for all of Judaism and for our very existence as Jews. As we say in our prayers, "For they are our life and the length of our days and in them we shall meditate day and night."

Ḥazak ḥazak v'nithazzek!

Be strong, be strong and let us summon up strength!